Technology Brands in the Digital Economy

This edited volume provides deep insight into theoretical and empirical evidence on how digital technologies and high-tech brands are interrelated. It traces the mutual links between these two phenomena, identifies the multidimensionality of interdependencies, and shows the reader how and why new technologies are the driving factors of creation and global dissemination of high-tech brands. In this context, it also refers to various types of economic and social networks that, on the one hand, are the products of digital technologies, while on the other enforce global visibility of high-tech brands.

The book contributes to the present state of knowledge, offering the reader broad evidence on how digital technologies impact the process of high-tech brands' nascence and how their growing role and global exposure influence networked economies and societies. It sets out to deliver a bridge between brand management and economical approaches to understanding how digital technologies and high-tech brands are interrelated. This multidisciplinary approach creates a complex compilation of different views and perspectives that sheds new light on the high-tech brands' phenomena of being an input and output of technology-driven economies.

Technology Brands in the Digital Economy is written for scholars and researchers from a wide variety of disciplines but especially for those addressing issues of brands and economic development and growth, social development, and the role of technological progress in broadly defined socio-economic progress. It will also be an invaluable source of knowledge for graduate and postgraduate students in a variety of areas such as economic and social development, information and technology, worldwide studies, social policy, and comparative economics.

Wioleta Kucharska is a professor in the Management Department of the Faculty of Management and Economics, Gdańsk University of Technology, Poland. She has 12 years of industrial experience in marketing management. Her latest book, *Personal Branding in the Knowledge Economy: The Interrelationship Between Corporate and Employee Brands*, published in 2022 by Routledge, provides a comprehensive picture of the phenomenon of personal branding in the network economy era by combining a solid scientific frame with branding practice.

Ewa Lechman is a professor of economics at the Faculty of Management and Economics, Gdańsk University of Technology, Poland. Since 2017, she has been Vice-Dean for Development and a PhD programme director. Her extensive research interests concentrate on economic development, ICT and technological progress, and ICT role in reshaping social and economic systems and various aspects of poverty and economics in developing countries.

RIOT!

Routledge Studies in Innovation, Organizations and Technology

Inclusive Innovation
Robyn Klingler-Vidra, Alex Glennie and Courtney Savie Lawrence

Organizational Change, Innovation and Business Development
The Impact of Non-Technological Innovations
Edited by Magdalena Popowska and Julita E. Wasilczuk

Public Innovation and Digital Transformation
Edited by Hannele Väyrynen, Nina Helander and Harri Jalonen

Innovation and Leadership in the Public Sector
The Australian Experience
Mahmoud Moussa, Leonie Newnham, Adela McMurray and Nuttawuth Muenjohn

Advancing Big Data Analytics for Healthcare Service Delivery
Tiko Iyamu

Open Labs and Innovation Management
The Dynamics of Communities and Ecosystems
Edited by Valérie Mérindol and David W. Versailles

Technology Brands in the Digital Economy
Edited by Wioleta Kucharska and Ewa Lechman

Business Models for Industry 4.0
Concepts and Challenges in SME Organizations
Sandra Grabowska and Sebastian Saniuk

For more information about this series, please visit: www.routledge.com/Routledge-Studies-in-Innovation-Organizations-and-Technology/book-series/RIOT

Technology Brands in the Digital Economy

Edited by Wioleta Kucharska
and Ewa Lechman

Routledge
Taylor & Francis Group
LONDON AND NEW YORK

First published 2023
by Routledge
4 Park Square, Milton Park, Abingdon, Oxon OX14 4RN

and by Routledge
605 Third Avenue, New York, NY 10158

Routledge is an imprint of the Taylor & Francis Group, an informa business

British Library Cataloguing-in-Publication Data
A catalogue record for this book is available from the British Library

ISBN: 978-1-032-02686-2 (hbk)
ISBN: 978-1-032-02687-9 (pbk)
ISBN: 978-1-003-18463-8 (ebk)

DOI: 10.4324/9781003184638

Typeset in Bembo
by Apex CoVantage, LLC

Contents

Contributors' bios

Hasret Balcioglu is an executive board member of YÖDAK and an expert in economics and business. She had an honorary doctoral dissertation supervisor at Harvard University. She has published many publications in leading international index journals and books. Prof. Dr. Hasret Balcioglu has the Young Researcher Award (USA), Business Plan Award (USA), and Best Paper Award (USA, Nigeria). She has worked in NASA, World Bank, and international and local projects. She has a Global Finalist Award organised by NASA, ESA, and JAXA. She has been in the expert pools of many leading Quality Assurance Agencies and Accreditation Institutions for education such as AQAS, CEEMAN, and EVALAG.

G. Scott Erickson is Charles A. Dana Professor and Chair of Marketing in the School of Business at Ithaca College, Ithaca, NY, where he has also served as Interim Associate Dean. In addition, he holds a position as Visiting Professor in the Dyson School of Management at Cornell University. He has published widely on big data, intellectual capital, and business analytics. He has received two Fulbright awards, serving as a visiting research chair at Queen's University, Kingston, ON, Canada and as a Fulbright/National Science Foundation Arctic Scholar at the University of Akureyri, Iceland. His recent book is *Marketing in a Digital World* published in 2021 by Flip Learning.

María Ángeles Alcaide González holds a PhD in the Business Administration and Management programme from UPV. She has lectured in the Department of Economics and Social Sciences (DECS) of the UPV since 2015, in the Master of Valuation and Appraisal, and in the Master of Science Real Estate accredited by the Royal International of Chartered Surveyors (RICS).

She has participated in several international conferences and has published scientific papers in prestigious international journals, especially in the area of valuation of intangibles, more specific brands, and also in the field of corporate social responsibility.

Dr. Xiufang (Leah) Li teaches, undertakes research, and supervises PhD students in public relations, digital communication, branding, journalism, media, and marketing. Her research focuses on the areas of international public relations and digital communication. Leah is a lecturer and former programme manager in the School of Media and Communication at RMIT University in Australia. Leah is engaged with private and public organisations to develop projects relating to communication and business strategies, user behaviours, and media production. She has a track record of over 35 peer-reviewed publications. Her recent work can be found in *Public Relations Review* and *European Journal of Cultural Studies*.

Mina Nasiri was a postdoctoral researcher at LUT University, School of Engineering Science, Department of Industrial Engineering and Management. Her research interests lie in the area of digitalisation, digital transformation, performance measurement and management, operations management, and sustainable strategies.

Tatjana Mamula Nikolić has been working as an associate professor at the Metropolitan University, where she lectures on marketing and management subjects. In her 25-year research career, she had managed a large number of quantitative and qualitative research projects, as a researcher and director of several marketing research companies. Her research interests are focused on management in a volatile time, business re-innovation, green economy, sustainable business, and generations Y and Z. In the last three years, Tatjana has published more than 25 papers in international journals covering these topics. In 2021, she published a book "Behavior of New Generation of Consumers and Leaders in the VUCA World."

Natividad Guadalajara Olmeda is a professor at the Polytechnic University of Valencia, Spain. She is also an academic member of the Royal Institution of Chartered Surveyors (RICS), specialising in the field of valuation, since 2012. Dr. Guadalajara has been the director of the master's degree in Appraisal and Valuation Engineering since its beginning in 1996. She has supervised 14 doctoral theses and a wide number of final master's theses. She has also published five books and more than 40 articles in prestigious scientific journals on asset valuation.

Karolina Perčić is an assistant professor at Modern Business School in Belgrade. She lectures courses on marketing research, consumer behaviour, and methodology of scientific research work. Her current research interests focus on marketing and education. She has a long-standing experience in the field of marketing research. Karolina is author of numerous papers published at national and international conferences, and in domestic and foreign journals. She received recognition for the best work of the IX International Scientific Conference "Sustainable Growth in Small Open Economies," organised by the Institute of Economic Sciences in Belgrade and the Faculty of Economics in University of Niš, in 2017.

Sanja Popović-Pantić is a senior research associate at the Institute Mihajlo Pupin, Science and Technology Policy Research Centre. Her main areas of expertise are entrepreneurship and innovation management. She has chaired Women's Entrepreneurship Sector Group within Enterprise Europe Network (EEN) since May 2015. As the leader of the largest national association of women entrepreneurs in Serbia and with an academic background, Sanja is considered a leading consultant in the field of women's entrepreneurship. Sanja has published numerous papers in international journals, mainly related to gender aspects of digitalisation, business in times of crisis, innovation, and access to supply chains.

Elena de la Poza Plaza holds a degree in Business Administration and Management from the Polytechnic University of Valencia (UPV) and a PhD in the Asset Valuation programme from the UPV. She is currently the strategy head of the UPV. Dr. de la Poza is a tenured associate professor in the Department of Economics and Social Sciences (DECS) of the UPV. She has published more than 40 scientific papers in prestigious international journals related to valuation, corporate social responsibility, and human behaviour modelling; she has edited four books and supervised three doctoral theses in the field of valuation.

Tero Rantala is a postdoctoral researcher at LUT University, School of Engineering Science. His current research focuses on performance management and measurement of university–industry collaborations. In addition, his current research interests involve different areas of performance management in digital business environments and sustainable business contexts. He has previously published in journals such as *European Journal of Operational Research*, *Journal of Cleaner Production*, *Information Technology & People*, and *Education and Work*.

Minna Saunila is an associate professor at LUT University, School of Engineering Science, Department of Industrial Engineering and Management. Since 2018, she is also a docent of the University of Jyväskylä School of Business and Economics. Her research covers topics related to sustainable operations and production, innovation, performance management, as well as service operations. Recently, her research projects have been related to digitisation of services and production. She has previously published in *Technovation*, *Computers in Industry*, *Journal of Engineering and Technology Management*, *Technology Analysis & Strategic Management*, and *Journal of Purchasing and Supply Management* among others.

Bruno Schivinski is a statistician, behavioural researcher, and senior lecturer in Advertising at RMIT University, Australia. He consults for online service providers, websites, and scientific institutions such as the Polish Ministry of Science and Higher Education (MNiSW) and the National Science

Centre (NCN). Schivinski specialises in problematic consumer behaviour, social media engagement, online branding, and user-generated content. His research has received international coverage in *Forbes Magazine* and *Google News*. His latest work can be found in academic journals such as the *Journal of Business Research*, *Journal of Advertising Research*, *Industrial Marketing Management*, *Journal of Strategic Marketing*, *Journal of Marketing Communications*, and *Journal of Clinical Medicine*.

Sariseelia Sore is a senior lecturer at LAB University of Applied Sciences, Faculty of Business. She is also the coordinator of the master's programme in digital solutions. Her research interests include areas of digital business operations and performance management, currently focusing on digital solution capabilities and digital business value.

Anna Ujwary-Gil is a professor at the Institute of Economics, Polish Academy of Sciences in Warsaw, Poland. She earned her PhD and habilitation in economics and management from the Warsaw School of Economics. She is also the founder and president of the Cognitione Foundation for the Dissemination of Knowledge and Science and an expert in the international think tank named Network Analysis Laboratory. Also, the editor-in-chief of the *Journal of Entrepreneurship, Management and Innovation* (JEMI). Her research interests include organisational network analysis, knowledge management, intellectual capital, resource-based views, and dynamic approaches to organisation and management.

Juhani Ukko is a professor at LUT University, School of Engineering Science, Department of Industrial Engineering and Management. He is also an adjunct professor at Tampere University. His current research focuses on performance measurement, operations management, digital transformation, digital services, and corporate sustainability performance. In recent years, he has managed and participated in research projects related to digital transformation in companies and society. His work has been published in journals such as *International Journal of Operations & Production Management*, *International Journal of Production Economics*, and *Journal of Cleaner Production*.

A.M. Alahmari is a PhD candidate in media and communication at RMIT University. He is a lecturer in Media and Communication at the Islamic University of Madinah, Saudi Arabia. Abdullah gained his BSc (Hons) in Public Relations from Umm Al-Qura University, Saudi Arabia; he then earned his MSc in Electronic Media Studies at Central Michigan University, USA. His research focuses on the areas of place branding, public relations, and social media. Abdullah is a public relations consultant for the public and private sectors such as the Islamic University of Madinah and Mina Real Estate.

Introductory words

Wioleta Kucharska and Ewa Lechman

This book is designed to provide deep insight into theoretical and empirical evidence on how digital technologies and high-tech brands are interrelated. Our intention is to demonstrate a variety of perspectives that emerge in the context of high-tech brands in a network society.

For readers interested exclusively in such evidence, this would constitute a great point of reference, a complex work, compilation of different views and perspectives. It allows for the dissemination of knowledge on the relationships between digital technologies and high-tech brands; it can have a critical impact on a growing body of literature covering a multitude of clearly focused papers, which are usually fragmented. Additionally, its coverage can serve as a best-suited stimulus for not previously published works of cutting-edge research and analysis in the areas of crucial and growing importance.

It entails a wide array of aspects dealing with broadly defined high-tech brands and digital society and economic issues; hence it may be claimed to have an international appeal. It traces the mutual links between these two phenomena, identifies the multidimensionality of interdependencies, and aims to show the reader how and why new technologies are the driving factor of the creation and global dissemination of high-tech brands. In this context, it also intends to refer to various types of economic and social networks that, on the one hand, are the "products" of digital technologies, while on the other, they enforce the global visibility of high-tech brands.

It also refers to the still observed gap in research concerning high-tech brands development, how their growing role and global exposure influence networked economies and societies, and how digital brands influence the global, local, and personal levels of growth. This book aims to deliver a bridge between a brand management approach and an economical approach to understand how digital technologies, brands, societies, and economies are interrelated. This multidisciplinary approach sheds new light on the high-tech brands' phenomena of being an input and output of technology-driven economies. Summing up, the relationship between brands and technology, society and economy, is an exciting line of research that reveals many factors, directly and indirectly, determining a value creation by TechBrands raised by this book.

DOI: 10.4324/9781003184638-1

Chapter 1 sets the general context and traces the links between TechBrands and digital economy. Next, Chapter 2, using historical methods, explores the essence of a technology brand's emergence and brings an understanding of TechBrands' impact on the economy of various countries through different business models' applications. So, this chapter brings some valuable lessons from the past.

Since today the best global brands are dominated by TechBrands and since top brands global are perceived as one of the most valuable companies and economies assets, Chapter 3 of this volume presents a network approach to value creation from intangible assets to expose the general essence of intangible assets contribution to entities and their economies in a networked world.

Continuing this line, Chapter 4 links the current methods of TechBrands' valuation with economic-financial and stock market information and exposes how the value of this valuable asset is measured. This chapter represents a considerable advance and contribution for valuation companies, investors, and professionals due to lack of homogeneity and trust in today's existing methods, and also given the need to obtain a more rigorous method for valuing this very valuable asset, especially for technology companies, and to know the contribution they make to society today. The presented study also acts as a step towards unifying quantitative criteria by complying with ISO 10668:2010. Finally, this chapter evidences that it is possible to apply the proposed method to value any technology brand on the stock market.

Chapter 5, on the contrary, explores the effects of digital business strategies and technology scanning on company performance. However, authors discovered that a digital business strategy alone negatively affects company performance, but at the same time, they revealed that technology scanning (collecting information via new digital channels and devices) acts as a mediator in the relation between digital business strategy and company performance. So, the knowledge from the chapter significantly improves our understanding of digital transformation by showing that a digital business strategy can positively impact company performance via technology scanning. Next, Chapter 6 stays in line with the previous chapter's findings, and exploring technology brands using digital media metrics exposes that higher value brands have higher and more consistent user interest. Furthermore, the authors of Chapter 7 exposed the cohort of Generation Z (GenZ)—digital natives use social media platforms and technology brands themselves most frequently and are also the most active brand co-creators. So, TechBrands equity and technology usage are key indicators of TechBrands' value.

In light of the above, Chapter 8 seems to clearly expose that technological image (TECH image) strongly drives TechBrands and any other technology-supported brands if only include the technological factor to their equity creation base as, for example, city brands do, can be more successful than brands that ignore technology as a common growth driver today. Specifically, the authors of Chapter 7 explore more in-depth exactly a concept of smart city-based place branding. Moreover, based on their comprehensive literature review, authors create a unified framework of intelligent city branding via social media. So, this final part is an excellent example of technology as one of the critical drivers of brands growth today.

Wioleta Kucharska and Ewa Lechman
(Editors)

1 Technology brands in the digitally-based and network economy

Setting the background

Wioleta Kucharska and Ewa Lechman

1.1. The context

Societies' and economies' development today is driven by technology. The overwhelming diffusion, adoption, and usage of digital technologies fundamentally reshaped world societies and economies recently. It is also widely acknowledged that digital technologies transform business models, good consumption and social, behavioural patterns, social norms, and attitudes then determine consumer preferences. Digital technologies enforce the emergence of cutting-the-edge changes. Technology and technological change do not just bring change or inventions to the economy and society, they enrich and shape socio-economic systems, enhancing their responsiveness and adaptability to further technological change. This demonstrates the interrelatedness of society, economy, and technology, driving home the point that none of these elements exists in isolation.

In that context, it is needless to claim that societies and economies are not digitally-neutral. Technological progress is a disruptive process that alters social and economic structures stimulating the emergence of a new *status quo*. The overwhelming diffusion, adoption, and usage of digital technologies fundamentally reshape world societies and economies. It is also widely acknowledged that digital technologies transform business, consumption and behavioural patterns, norms, and attitudes, and consumer preferences. Digital technologies enforce the emergence of cutting-the-edge changes, but above all, they generate the emergence of various networks in which transformative power is demonstrated through different channels. One of these channels of impact is digitally-native and digitally-born high-tech brands. The profound connections between the positive and negative effects of exponentially growing digital technologies on emerging network economies and societies are unquestionable. Therefore, high-tech brands' rapid growth and impact on the networked world are observed; they unleash the full potential of digitally-led economies and network societies. This strong relationship between digital technologies and high-tech brands is bi-directional. On the one hand, high-tech brands are an exquisite demonstration of the unique power and opportunities that digital technologies brought to economies and societies, while on the other, unique

DOI: 10.4324/9781003184638-2

economic and social networks that emerged due to the digital technologies promote high-tech brands globally, enforcing their value growth and increasing visibility.

Still, above all, they energise the emergence and support existing business development and stimulate social networks progression in which transformative power is visible. Technological progress is a process that alters social and economic structures, facilitating constant change, for example, technology-supported businesses and social networks expand rapidly in reality and virtuality and reshaped the way we work and live. Therefore, the current economic conditions expose strongly overall-existing tightly networked interdependencies where everything and everybody depend on everything and everyone. It creates a pokey network of ties cooperating thanks to the common system of values of business partners, customers, and company employees. Technology serves in networked reality as an infrastructure supporting all kinds of relations among individuals and entities. Therefore, the current, networked reality of business sees technology as one of the keys, next to relations, knowledge, and intellectual capital growth facilitators (Powell, 2003; Tapscott, 1999). Networks dominate as a form of infrastructure and a new way of market coordination. Digital reality determines a network-coordinated economy where the network transcends markets and a hierarchy of relationships that largely determine the way for the operation of all market actors: individuals and entities. In this context, digital technologies represented by technology brands create enormous value.

1.2. Digital technologies

Digital technologies are claimed as General Purpose Technologies; hence, they generate path-breaking innovations and are recognised as fundamental factors in long-run technological progress and deep-going structural and qualitative shifts in economies and societies (Sahal, 1981; Bresnahan, 2010; Coccia, 2017). As argued by Rosenberg and Trajtenberg (2004), digital technologies are "epochal innovations" as they demonstrate the capacity to radically reshape the contours of the world economies, ways of doing business enforce the emergence of new industries and services. Digital technologies (ICT) are widely acknowledged as the critical drivers for knowledge and information acquisition, labour and capital productivity, and social, political, and economic empowerment (Graham, 2019). Digital technologies, due to strong network effects (Katz & Shapiro, 1985) that they generate, enable the emergence of various networks reshaping the way that businesses are run, trading and consumption patterns, economic and social behaviours, social norms, and attitudes (Graham & Dutton, 2019). The network economy emerges as the economy that is driven by digital technologies. Henceforth, tracing and understanding existing relationships between society-wide adoption and usage of digital technologies and economic development deserve special attention. Not only to claim that it deepens our knowledge on how economies work, but the state policy perspective that shapes institutional and economic environment is of seminal importance in this case (Stiroh, 2002; Gilbert, 2020).

Evidently, empirical researches tracing societies' and economies' sensitivity to the introduction of digital technologies discuss a variety of channels of impact between and interrelations between these two. Earlier studies concentrated predominantly on creating network societies and economies (Shapiro et al., 1998; Castells, 2000, 2011; Johansson et al., 2012; Van Dijk, 2020), information societies (Mossberger et al., 2007; Beniger, 2009; Lyon, 2013; Buckland, 2017; Martin, 2017) where structural changes are driven by strong network externalities (Katz & Shapiro, 1985), and unlimited access to all types of information and knowledge usually at negligible marginal cost. Other studies put emphasis on the purely technical side of technological progress that changes the structure of production and, consequently, the consumption side (Joyce et al., 2019). The effects of technological progress on both supply and demand sides of the economy are rather direct and immediate, while changes in ways of doing business and trading patterns (Rodríguez-Crespo & Martínez-Zarzoso, 2019), education and skills (Livingstone, 2012), labour markets and labour force (Falk & Biagi, 2017), people's economic engagement, or—more broadly—productivity shifts or poverty alleviation seem to be more hidden, indirect, and unveiled in a long-term perspective. Theoretical and empirical academic contributions highlight different positive effects that digital technologies may generate, contributing to the general welfare of individuals, companies, businesses, and whole societies by offering them new opportunities in education and skills improvements, setting up a new business, or improving those already existing and arising from gradually increasing the use of ICT worldwide. Starting from contributing works of, for example, Abramovitz (1986), Dosi et al. (1988), Freeman and Soete (1990), Fagerberg (1994, 1995), and Fagerberg et al. (1994) to more recent evidence like, for instance, works of Bilan et al. (2019), Loh and Chib (2019), Tchamyou et al. (2019), Adam (2020), Ali et al. (2020), Nair et al. (2020) or Vu et al. (2020), massive literature documents both conceptual frameworks and empirical evidence regarding ICT impact on social and economic development.

Moreover, various types of social and economic networks that emerge due to digital technologies deployment (Castells & Cardoso, 2006) generate economic advantages like, for instance, the economics of scale (Economides, 1996), which are closely related to the network effects, the "domino effects," and the network externalities (Katz & Shapiro, 1985), also labelled the "bandwagon effect" (Katz & Shapiro, 1994) that generate benefits for both sides of the market due to growing number of users, consumers, and adopters of certain technologies. The latter strengthens the process of, for example, high-tech solutions growing adoption and usage across heterogeneous societies, which undoubtedly is closely associated with specific behaviour by consumers, permanent status, and benefits-seeking in connection with the acquisition of technological novelties (Kaur et al., 2017; Lechman, 2017), shifts in consumption modes and patterns, strengthening the demonstration effects especially when modern and high-tech brands are considered. If positive externalities are triggered, the process of high-tech brands' (TechBrands) global recognition accelerates, which usually generates disorder in well-established business systems.

1.3. Technology brands (TechBrands)

Brands are defined as unique, usually legally protected symbols called a logo: a symbol, name, graphic, or sound design that identifies one seller's good or service as distinct from those of other sellers (AMA, 2020). The legally protected brand name is called a trademark, while a trademark as a symbol does not create value. The ability to generate value and revenue by the brand is determined by the brand's equity interpreted as the impressions, associations, attitudes, beliefs, and values in an ideological sense created in the minds of consumers and related to an individual trademark (Aaker, 1996; Keller, 2003). The particular brand's equity, in combination with a specific market situation, determines the financial value of a brand and, as a result, of the company that owns it (Aaker, 1991, 1996). Simplifying, brand value is a full result of brand strategy in the given period in the sector forecasts context. It is an objective measure of efficiency and effectiveness of all organisation market efforts to win customers' attention and preference above competitors in particular market conditions. Therefore, brand value is an objective financial representation of brand equity according to the adopted valuation method, from the company perception, the brand asset value is the essence of creating, owning, and investing in the brand equity (incurring expenditures) in order to generate further revenue. Therefore, the interest of the business in assessment of the brand value is its growth. Brand value is an indicator of the whole organisation's marketing activities efficacy, and it is the key challenge for brand managers nowadays. Brand value can be used as a brand management metric, and a supportive indicator for market decision-making for management.

So, the brand enables individuals and organisations to generate future revenues, which often makes them the most valuable asset on the company's balance sheets (Barwise et al., 1990; Simon & Sullivan, 1993). Brand as an asset may also be the subject of a sale or purchase transaction. It is subject to valuation similar to other intangible and legal assets and it is considered to be the most valuable intangible assets of companies (Barwise, 1993; Barwise et al., 1989, 1990).

Also, we found relevant literature linking economic geography and brand management, which supports the fact that intangibles being—to a large extent—the "effect" of digital innovations and solutions, such as brands, can strongly influence economic growth (Pike, 2009, 2011, 2015; Kucharska et al., 2018). Moreover, for economies like, for example, the US, South Korea, and Japan, electronics and software engendering images of their counties are causally linked with the pictures of key sectors existing in these countries (Ferilli et al., 2016). Moreover, Schoenfelder and Harris (2004) noted that digital technologies and high-tech sectors regularly deliver innovative tools for both corporations' and individuals' growth. Therefore, high-tech corporate branding coexists with high-tech national, local, or personal branding. In the recent decade, the network economy has changed and continues to change how value is perceived, produced, and monetised, primarily through brand models of value creation. Social media and, specifically, online brand communities (Kucharska, 2019) significantly contribute to, for example, the new business models.

Technological brands achieve spectacular results in the global market (Brand Finance, 2020). So, what is the contribution of high-tech brands in the development of economies, given their significant contribution to the development of companies (Barwise, 1993; Barwise et al., 1989, 1990)? This contribution can be defined and considered in direct financial terms, but also in indirect terms through the contribution to the improvement of the quality of life. In the case of public figures and celebrities, the opportunities for social impact can be truly profound. Especially, in a networked economy, not only enterprises but also individuals are value producers.

Knowledge workers, that is, key producers of intangible assets, have transformed the importance of the role of an employee for a corporation and its environment. And it does not surprise at all that such famous knowledge workers as, for example, Steve Jobs, Bill Gates, Richard Branson, Larry Page, Sergey Brin, Jeff Bezos, or Mark Zuckerberg are the most recognised human brands aroused thanks to their contribution to such global technological giants as Apple, Facebook, Microsoft, Google, Amazon, or Virgin. It all together creates a fascinating perspective for studies about technological brands as a source of global wealth today, following the idea of Stewart (1997), who stressed that intangible assets driven by intellectual capital are a source of wealth. Therefore, both human brands and companies' owned technological brands are worth to be more-in-depth investigated in the context of their contribution to economies and societies today. Stakeholders are interested in continually increasing the value of their brands. The key to this is constantly delivering new values to the market and continuously looking for a new way of monetising it. Sustainable business models based on technology are at the centre of attention not only of high-tech brands but also of all brands that perceive technology adaptation as an opportunity to grow. The global and information-rich environment that digital technologies create constituted an ideal enabler for high-tech brands' creation, value, global visibility, and recognition growth.

The technology sector drives the top 500 brand value annual ranking powered by Brand Finance in 2020 and 2021. Accounting for 14% of total brand value in the 2021 ranking, TechBrands remains the most valuable sector representation in the Brand Finance Global 500 (Branddirectory, 2021–2018b), with 47 brands represented and a combined brand value of US$998.9 billion. In 2020, it was also 14% of the top 500, represented by 46 brands and valued at US$986.5 billion. The expanded Tech 100 Best Global Brands Annual Report (Branddirectory, 2021–2018a) includes such TechBrands giants as Apple, Amazon, Google, Microsoft, Samsung, Facebook, WeChat, Tencent, YouTube, Huawei, Taobao, Oracle, SAP, and others from such sectors as electronics

26.8%, software 20.9%, electronic retail 18.7%, media and games 17.7%, and others 15.9%. All these sectors, in recent years, epitomised by everywhere observed global lockdowns (COVID-19 pandemic), support a new standard of working/learning/shopping/entertaining from home. Virtuality became the new reality thanks to the unprecedented reliance intensity of the digital human interactions environment: digital chatting, working, learning, communicating, shopping, and entertaining. So, technology's contribution to human life is higher than ever before. All human activities are supported by technological solutions delivered by technological giants. Therefore, the observed growing trend of the TECH brand's value will probably be continued, successfully leveraging technological innovations in all areas where technology affects the quality of human life. So, there is a huge chance that the TECH brand's contribution to the economic growth of their countries of origin will also constantly increase thanks to delivering new, innovative solutions leveraging conditions of societies and economies worldwide. Therefore, it is easy to assume in light of the previous paragraph that technology brands have a strong influence on the economies, and everything indicates that this trend will instead be continued.

Best global brands contribute to a condition of economies of their countries of origin (Flisikowski & Kucharska, 2018; Gupta et al., 2020; Kucharska et al., 2018; Ökten et al., 2019). Top global brands positively influence not only economic growth but also promote a positive image of their countries of origin (Ferilli et al., 2016), and regions or cities (Pike, 2011; Cleveland et al., 2011; Scarborough & Crabbe, 2021). Following Lechman (2015, 2018), who proved that technology drives economic growth, technology brands (TechBrands) seem in this context to be a fascinating object of studies as a potential source of economic wealth in the current more and more networked economy. Network as a dominated structure of markets organisation is strongly supported by technology. In the networked reality, TechBrands position is dominated in the global rankings of top brands (Brand Finance, 2022; Interbrand, 2021; BrandZ, 2021). The relation between TechBrands and technology is even more fascinating if taken into account that the ability of value creation today strongly depends on intellectual capital (Li et al., 2021). So, both technology (Mahmood & Mubarik, 2020) and brands development (Mohammad Shafiee, 2021; Liu & Jiang, 2020) are driven by intellectual capital. Therefore, linking economic geography and brand management, it is the fact that intangibles being—to a large extent—the "effect" of digital innovations and solutions, such as brands, can strongly influence economic growth (Pike, 2009, 2015; Kucharska et al., 2018). Moreover, for economies like, for example, the US, South Korea, and Japan, electronics and software engendering images of their counties are causally linked with the pictures of key sectors existing in these countries (Ferilli et al., 2016). Moreover, Schoenfelder and Harris (2004) noted that digital technologies and high-tech sectors regularly deliver innovative tools for both corporations' and individuals' growth. Therefore, high-tech corporate branding coexists with high-tech national, local, or personal branding. In the recent decade, the network economy has changed and continues to change how value is perceived, produced, and monetised, primarily through brand models of value creation. Social media and, specifically, online brand communities (Kucharska, 2019) significantly contribute to, for example, the new business models. Online communities can offer tangible and intangible values to businesses. The first ones are primarily financial and relate to the sales of products and services. The latter may include positive word-of-mouth, creating more effective market segments, increasing website traffic, providing better product support and service delivery, or co-creating brand production thanks to strong bonding with users' personal brands (Confente & Kucharska, 2021; Kucharska, 2022). The profound connections between the positive and negative effects of exponentially growing digital technologies on emerging network economies and societies are unquestionable. Therefore, high-tech brands' rapid growth and impact on the networked world are observed; they unleash the full potential of digitally-led economies and network societies. This strong relationship between digital technologies and high-tech brands is bi-directional. On the one hand, high-tech brands are an exquisite demonstration of the unique power and opportunities that digital technologies brought to economies and societies, while on the other, unique economic and social networks that emerged due to digital technologies promote high-tech brands globally, enforcing their value growth and increasing visibility.

1.4. Summary of conceptualisation

Summing up all the above, brand is one of the most valuable intellectual assets of a company and is also a vital asset for the economies of their country of origin. The core point of any brand value creation is brand equity. Brand equity factors result directly from the cumulated intellectual capital of the parent company (brand owner). Brand authenticity and trust are other proprietary assets and brand associations components of brand equity essential for TechBrands value growth. Besides, the embedded TechBrands' constant and innovative contribution to human life, brand authenticity, brand associations, and other proprietary assets are created thanks to the cumulated, organisational intellectual capital (Kucharska, 2022; Ujwary-Gil, 2019). Since brand equity is a proxy for brand value, brand equity is created thanks to the cumulated intellectual capital. Therefore, cumulated organisational intellectual capital can be perceived as a strong brand value predictor. Similarly, cumulated national intellectual capital is perceived as a GDP proxy. So, it does not surprise that in the centre of discussion today are technological (high-tech) brands with remarkable meaning in the networked, digitally-led economy. The "network economy" based on knowledge has significantly contributed to economic growth in recent years (Malik et al., 2014). According to the World Bank estimates (Hamilton et al., 2005), intangible capital constitutes approximately 78% of the world's wealth. In developing countries, intangible capital accounts for 59% of assets, while in OECD countries, it is around 80%. Intangible assets are the basis of the "new economy" (De, 2014; Crouzet & Eberly, 2018). In such a context, the perception of TechBrands as a facilitator of enormous value of technology's contribution to human life quality, the financial conditions of these brands owners, as well as the entire economies inspire such interesting further themes as

- channels of digital technologies impact global high-tech industries,
- role of digital technologies in creating and promoting high-tech brands,
- identifying network intensities in creating global exposure of high-tech brands,
- case-based evidence on digital technologies versus high-tech brands,
- high-tech brands and sustainable digital business models creation,
- the interrelationship between corporate TechBrands and employee brands (CEOs and knowledge workers).

The proposed topics create an exciting perspective for further studies and discussion about the place of technology brands in modern and technology-driven economies and societies' running modes—both in economic and managerial terms.

References

Aaker, D. A. (1991). *Managing brand equity*. Free Press.

Aaker, D. A. (1996). *Building strong brands*. Free Press.

Abramovitz, M. (1986). Catching up, forging ahead, and falling behind. *Journal of Economic History*, 385–406.

Adam, I. O. (2020). ICT development, E-government development and economic development: Does institutional quality matter? *Information Technologies & International Development, 16*, 19.

Ali, M. A., Alam, K., Taylor, B., & Rafiq, S. (2020). Does ICT maturity catalyse economic development? Evidence from a panel data estimation approach in OECD countries. *Economic Analysis and Policy*. https://doi.org/10.1016/j.eap.2020.09.003

AMA. (2020). *Brand—definition*. Retrieved July 22, 2020, from www.ama.org/topics/branding/

Barwise, P. (1993). Brand equity: Snark or boojum? *International Journal of Research in Marketing, 10*(1), 93–104.

Barwise, P., Higson, C., Likierman, A., & Marsh, P. (1989). *Accounting for brands*. London Business School and The Institute of Chartered Accountants in England and Wales.

Barwise, P., Higson, C., Likierman, A., & Marsh, P. (1990). Brands as "separable assets". *Business Strategy Review, 1*(2), 43–59.

Beniger, J. (2009). *The control revolution: Technological and economic origins of the information society*. Harvard University Press.

Bilan, Y., Mishchuk, H., Samoliuk, N., & Grishnova, O. (2019). ICT and economic growth: Links and possibilities of engaging. *Intellectual Economics, 13*(1), 93–104.

Branddirectory. (2021–2018a). *Tech100 best global brands ranking*. Retrieved June 3, 2021, from http://brandirectory.com

Branddirectory. (2021–2018b). *The most 500 valuable global brands ranking*. Retrieved June 3, 2021, from http://brandirectory.com

Brand Finance. (2020). *Global 500, 2020.* Retrieved July 20, 2020, from https://brandfinance.com/images/upload/brand_finance_global_500_2020_preview.pdf

Brand Finance. (2022). *Global 500 2022: The annual report on the world's most valuable and strongest brands.* Retrieved January 30, 2022, from https://brandirectory.com/rankings/global

BrandZ. (2021). *Kantar BrandZ most valuable global brands 2021.* Retrieved January 30, 2022, from www.kantar.com/campaigns/brandz-downloads/kantar-brandz-most-valuable-global-brands-2021

Bresnahan, T. (2010). General purpose technologies. *Handbook of the Economics of Innovation, 2*, 761–791.

Buckland, M. (2017). *Information and society*. MIT Press.

Castells, M. (2000). Toward a sociology of the network society. *Contemporary Sociology, 29*(5), 693–699.

Castells, M. (2011). *The rise of the network society* (Vol. 12). John Wiley & Sons.

Castells, M., & Cardoso, G. (Eds.). (2006). *The network society: From knowledge to policy* (pp. 3–23). Johns Hopkins Center for Transatlantic Relations.

Cleveland, M., Papadopoulos, N., & Laroche, M. (2011). Identity, demographics, and consumer behaviors: International market segmentation across product categories. *International Marketing Review, 28*(3), 244–266.

Coccia, M. (2017). Sources of technological innovation: Radical and incremental innovation problem-driven to support competitive advantage of firms. *Technology Analysis & Strategic Management, 29*(9), 1048–1061.

Confente, I., & Kucharska, W. (2021). Company versus consumer performance: Does brand community identification foster brand loyalty and the consumer's personal brand? *Journal of Brand Management, 28*(1), 8–31.

Crouzet, N., & Eberly, J. (2018). *Understanding weak capital investment: The role of market concentration and intangibles.* Jackson Hole Symposium. Retrieved July 20, 2020, from www.kansascityfed.org/~/media/files/publicat/sympos/2018/papersandhandouts/824180816crouzeteberlyhandout.pdf?la=en

De, S. (2014). Intangible capital and growth in the "new economy": Implications of a multi-sector endogenous growth model. *Structural Change and Economic Dynamics, 28*. http://dx.doi.org/10.1016/j.strueco.2013.11.003

Dosi, G., Freeman, C., Nelson, R., Silverberg, G., & Soete, L. (1988). *Technical change and economic theory*. Laboratory of Economics and Management (LEM), Sant'Anna School of Advanced Studies.

Economides, N. (1996). The economics of networks. *International Journal of Industrial Organization, 14*(6), 673–699.

Fagerberg, J. (1994). Technology and international differences in growth rates. *Journal of Economic Literature, 32*(3), 1147–1175.

Fagerberg, J. (1995). Convergence or divergence? The impact of technology on "why growth rates differ". *Journal of Evolutionary Economics, 5*(3), 269–284.

Fagerberg, J., Verspagen, B., & von Tunzelmann, G. N. (1994). *The dynamics of technology, trade and growth*. Edward Elgar Publishing.

Falk, M., & Biagi, F. (2017). Relative demand for highly skilled workers and use of different ICT technologies. *Applied Economics, 49*(9), 903–914.

Ferilli, G., Sacco, P. L., Teti, E., & Buscema, M. (2016). Top corporate brands and the global structure of country brand positioning: An AutoCMANN approach. *Expert Systems with Applications, 66*, 62–75.

Flisikowski, K., & Kucharska, W. (2018). The condition of economies: Do most valuable global brands matter? *Equilibrium Quarterly Journal of Economics and Economic Policy, 13*(2), 251–264.

Freeman, C., & Soete, L. (1990). Information technology, and the global economy. In *The information society: Evolving landscapes* (pp. 278–294). Springer.

Gilbert, R. J. (2020). *Innovation matters: Competition policy for the high-technology economy*. MIT Press.

Graham, M. (Ed.). (2019). *Digital economies at global margins*. MIT Press.

Graham, M., & Dutton, W. H. (Eds.). (2019). *Society and the internet: How networks of information and communication are changing our lives*. Oxford University Press.

Gupta, S., Gallearb, D., Ruddc, J., & Foroudid, P. (2020). The impact of brand value on brand competitiveness. *Journal of Business Research, 12*, 210–222.

Hamilton, K., Ruta, G., Bolt, K., Markandya, A., Pedroso-Galinato, S., Silva, P., Ordoubadi, M. S., Lange, G. M., & Tajibaeva, L. (2005). *Where is the wealth of nations?: Measuring capital for the 21st century*. The World Bank.

Interbrand. (2021). *Best global brands 2021*. Retrieved January 30, 2022, from https://interbrand.com/best-brands/

Johansson, B., Karlsson, C., & Westin, L. (Eds.). (2012). *Patterns of a network economy*. Springer Science & Business Media.

Joyce, P. J., Finnveden, G., Håkansson, C., & Wood, R. (2019). A multi-impact analysis of changing ICT consumption patterns for Sweden and the EU: Indirect rebound effects and evidence of decoupling. *Journal of Cleaner Production, 211*, 1154–1161.

Katz, M. L., & Shapiro, C. (1985). Network externalities, competition, and compatibility. *The American Economic Review, 75*(3), 424–440.

Katz, M. L., & Shapiro, C. (1994). Systems competition and network effects. *Journal of Economic Perspectives, 8*(2), 93–115.

Kaur, H., Lechman, E., & Marszk, A. (2017). *Catalyzing development through ICT adoption*. Springer.

Keller, K. L. (2003). *Strategic brand management: Building, measuring, and managing brand equity*. Prentice Hall.

Kucharska, W. (2019). Online brand communities' contribution to digital business models social drivers and mediators. *Journal of Research in Interactive Marketing, 13*(4), 437–463.

Kucharska, W. (2022). *Personal branding in the knowledge economy: The inter-relationship between corporate and employee brands*. Routledge.

Kucharska, W., Flisikowski, K., & Confente, I. (2018). Do global brands contribute to the economy of their country of origin? A dynamic spatial approach. *Journal of Product and Brand Management, 27*(7), 768–780.

Lechman, E. (2015). *ICT diffusion in developing countries*. Springer.

Lechman, E. (2017). *The diffusion of information and communication technologies*. Routledge.

Lechman, E. (2018). Networks externalities as social phenomenon in the process ICT diffusion. *Economics and Sociology, 11*(1), 22–43. https://doi.org/10.14254/2071-789X.2018/11-1/2

Li, X., Nosheen, S., Ul Haq, N., & Gao, X. (2021). Value creation during fourth industrial revolution: Use of intellectual capital by most innovative companies of the world. *Technological Forecasting & Social Change, 163*, 120479.

Liu, C. H., & Jiang, J. F. (2020). Assessing the moderating roles of brand equity, intellectual capital and social capital in Chinese luxury hotels. *Journal of Hospitality and Tourism Management, 43*, 139–148.

Livingstone, S. (2012). Critical reflections on the benefits of ICT in education. *Oxford Review of Education, 38*(1), 9–24.

Loh, Y. A. C., & Chib, A. (2019). Tackling social inequality in development: Beyond access to appropriation of ICTs for employability. *Information Technology for Development, 25*(3), 532–551.

Lyon, D. (2013). *The information society: Issues and illusions.* John Wiley & Sons.

Mahmood, T., & Mubarik, M. S. (2020). Balancing innovation and exploitation in the fourth industrial revolution: Role of intellectual capital and technology absorptive capacity. *Technological Forecasting & Social Change, 160,* 120248.

Malik, K. Z., Ali, S. Z., & Khalid, A. M. (2014). Intangible capital in a real business cycle model. *Economic Modelling, 39.* http://dx.doi.org/10.1016/j.econmod.2014.02.018

Martin, W. J. (2017). *The global information society.* Taylor & Francis.

Mohammad Shafiee, M. (2021). Competitive advantage via intellectual capital: A moderated mediation analysis. *Journal of Intellectual Capital.* https://doi.org/10.1108/JIC-05-2020-0152

Mossberger, K., Tolbert, C. J., & McNeal, R. S. (2007). *Digital citizenship: The internet, society, and participation.* MIT Press.

Nair, M., Pradhan, R. P., & Arvin, M. B. (2020). Endogenous dynamics between R&D, ICT and economic growth: Empirical evidence from the OECD countries. *Technology in Society, 62,* 101315.

Ökten, Z., Okan, E. Y., Arslan, Ü., & Güngör, M. Ö. (2019). The effect of brand value on economic growth: A multinational analysis. *European Research on Management and Business Economics, 25,* 1–7.

Pike, A. (2009). Brand and branding geographies. *Geography Compass, 3*(1), 190–213.

Pike, A. (2011). *Brands and branding geographies.* Edward Elgar Publishing.

Pike, A. (2015). *Origination: The geographies of brands and branding.* John Wiley and Sons.

Powell, W. (2003). Neither market nor hierarchy. *The Sociology of Organizations: Classic, Contemporary, and Critical Readings, 315,* 104–117.

Rodríguez-Crespo, E., & Martínez-Zarzoso, I. (2019). The effect of ICT on trade: Does product complexity matter? *Telematics and Informatics, 41,* 182–196.

Rosenberg, N., & Trajtenberg, M. (2004). A general-purpose technology at work: The Corliss steam engine in the late-nineteenth-century United States. *The Journal of Economic History, 64*(1), 61–99.

Sahal, D. (1981). *Patterns of technological innovation.* Addison-Wesley.

Scarborough, W., & Crabbe, R. (2021). Place brands across US cities and growth in local high-technology sectors. *Journal of Business Research, 130,* 70–85.

Schoenfelder, J., & Harris, P. (2004). High-tech corporate branding: Lessons for market research in the next decade. *Qualitative Market Research,* 7(2), 91–99.

Shapiro, C., Carl, S., & Varian, H. R. (1998). *Information rules: A strategic guide to the network economy.* Harvard Business Press.

Simon, C. J., & Sullivan M. W. (1993). The measurement and determinants of brand equity: A financial approach. *Marketing Science, 12,* 28–52.

Stewart, T. A. (1997). *Intellectual capital: The new wealth of organizations.* Doubleday/Currency.

Stiroh, K. J. (2002). Are ICT spillovers driving the new economy? *Review of Income and Wealth, 48*(1), 33–57.

Tapscott, D. (1999). *Creating value in the network economy.* Harvard Business Review Book.

Tchamyou, V. S., Erreygers, G., & Cassimon, D. (2019). Inequality, ICT and financial access in Africa. *Technological Forecasting and Social Change, 139,* 169–184.

Ujwary-Gil, A. (2019). *Organizational network analysis*. Routledge.
Van Dijk, J. (2020). *The network society*. Sage Publications Limited.
Vu, K., Hanafizadeh, P., & Bohlin, E. (2020). ICT as a driver of economic growth: A survey of the literature and directions for future research. *Telecommunications Policy*, *44*(2), 101922.

2 The history of technology brand emergence

Hasret Balcioglu

2.1. Introduction

It is known that "information technology (IT)" is the use of any computer, storage, network, infrastructure, and process to create, store, protect, and exchange all forms of electronic data. It builds communication networks for a business, creates and administers databases, protects data and information, and helps employees solve problems with their computers/mobile devices to enable efficiency and information security of the company. Some examples of types of information technology are telephone and radio equipment; personal computers; video conferencing equipment; performance management software for managing goal setting and performance appraisal; and content management software for blogging and collaboration.

Today, with the rapid development of information technology, the economy is undergoing fundamental changes (Lechman & Anacka, 2022; Kaur et al., 2017). The development of informatics and its products based on Internet technology provides opportunities for the application of information technology in the business environment of the new economy or the digital economy era. Therefore, the digital economy has an important positive impact on business transformation and the creation of new digital businesses, especially small- and medium-sized enterprises. To remain competitive in the market over the past 10–15 years, companies should improve business processes and develop new methods to provide products and services to consumers.

Information technology is more and more important because it enables the development of communication in remote areas, a widespread and simple education system, public engagement in governing and policymaking, the spread of e-governance facilities, and fast economic development (Lechman, 2015).

Companies invest in innovation to build knowledge and thereby increase competitive advantage (Kucharska, 2022). The technology development process is the directional process of developing new knowledge, skills, and artefacts, which in turn promotes platform development (Halman et al., 2003; Kucharska, 2019), which is a leader in product/process development (Högman & Johannesson, 2013). By definition, the technical results of this process are new, different, and unpredictable (Ajamian & Koen, 2002; Eldred &

DOI: 10.4324/9781003184638-3

McGrath, 1997). Opportunity-driven and idea-driven processes are the sources of all innovations and make great contributions to potential (Goffin & Mitchell, 2016); however, not all innovations can be achieved, and a structured technology development process is usually required to determine the best of them and the future steps (Cooper et al., 2001; Cooper & Mills, 2005).

Bearing in mind the strong interdependence between brands, especially technology brands' values and the GDP of their origin countries (Kucharska et al., 2018; Flisikowski & Kucharska, 2018). To better understand and realise the emergence and origin of technology brands, this chapter adopts historical methods to explore them. The application of the historical method in this chapter looks at technology brands by answering the following questions: a. How did the biggest tech giants emerge and choose to present themselves to customers? b. What methods will help keep them on the market?

A literature review section will follow the introduction and then a section mentioning some of the significant technology brands such as AT&T, International Business Machines Corporation (IBM), General Electric, Xerox, Hewlett-Packard, Intel, Microsoft, Apple, Google, and Facebook will be presented in the study. After explaining the dynamics from the perspective of technology brands, conclusions and recommendations will be the last section of this chapter.

2.2. Literature review

Branding and the branding process are as old as the civilisation of human beings. The term brand is derived from the word "brand" which means "to burn" and originates from the ancient North Scandinavian language (Khan & Mufti, 2007). Centuries ago, there was certain symbols/drawings representative of the animals where the trade/sale of the animals has taken place. International trade has spread since the 14th century and many forms of branding have been created/developed for products, services, placemarks, etc. In 2012, Yang et al. pointed out that the brand had similar definitions with the mark, but the similar meaning was on the surface, as the mark has been used in the date that goes back to 5000 BC and the birth of the brand was much later.

Innovation is a hybrid concept that evolves and adapts to changing conditions (Fagerberg et al., 2006). It plays an important role in the growth and economic competitiveness of companies, industries, and countries (Gardiner, 2010). The definition of innovation varies from environment to environment, but it can be defined as the introduction of new things, ideas, or ways of doing something (Venuvinod, 2010). Over time, the understanding of innovation has continued to develop and has been recognised by Joseph Schumpeter. He believes that innovation is the introduction of a good product and a new production method for a specific industry branch. The innovation is seen also as an opening of new markets, the use of new sources of supply, or new forms of competition (Schumpeter, 1934). Innovation can also be defined as the improvement of technology and better ways or methods of doing things, or the application of new ideas to the company, regardless of whether the new ideas are reflected in the products, processes, or services (Grant, 2012). Fagerberg et al. (2006) believe that the function of innovation is to introduce novelty into the economic field, which is essential for long-term economic growth.

The term information technology first appeared in an article published by Harold J. Leavitt and Thomas L. Whisler in 1958 in the "Harvard Business Review." The author interprets this term as "the new technology does not yet have an established name. We should call it information technology (IT)."

The first message was invented by Guglielmo Marconi in 1894 and was the first radio developed. This invention led to great advances in the field of information technology. The first large-scale automatic digital computer used in the United States was the Mark 1 created by Harvard University in the 1940s.

The Internet originated in the 1970s (Kim, 2005). For more than a decade, it was only known to university researchers. The creation of the World Wide Web in the 1990s has transformed the Internet into an accessible information-sharing tool. At the beginning of the 21st century, companies have adopted the World Wide Web as a means of communication and sales. Since 2010, the fastest growth has been the adoption of cloud computing.

2.3. Emergence of technology brands

American Telephone and Telegraph Co. (AT&T), est. 1885

AT&T has begun to merge several companies to control Alexander Graham Bell's patent rights. It played an important guiding role in the development of the telephone and telegraph. AT&T created a new department called Bell Telephone Laboratories in 1925 (Peck & Scherer, 1962). The R&D unit has achieved success in transistors, photovoltaic cells, radio astronomy, Unix operating systems, and C programming language. In the 1940s, AT&T invented the transistor, laying the foundation for cellular phones and achieving broadband transmission for the first time. The company has been positioned as a natural monopolist of local telephone services in the United States for many years. In 1956, this monopoly position was eroded for the first time. Hush-A-Phone v. United States ruled to allow third-party devices to be connected to lease phones owned by AT&T. In 1968, Carterfone decided to connect third-party devices to the AT&T telephone network. With the influence of cheap microwave communication equipment, new competitors began entering the market in the 1970s. Microwave Communications, Inc. has positioned itself in a market that sells communication services to large enterprises. AT&T's monopoly continued for another 15 years, until the fibre optic revolution began, which was considered the end of microwave-based long-distance telephony.

AT&T had monopoly power in the market until the antitrust regulator agreed to allow AT&T to retain Western Electric and to enter the general industry to manufacture computers and to sell them in exchange for its proposal to split the Bell system. In 1982, this method was successful because it deprived Bell operating companies (such as Bell Telephone Company in Illinois) of ownership. In 1991, AT&T decided not to provide telegram services (web.archive.org/). In 2005, one of the regional Bell operating companies acquired AT&T, and the combined company was renamed AT&T.

Randall Stephenson (new chairman and CEO) once stated that wireless services were at the core of "The New AT&T" in 2007 (Johnson, 2007). AT&T has launched various new media such as Video Share and U-verse. These new media enable the reach of high-speed Internet to rural areas across the country. With this introduction, sales of traditional home phone lines have fallen. AT&T acquired Interwise, which is a leading global provider of network, video conferencing, and voice services for enterprises. In the next few months of 2007, AT&T purchased 12 MHz of the 700 MHz main frequency band from Aloha Partners (Antonio, 2008). In 2008, AT&T bought Edge Wireless. In 2013, AT&T got Cricket to provide customers with more mobile Internet services. The company acquired Lusacell and Nextel Mexico in 2015. In 2015, the company purchased DIRECTV and became the world's largest pay-TV provider.

As a concluding remark, AT&T provides the most advanced and efficient telecommunications in the United States. Up to this time, the company achieved great success in providing many major technological advancements for telephone services, switching systems, and signal transmission. The company installed an early warning radar system and created the Telstar satellite communication system for the US Department of Defense.

International Business Machines (IBM), est. 1888

As we all know, IBM entered the market as an international time recording company and made major innovations in computing, especially in the 1960s. In 1911 and 1924, the company diversified its business and acted as a calculation-tabulation-recording company and an international business machine company. IBM invented floppy disks, automated teller machines (ATM), hard drives, magnetic stripe cards, relational databases, SQL programming languages, UPC bar codes, and dynamic random access memory (DRAM). In the 1960s and 1970s, the IBM mainframe was the main computing platform. For example, System/360. IBM personal computer was the first computer in the IBM PC model series, which was introduced to the market in 1981 (Pollack, 1981). With this computer, IBM has transformed its business operations into a more valuable and profitable one. The company has switched from spin-off printer manufacturer Lexmark in 1991. In 2002, IBM acquired companies such as PwC Consulting. In the following years, the company began selling personal computers and switched from an x86-based server business to Lenovo in 2005 and 2014, respectively. IBM purchased SPSS (2009), the Weather Company (2016), and Red Hat (2019). In 2015, IBM continued its fabless manufacturing, and in 2020, the company has turned into a by-product of the managed infrastructure services division of its global technical services division. It can be summarised as IBM's production and sales of computer hardware, middleware, and software. IBM is also a major research organisation. As of 2020, it has the most annual US patents generated by companies.

General Electric (GE), est. 1890

In the late 19th century, Thomas Edison found himself in control of more than one company. They are Edison Lamp Company, Edison Machinery Plant, and Edison Electric Light Company. Then, he decided to merge them into General Electric. General Electric created television technology and aircraft turbochargers. In the 1960s, the company has been a leader in computing. In 2000, GE's revenue was close to 130 billion US dollars. The company had worked as an electrical appliance manufacturer, a lender, a media giant (with NBC Universal), and a healthcare provider. The company has core businesses such as aviation, power and renewable energy, additives, capital, and digital. GE's crown jewel was negatively affected by the 2008 financial crisis and has not returned to normal since then. GE is recognised as one of the largest jet engine manufacturers in the world. Jet engines are used in commercial and military aircraft. The company produces GEnx for the Boeing 787 Dreamliner and Boeing 747-8. GE also manufactures GE90 for Boeing 777 and CF6. These powerful engines are used in Airbus and Boeing flights. The company produces one-third of the world's electricity by using natural gas power plants, steam, nuclear power, and grid services.

GE Renewable Energy utilises onshore and offshore wind and hydropower technologies as well as concentrated solar power generation. The company's digital department was established in 2015. The digital department included the company's software centre, GE's IT, business software team, and the technology of the network security company "Wurldtech." In 2016, GE invested heavily in additive manufacturing, such as 3D printers. GE sold its biopharmaceutical business in 2018. Currently, the company's product lines include motors, aircraft engines, energy, finance, medical care, wind turbines, and software.

Xerox, est. 1906

Xerox, in its initial form, was the Haloid Photographic Company that has been producing photographic paper. The company had changed its name from "Haloid Xerox" to "Xerox" in the 1950s. In 1947, the firm has got the commercial rights for the electrophotography invented by Chester Carlson. The company has introduced the 914 xerographic copiers to the market in 1959. During the 1960s, Xerox opened branches in Europe, Mexico, and Australia. It also joined with Fujifilm in Japan to locate the product lines in the Asian market.

In the 1970s and 1980s, Xerox has invented the graphical user interface, the mouse, and the Internet. The company has developed word-processing machines in 1974, laser printers in 1977, and Ethernet in 1979, respectively. In

1985, Xerox sold its publishing firms. Digital photocopiers were new products in the 1990s. In 2006, the company got a patent for photosensitive erasable paper. Another successful investment occurred in 2007 when Xerox acquired Global Imaging Systems. In 2010, Xerox acquired Affiliated Computer Services (ACS) and outsourced business services. With this attempt, the focus of the company has been changed to services than products. In 2017, Xerox has formed an independent company. Xerox consumed the colour imaging and printing segment of Tektronix at the turn of the last century. Whenever the purchase has been done, Xerox has gained the second-highest market share in the USA for colour laser printers and has been the follower of Hewlett-Packard.

Currently, copiers, printers, digital print production press, the software, and systems support needed for the production of the document are the product lines of Xerox. It can be concluded that Xerox has located itself within the market with the strategy of developing and acquiring the necessary products for office technology without moving to sub-different product lines.

Hewlett-Packard, est. 1939

The company has been founded in the year of 1939. An audio oscillator was the first product of Hewlett-Packard (HP). In 1951, HP invented the 524A counter. The signal-measuring product has enabled the company to gain a huge revenue in the following years. HP established facilities in Switzerland and Germany in 1959 to become more international. HP invented a frequency synthesiser in 1963. It is used for deep-space vehicles. The atomic clock has been created the following year. In the 1960s, they engaged in the semiconductor game. HP introduced the HP 2116A to the computer market and invented light-emitting diodes (LEDs) in 1966. The company created a personal computer in 1968. Stanford graduates, William Hewlett and James Packard have extended their business by producing calculators, printers, scanners, and more since then. HP offered the world's first programmable pocket calculator to the market in 1974. In 1980, HP has created the HP-85, the first PC. The PC could communicate with other computers. The company has offered the HP-150 to the market in 1983, which has let the consumers reach the interface by touching the screen. The first HP LaserJet was manufactured in the year of 1984 and become the most popular laser printer in the world. In 1991, HP created HP DeskJet 500C, an affordable colour printer. The company manufactured the HP OfficeJet that could print, fax, and copy three years later. In 2001, HP launched Itanium architecture for enterprise servers and high-performance computing systems to improve computers from 32 to 64 bits. HP has developed an image-compression algorithm in 2004. The algorithm used by NASA for Spirit rover has high-resolution images of Mars. An image-compression algorithm developed by HP Labs was used by NASA to create high-resolution images of Mars transmitted by NASA's Spirit rover. The HP Photosmart Premium with TouchSmart Web was introduced by the company in the year of 2010. It was the first web-connected printer used globally. In 2012, HP has opened its doors to the first net-zero energy data centres. The data centre has used/uses solar energy and other renewable sources. It was a good example for other data centres to increase the quality of air and to protect the environment (Nandakumar, 2012). In 2014, HP announced that they would have two separate companies as personal computer and printer businesses. Six years after the introduction of HP Photosmart Premium, HP launched the first 3D printer HP Jet Fusion.

It can be shown that the company contributes to the market with the product line of computing (software and computer services).

Intel, est. 1968

In 1957, a group of engineers has founded "Fairchild Semiconductor." In 1968, Gordon Moore has, one of those engineers, established his own microprocessor company named Intel. Intel had a problem whenever it wanted to be integrated into the market. All of its products were inside the computer so the consumers could not observe/see the products. To find a solution to this problem, the company has agreed with PC producers to put a sticker with the logo of Intel to show that Intel's microprocessors were used. With this policy, Intel has achieved to be visible in the market in 1991 (Goodin, 1998). Memory chips were Intel's initial products. These chips have the world's first metal oxide semiconductor (1101). 1101 was not demanded very much but its sibling, 1103, a one-kilobit dynamic random access memory (DRAM) chip, has been successful in the market with the capacity of keeping an important amount of information. In 1970, the American technology company Honeywell Incorporated has consumed it. The main aim of the company is to replace the core memory technology in its computers. The advantages of DRAMs were being cheaper and using less power than core memory. They are quickly accepted in the computer world as standard memory devices. After this successful location in the market, Intel has been a public company in 1971. Intel offered the erasable programmable read-only memory (EPROM) chip to the market. This product has been the most demanded one among the products until 1985. In 1972, Intel opened its first international manufacturing facility in Malaysia, semiconductor plants in Singapore and Jerusalem in the early 1980s, and manufacturing centres in China, India, and Costa Rica in the 1990s (Intel, 2003).

In 1993, Intel introduced the Pentium microprocessor. The microprocessor was the first Intel chip for PCs to use parallel/superscalar processing. The higher performance Pentium machines have empowered PCs for applications of multimedia graphs such as games that needed more processing power. Intel was selling more than 10 million motherboards to PC makers, approximately 40% of the overall PC market in 1995. The Taiwan-based manufacturer ASUSTeK had produced more PC motherboards than Intel in the early 21st century. In 2005, Apple has decided to use Intel CPUs. The company has become the largest CPU supplier in the market in the early 21st century.

Microsoft, est. 1975

In 1972, Bill Gates and Paul Allen established a company named "Traf-O-Data." Their purpose was to utilise computers to analyse automobile traffic data. Then, they made microprocessor software called "Microsoft." They introduced Windows and Office into the market and became competitors to the company Apple in 1980. Microsoft released Microsoft Windows in 1985 as a graphical extension for MS-DOS and version OS/2 in 1987, respectively. In 1990, Microsoft introduced the Microsoft Office suite, which combined separate applications such as Microsoft Word and Microsoft Excel. In the same year, Microsoft released Windows 3.0 with smooth user interface graphics and enhanced protection mode feature for the Intel 386 processor.

In 1995, Microsoft began redefining its offerings and expanding its product line to computer networks and the World Wide Web. Except for a few start-ups like Netscape, Microsoft has been the only big and established company to move fast enough to be part of the World Wide Web. It achieved market dominance since other companies such as IBM, WordPerfect, Novell, Borland, and Lotus were much slower to adapt to the new situation.

In 1995, the company released Windows 95. This program included pre-emptive multitasking, an entirely new user interface with a new start button, and 32-bit compatibility. It provided the Win32 API. Windows 95 came with MSN, the online service that was originally intended to rival the Internet. Internet Explorer was excluded from retail Windows 95 boxes because the boxes were printed before the team finished the Web browser and was included in Windows 95 Plus instead. Microsoft and General Electric's NBC division, which expanded into new markets in 1996, created a new 24/7 cable news channel, MSNBC. Microsoft has launched Windows CE 1.0, a new operating system designed for devices with low memory and other limitations such as personal digital assistants, to the market. Various companies, including Microsoft, formed the Trusted Computing Platform Alliance in 1999 to improve security and to protect intellectual property by identifying changes in hardware and software. In 2001, Microsoft released Windows XP, which combined the mainstream and NT lines of the operating system under the NT codebase. The company launched the Xbox in the same year and entered the video game console market dominated by Sony and Nintendo. Increasingly involved in the hardware business after the Xbox, Microsoft launched its Zune line of digital media players in 2006, the successor to its previous software platform Portable Media Center. These attempts expanded on Microsoft's previous hardware commitments by following the original Microsoft Mouse of 1983. As of 2007, the company sold the best-selling wired keyboard, mouse, and desktop webcam in the United States. That year, the company also released the digital chart, which was later renamed PixelSense.

Vista, the next version of Windows, was released in January 2007, and focused on features, security, and a redesigned user interface called Aero. Azure Services Platform, the company's entry into the cloud computing market for

Windows, was released in 2008. In 2009, Microsoft announced its intention to open a chain of Microsoft-branded retail stores, and in 2009, the first retail Microsoft Store was opened in Scottsdale, Arizona. Windows 7 was also officially released to the public on the same day. The focus of Windows 7 was to improve Vista with ease-of-use features and performance improvements, rather than an extensive rework of Windows. As the smartphone industry boomed in the late 2000s, Microsoft struggled to keep up with its competitors in providing a modern smartphone operating system, falling behind Apple and Google-sponsored Android in the United States. As a result, in 2010, Microsoft replaced its ageing flagship mobile operating system, Windows Mobile, with the new Windows Phone operating system, which was released in October of that year. It used a new user interface design language code-named "Metro," which uses the notion of minimalism and distinctively simple shapes, typography, and iconography. Microsoft has implemented a new strategy for the software industry that provides a consistent user experience across all smartphones running the Windows Phone operating system.

Microsoft gradually rebranded its product line throughout 2011 and 2012 after it has launched Windows Phone. Then, the company's logos, products, services, and websites adopted the principles and concepts of the Metro design language. Microsoft introduced Windows 8, an operating system designed to power both personal and tablet computers, in Taipei in June 2011. In the following months, Microsoft acquired the social network Yammer. On 31 July, they launched the Outlook.com webmail service to compete with Gmail. On 4 September 2012, Microsoft released Windows Server 2012. To cope with the potential for increased demand for products and services, Microsoft has opened a series of "holiday stores" across the USA to complement the growing number of "real venue" Microsoft stores that opened in 2012. On 29 March 2013, Microsoft launched a Patent Tracker. On 25 April 2014, Microsoft acquired Nokia Devices and Services. This new subsidiary was renamed Microsoft Mobile. On 15 September 2014, Microsoft acquired Mojang, the video game development company known for Minecraft, for $2.5 billion. On 8 June 2017, Microsoft acquired Hexadite, an Israeli security firm, for $100 million. On 21 January 2015, Microsoft announced the release of their first Interactive whiteboard, Microsoft Surface Hub. Windows 10 was released on 29 July 2015. In September 2016, the market was introduced to Windows Server 2016. On 4 June 2018, Microsoft officially announced that it had acquired GitHub for $7.5 billion, a deal that expired on 26 October 2018. On 10 July 2018, Microsoft announced the Surface Goes platform to the public. Later in the month, it converted Microsoft Teams for free. In August 2018, Microsoft released two projects called Microsoft AccountGuard and Defending Democracy. It also announced Snapdragon 850 compatibility for Windows 10 on the ARM platform.

In August 2018, Toyota Tsusho started a partnership with Microsoft to build fish farming tools using the Microsoft Azure application suite for water management-related Internet of Things (IoT) technologies (Foley, 2018). Developed in part by researchers from Kindai University, water pump mechanisms use artificial intelligence to count the number of fish on a conveyor belt, analyse the number of fish, and infer the efficiency of water flow from the data provided by the fish. The specific computer programs used in the process included the Azure Machine Learning and Azure IoT Hub platforms. In September 2018, Microsoft discontinued producing Skype Classic programs. In November 2018, Microsoft agreed to supply 100,000 Microsoft HoloLens headsets to the US military to "increase lethality by improving the ability to detect, decide, and respond before the enemy." In December 2018, Microsoft announced Project Mu, an open-source version of the Unified Extensible Firmware Interface kernel used in Microsoft Surface and Hyper-V products. In the same month, Microsoft announced the open-source implementation of Windows Forms and the Windows Presentation Foundation (WPF), which will allow the company to move further towards the transparent publication of the core framework used in the development of Windows desktop applications and software.

On 20 February 2019, Microsoft Corp has launched its cyber security service AccountGuard in 12 new markets in Europe, including Germany, France, and Spain, to close security vulnerabilities and protect political customers from hacking.

On 26 March 2020, Microsoft announced that it had acquired Affirmed Networks. When the COVID-19 outbreak occurred, Microsoft closed all retail stores indefinitely due to health concerns. On 22 July 2020, Microsoft announced that it plans to shut down the Mixer service, with plans to migrate existing partners to Facebook Gaming. On 31 July 2020, Microsoft was reportedly in talks to acquire TikTok after the Trump administration ordered ByteDance to transfer the ownership of the application to the USA. On 3 August 2020, Microsoft acquired the application.

On 22 September 2020, Microsoft announced that OpenAI has an exclusive license to use the GPT-3 artificial intelligence language generator. On 10 November 2020, Microsoft released the Xbox Series X and Xbox Series S video game consoles.

On 9 March 2021, Microsoft completed the acquisition of ZeniMax Media and ZeniMax Media became part of Microsoft's Xbox Game Studios division.

In 2021, Microsoft's valuation approached $2 trillion, in part due to strong quarterly earnings spurred by the COVID-19 pandemic. The increasing requirement for remote work and distance education has increased the demand for cloud computing services and boosted the company's game sales. On 24 June 2021, Microsoft announced Windows 11 during a live stream. It can be concluded that a high-profile marketing campaign was the success of Microsoft. The company has followed the demands of the market and differentiated the products in the required way.

Apple, est. 1977

Apple was founded in 1976 by Steve Jobs, Steve Wozniak, and Ronald Wayne. The main idea is to develop and sell personal computers. Steve Jobs and

Steve Wozniak visited the Homebrew Computer Club and made the Apple I (Schlender & Tetzeli, 2016) in the same year. After the unexpected success of Apple I, Jobs considered a further investment to expand the product line of the business. The bank was not very active in lending him the necessary money, because, in that era, the idea of providing computers to ordinary people was not an ordinary method (Linzmayer, 2004). Markkula hired Michael Scott from National Semiconductor as the CEO of Apple Computer in 1977 (Isaacson, 2011). Wozniak resigned from HP to become a full-time employee at Apple. Apple II models used ordinary cassette tapes for storage.

In 1978, a 5 + 1/4-inch floppy disk drive and interface called Disk II replaced ordinary cassette tapes. In 1984, Apple was seen as the only alternative competitor to IBM. In 1993, after the total sales of the Apple II series reached 6 million units, it was decided not to produce it (Isaacson, 2011). Between 1988 and 1989, Apple acquired software companies Network Innovations, Styleware, Nashoba Systems, Coral Software, and satellite communications company Orion Network Systems (Julie, 1988). In 1991, Apple decided to cooperate with IBM and Motorola to form the AIM alliance. In 1993, Apple introduced a new product to the market, Newton, an early personal digital assistant (PDA). Apple launched eWorld in 1994 to replace AppleLink, which closed in 1996. In 1995, the company began to license Mac OS and Macintosh ROM to third-party manufacturers. Third-party manufacturers begin to produce Macintosh "clones." Apple launched the Apple Store in 1997. Apple Store is an online retail store based on the WebObjects application server (Harreld, 1997). In 1999, Apple created the Power Mac G4 as its flagship processor series. Apple introduced Mac OS X in 2001. Mac OS X is an operating system based on NeXT's NeXTSTEP and has part of the FreeBSD kernel (Amit, 2001). Apple introduced the first iPod portable digital audio player in October 2001. The company's share of the entire portable music device market in 2005 was 76% (Apple, 2005). In 2007, Apple introduced the first iPhone in selected markets. The Apple iPad was launched in 2010. Apple acquired PrimeSense and Beats Electronics as music servers in 2013 and 2014, respectively. In 2017, Apple introduced iOS 11, new versions of macOS, watchOS, and tvOS. The information provided by Tim Cook indicates that his company has completed the transition from Intel processors to Mac chips in 2020.

In 2020, the iPhone 12, 12 Pro, and 12 Pro Max were launched. They are the first iPhones to support 5G. In 2021, the M1-driven iPad and the new M1-driven iMac with 7 colours were produced. In summary, Apple's product line can be said to be consumer electronics, personal computers, servers, computer software, and media content (it acts as a distributor).

Google, est. 1998

While studying for a PhD at Stanford University, Larry Page and Sergey Brin started Google as a research experiment called "BackRub." Then they converted the name to "Googol." They decided to improve the search engine algorithm by ranking pages based on the number of backlinks rather than keyword density. Google was developed in 1997. In 2011, Google launched "Google Voice Search" to search spoken languages. The following year, Google launched a semantic search function for knowledge graphs in the United States. Since mid-2016, Google's search engine has begun to rely on deep neural networks. In 2017, Google provided a new "personal" tab in Google Search, enabling users to search for content in various services in their Google account, such as emails from Gmail and photos from Google Photos (Gartenberg, 2017). In 2018, Google's Danny Sullivan explained that there was an extensive core algorithm update. The update is about deleting medical and health-related websites. They are not user-friendly, nor do they provide a good user experience.

Facebook, est. 2003

In 2003, Mark Zuckerberg founded "Facebook" with the help of Harvard classmates Eduardo Saverin, Dustin Moskowitz, and Chris Hughes. In 2012, the company acquired Instagram, in 2013, it acquired the Israeli mobile web analytics company Onavo (2013, Lunden, 2013), and in 2014, it acquired WhatsApp and Oculus. In 2019, Facebook acquired game developer Beat Games, which developed the most popular VR game of the year, Beat Saber. In 2020, it also acquired Giphy and Mapillary, as well as a 9.99% stake in Jio Platforms (New York Times, 2020). By 2021, Facebook's monthly users have reached 2.9 billion.

2.4. Dynamics from the perspective of technology brands

Dynamics from the perspective of technology brands define a comprehensive approach to examine how technological innovation gives away to the firm's know-how through its dynamic and commercialisation of the products. The gathering of knowledge realises the innovation of products and processes leading to efficient productivity, customer satisfaction, and opportunity for reinvestment from the gained profits.

Research and development show that technological innovation and the development of new technology encourage the productivity of firms and customer satisfaction. It has been understood that industrial innovation characteristics and the relationship between the innovation and the performance of the firm are thought to be the base for the business activity so that a company manages its mission and has the right policy. Therefore, it has to recognise the characteristics of technological innovation which are the dynamic processes that affect each innovation, and the economic and political factors that focus on the technological innovation.

Allocation of resources changes the technological level, encourages the proliferation of new products, and impacts the related industries. Business profits from the sale of new products/services are reinvested in research and development activities.

Kline and Rosenberg (1986) have pointed out that the growth of a business entity through technological innovation creates a motivation to go for research and development activities. Therefore, the companies feel very much comfortable making investments in new innovative technologies. Pursuing an investment through research and development will lead to a price advantage due to the technologically improved products and increased market share. As a result, this approach allows a business model and location of the brand in the market.

Companies have, on the other hand, had to find solutions for two inconsistent issues: i. developing unique brands and ii. making them fundamental in their class. These issues shape category dynamics such as consumer preferences, pricing, and pursuit of innovation. Distinctive brands locate themselves in the market in a way that they are noticeable among other brands and do not have direct competition with other popular brands. Choices of companies influence the location of the brand in the market, as well as the selling amount, the price level, and the obtained profit. Companies have traditionally considered the positioning of the brand and the performance of the business independently (Haley, 2022). Companies have used positioning maps for discovering gaps in the market and finding loyal people for their brands. Positioning maps have revealed consumers' insights about brands. Companies have also used different strategic tools near positioning maps to get more information about the performance of their products and services such as market share, growth rate, and profitability.

There are also multi-brand companies such as Facebook and Apple. It is more difficult for them to pursue a strategy for branding or for having different categories of brands. Facebook has started as a single application and then offered services that made people connect to different communities and develop their businesses. There are advantages and disadvantages to having multi-product strategies for different brands. Advantages are reputation (awareness of customers with different brands in the same company may not be so obvious, one negatively affected brand will not make any negative impact on the other brands in the same company); capacity to position the brand in the market (if there is an experience about one brand and a good number of loyal customers, followed up by a different brand will make people trust the company because of having experience before); effective shelf space (less room for the other products if a company has different types of the same products on the shelf); and giving opportunities for people who like to switch to other brands.

Disadvantages are brands overlapping with each other (some customers are not satisfied with many options); one product can have more preference than others; wastage of resources with different products in the same brand to reach the necessary amount of profit; not having the expected standard for the customers; and credibility loss for the company will negatively affect all of the products.

It has been understood from the technology brands in this chapter that they work with different innovative business models. AT&T works through three main business segments. The segments are communications, WarnerMedia, and Latin America. AT&T obtains revenue from these segments and uses operating income for each of the segments. The business model of IBM is based on computer hardware and software, cloud computing, and AI. Its talent to renew itself, make continuous innovations, and create new markets makes the company unique. GE operates through the segments like AT&T. The difference is the number of segments: aviation, power, renewable energy, and healthcare. Xerox's business operations are mainly based on cross-selling (attracting new customers besides keeping the customers loyal), customer relationship (sales growth is important while increasing the cost level to reach additional customers), archetype business model (having many business personalities working independently), rent rather than purchasing, and aikido (finding weaknesses in the strategic position of the competitors). Hewlett-Packard has a mass-market business model. The mission behind their strategy is that there are no significant differences between customers. The business model of Intel requires designing, developing, and manufacturing the products. The company has high standards for global technology firms to pursue with zero hazardous waste. Microsoft has a diversified business model. A diversified business model focuses on a development strategy in which a company makes new products, offers new services, or enters new markets. The business partnership of Apple focuses on the strategy of design, development, manufacturing, and sales. Google's business model is a multinational product and service model that depends on advertising. The business model of Facebook is based on rolling out its tools and services to billions of users for free and then making money by allowing companies to advertise to Facebook users. The price that advertisers pay to Facebook is determined through an auction based on demand and supply.

Table 2.1 summarises the technical brand model which explains the brand's success, appropriate applications, the role of the holder, and the value to consumers, all of which are included in the brand's position in the market mentioned in the section of "Emergence of Technology Brands."

Mainly used business models are included to understand the innovative sustainable strategy put forward by the well-known considered brands.

2.5. Conclusions and recommendations

This research explores the history of the emergence of technology brands through historical methods to better understand and realise the emergence and origin of technology brands. The brands discussed include American Telephone and Telegraph Company (AT&T), International Business Machines Corporation (IBM), General Electric (GE), Xerox, Hewlett-Packard (HP), Intel, Microsoft, Apple, Google, and Facebook. All these brands have had a

Table 2.1 Technology brand model

Name of technology brand	*Product lines*	*Business model and location of the brand in the market*
AT&T	Long-distance telephone and other telecommunication services	Starting from a monopoly, it has been a competitive company. It has a differentiated product line and a strategy of acquiring similar companies to expand its business and achieve success in the market according to customer needs
IBM	Mainframe, personal computers, nanotechnology, digital data management, virtualisation, and cloud services	The business model of IBM is based on direct sales, PR, and advertisement
GE	Aviation, power and renewable energy, additive, capital, and digital	GE business model creates value by sharing capabilities between different businesses
Xerox	Office technology	Open innovation partnerships to develop product lines and position them in the market
Hewlett-Packard	Computer, printer, 3D printer, AI, VR, and gaming	HP has a mass-market business model. The strategy is that there are no significant differences between customers. The company's customer base is consumers, small and medium enterprises, and large enterprises dealing with education, health, and government departments
Intel	Central processing units, motherboard chipsets, microprocessors, Integrated graphics processing units (GPU), systems-on-chip (SoCs), network interface controllers, modems, mobile phones, solid-state drives, Wi-Fi and Bluetooth, chipsets flash memory, and vehicle automation sensors	Intel's business model is to design, develop, and manufacture its products
Microsoft	Client, server, Information Worker, Microsoft business solutions, MSN, mobile and embedded devices, home and entertainment	Microsoft has a diversified business model, including office products, hardware, Windows, games, search ads, LinkedIn, and cloud

Name of technology brand	*Product lines*	*Business model and location of the brand in the market*
Apple	Consumer electronics, personal computers, servers, computer software, and media content	Business partnership based on the design, development, manufacturing, and sales of computer software, consumer electronics, and online services
Google	Gmail, Google Contacts, Google Calendar, Google Docs Editors, Google Sites, Google Meet, Google Chat, Google Cloud Search	It depends on the advertising business model. In this model, the company focuses on an advertising network called AdWords
Facebook	Facebook, Messenger, Instagram, portal-branded devices, Oculus products, Facebook Shops, Spark AR, Audience Network, and NPE Team apps	The business model is based on rolling out its tools and services to billions of users for free and then making money by allowing companies to advertise to Facebook users. The price that advertisers pay to Facebook is determined through an auction based on demand and supply

Source: Author's elaboration.

significant impact on the commercial products and economy of various countries by using sustainable strategies in the market.

Another important point that has been discussed is that dynamics from the perspective of technology brands examine how technological innovation gives away to the firm's know-how through its dynamic and commercialisation of the products. The gathering of knowledge comprehends the innovation of products and processes leading to efficient productivity, customer satisfaction, and opportunity for reinvestment from the gained profits. Distinctive brands locate themselves in the market in a way that they are noticeable among other brands and do not have direct competition with other popular brands. Choices of companies influence the location of the brand in the market, as well as the selling amount, the price level, and the obtained profit. Companies have also used different strategic tools near positioning maps to get more information about the performance of their products and services such as market share, growth rate, and profitability. Multi-brand companies such as Facebook and Apple should have multi-brand strategies to be able to survive in the competitive markets with the brands in the same pool. There are advantages and disadvantages to having multi-product strategies for different brands. Advantages are reputation; capacity to position the brand in the market; effective shelf space and giving opportunities for people who like to switch to other brands. Disadvantages are brands overlapping with each other; one product can have more preference than others; wastage of resources with different products in the same brand to reach the necessary amount of profit; not having the expected standard for the customers, and credibility loss for the company will negatively affect all of the products. All this gathering of information leads the technology brands to create different innovative business models.

Whenever people read this chapter, they will be aware of the company's creation and market positioning. The understanding of becoming a brand and the sustainability of the product line will be the guide. Therefore, for technology companies, understanding how to build a brand and its importance to the country and society may be a good guide.

References

Ajamian, G. M., & Koen, P. A. (2002). Technology stage-gate: A structured process for managing high-risk new technology projects. In *The PDMA toolbook for new product development* (pp. 267–295). John Wiley & Sons.

Amit, S. (2001). *What is Mac OS X?—XNU: The Kernel.* Mac OS X Internals. Retrieved May 25, 2017.

Antonio, S. (2008). AT&T completes buy-out of edge wireless. *American City Business Journals.* Available at: https://www.bizjournals.com/sanantonio/stories/2008/04/14/daily37.html (accessed November, 16, 2022)

Apple. (2005). *Apple reports second quarter results* [Press release]. Apple Inc.

AT&T Exits Telegraph Business. (1991). *AT&T* [Press Release]. https://web.archive.org/web/20121209103153/www.baudot.net/docs/att-exits-telegraph-biz.pdf

Cooper, R. G., Edgett, S. J., & Kleinschmidt, E. J. (2001). Portfolio management for new product development: Results of an industry practices study. *R&D Management (Industrial Research Institute, Inc.), 13*(4), 1–39.

Cooper, R. G., & Mills, M. S. (2005). Succeeding at new product development the P&G way: A key element is using the "innovation diamond". *PDMA Visions, 29*(4), 8–17.

Eldred, E. W., & McGrath, M. E. (1997). Commercializing new technology I. *Research-Technology Management, 40*(1), 41–47.

Fagerberg, J., Mowery, D., & Nelson, R. (2006). *The oxford handbook of innovation* (1st ed.). Oxford University Press.

Flisikowski, K, & Kucharska, W. (2018). The condition of economies: do most valuable global brands matter? *Equilibrium, 13*(2), 251-264.

Foley, M. J. (2018). Microsoft's Azure IoT Edge, now generally available, is key to Redmond's IoT strategy | ZDNet. *ZDNet.*

Gardiner, C. (2010). Evaluation and selection of coagulometers. *International Journal of Laboratory Hematology, 32*, 1–85.

Gartenberg, C. (2017). Google adds a new personal tab to search results to show Gmail and photos content. *The Verge.* Vox Media.

Goffin, K., & Mitchell, R. (2016). *Innovation management: Effective strategy and implementation.* Springer. ISBN-13978-1137373434.

Goodin, D. (1998). Microsoft's holy war on Java. *CNET.* Archived from the original on January 16, 2013.

Grant, R. M. (2012). *Contemporary strategy analysis: Text & cases* (p. 8). Wiley & Sons.
Haley, A. (2022). *Positioning in marketing: Definition, types, examples, benefits & how to*. www.mageplaza.com/blog/positioning-in-marketing.html
Halman, J. I. M., Hofer, A. P., & Van Vuuren, W. (2003). Platform-driven development of product families: Linking theory with practice. *Journal of Product Innovation Management, 20*(2), 149–162.
Harreld, H. (1997). Apple gains tech, agency customers in the next deal. *Federal Computer Week*. Archived from the original on December 6, 2008.
Högman, U., & Johannesson, H. (2013). Applying stage-gate processes to technology development—experience from six hardware-oriented companies. *Journal of Engineering and Technology Management, 30*(3), 264–287.
Intel. (2003). *Intel: 35 years of innovation (1968–2003)*. https://www.intel.com/pressroom/archive/releases/2003/20030715corp.htm
Isaacson, W. (2011). *Steve Jobs*. Simon and Schuster. ISBN 9781451648546.
Johnson, K. C. (2007). AT&T's new chief dialed in. *Chicago Tribune*.
Julie, P. (1988). Apple buys Orion, aims to mine SNA. *Computerworld, 22*(24), 18.
Kaur, H., Lechman, E, & Marszk, A. (2017). *Catalyzing development through ICT adoption*. Springer.
Khan, S., & Mufti, O. (2007). The hot history & cold future of brands. *Journal of Managerial Sciences, 1*(1), 75–87.
Kim, B. (2005). *Internationalizing the internet the co-evolution of influence and technology* (pp. 51–55). Edward Elgar. ISBN 978–1845426750.
Kline, S. J., & Rosenberg, N. (1986). An overview of innovation. The positive sum strategy. *Harnessing technology for economic growth, 14*, 640.
Kucharska, W. (2022). Tacit knowledge influence on intellectual capital and innovativeness in the healthcare sector: A cross-country study of Poland and the US. *Journal of Business Research, 149*, 869-883.
Kucharska, W. (2019). Online brand communities' contribution to digital business models: Social drivers and mediators. *Journal of Research in Interactive Marketing, 13*(4), 437-463.
Kucharska, W., Flisikowski, K., & Confente, I. (2018). Do global brands contribute to the economy of their country of origin? A dynamic spatial approach. *Journal of Product & Brand Management, 27*(7), 768-780.
Lechman, E., & Anacka, H. (2022). Digitalization Process and Its Impact on Economic Growth. In Ben Ali, M.S. (Ed.) *Digitalization and Economic Development: Insights from Developing Countries* (1st ed.). Routledge. ISBN 9781003198284.
Lechman, E. (2015). *ICT Diffusion in Developing Countries*. Springer.
Leavitt, H. J., & Wisler, T. L. (1958). *Management in the 1980s*. Harvard Business Review as quoted on Wikipedia.
Linzmayer, O. W. (2004). *Apple confidential 2.0: The definitive history of the world's most colorful company*. No Starch Press. ISBN 9781593270100.
Lunden, I. (2013). *Facebook buys mobile data analytics company Onavo, reportedly for up to $200M . . . and (finally?) gets its office in Israel*. TechCrunch.
Nandakumar, I. (2012). PC-maker HP unveils its first net-zero energy data center. *The Times of India*.
New York Times (2020). Facebook Invests $5.7 Billion in Indian Internet Giant Jio. Available at: https://www.nytimes.com/2020/04/21/technology/facebook-jio-india.html (accessed November, 16, 2022)
Peck, M. J., & Scherer, F. M. (1962). *The weapons acquisition process: An economic analysis* (p. 619). Harvard Business School.

Pollack, A. (1981). Big I.B.M.'s little computer. *The New York Times*, p. D1. ISSN 0362–4331.

Schumpeter, J. (1934). *The theory of economic development*. Transaction Publishers.

Schlender, B., & Tetzeli, R. (2016). *Becoming Steve Jobs: The evolution of a reckless upstart into a visionary leader* (reprint ed.). Crown Business. ISBN 9780385347426.

Venuvinod, P. K. (2010). *Technology, innovation and entrepreneurship part I: My world, my nation*. Smashwords.

Yang, D., Sonmez, M., & Li, Q. (2012). Marks and brands: Conceptual, operational and methodological comparisons. *Journal of Intellectual Property Rights, 17*, 315–323.

3 A network approach to value creation from intangible assets

Anna Ujwary-Gil

3.1. Introduction

Value creation depends to a greater extent on intangible assets and is observed in studies on the modern economy, which, especially in developing countries, becomes network economy (e.g., Chen, 2020; Jabłoński et al., 2020), digital economy (e.g., Bertani et al., 2021; Rakhimova et al., 2020; Skvarciany & Jurevičienë, 2021; Sorescu & Schreier, 2021), or Industry 4.0 (e.g., Rymarczyk, 2021; Gajdzik et al., 2021; Giza & Wilk, 2021; Křenková et al., 2021). Networks are part of our reality; they permeate science, technology, and business. Moreover, networks are everywhere, and basically, every aspect of an organisation's functioning (and not only) can be analysed through the prism of a network of relations, interactions, and cause-and-effect relationships. Many contemporary trends in the economy point to network analysis as the basic tool for researching and measuring the network economy, digital economy, and organisational behaviour. Nowadays, network research is one of the most knowledge-forming areas of analysing the behaviour of a complex community thanks to quantitative tools for measuring relations, interactions, interdependence, or understanding the cause–effect mechanisms of the functioning of a given community. In order to understand how organisations work from the perspective of a network of relations and how value is created in an organisation, it is necessary to look at the examined entity through the prism of interactions and connections in a multimodal network, going beyond the traditional social network consisting only of social actors (organisations), and their intra- and inter-organisational relationships.

A network will be any relationship between at least two actors (e.g., employees and organisations), which we call a dyad. A good example is the value chain that can be shown from the perspective of a network of relationships, interactions, or interdependencies between organisations and the creation of digital value (Miao, 2021; Ya et al., 2021) or digital innovation (Florek-Paszkowska et al., 2021). A network is also a group or system of interconnected organisations (e.g., as part of a technology park, clusters, or national innovation systems) based on specific (formal and/or informal) types of relationships between them, where value is created within such an ecosystem (Alberti & Belfanti,

DOI: 10.4324/9781003184638-4

2021). According to this perspective, organisations are embedded in relationships that influence the actors' behaviour. The network approach focuses on relationships and interaction patterns and not on the individual characteristics of individual organisations or employees. Such a network approach to the organisation and employees (social actors) allows for modelling the structure of relations between and within organisations. And also, to study the impact of this structure on the organisation's functioning and examine the possibilities or limitations of individual activities of each organisation and employee in the network. The organisational network, which we call the network ecology (cf. Carley, 1999; Kurbanov et al., 2019), is, therefore, a form of informal cooperation between many independent organisations or employees, which is based on the division of tasks, knowledge, resources, and the creation of value based on synergy. Changes to any part of this network ecology affect all other parts, and the entire system's behaviour determines de facto how these organisations (employees) are networked together. Networks understood in this way have a significant impact on many areas, including value creation (Ujwary-Gil & Potoczek, 2020), speed of information diffusion (Buskens, 2020; Tsuda & Tsugawa, 2021), knowledge sharing in an organisation (Han et al., 2020; Su, 2021), inter-organisational knowledge transfer (Kubsch et al., 2020; Moon et al., 2019) creating innovation (Tamburis & Bonacci, 2019; Valente, 2010), or the ability of an organisation to acquire and use resources (Ujwary-Gil, 2020, 2019).

This chapter tries to link value creation with the employees of the ICT sector organisation in which intangible assets (i.e., software) and digital technologies play a key role. In addition, it presents the so-called meta-network (multimodal) approach to organisation, which is a promising approach to understand value creation based on complex relationships in an organisational network based on social actors, knowledge and resource use, and task performance. The main research questions (RQs) that this chapter addresses are as follows:

RQ1: What is the meta-network approach to the organisation, value creation, and its intangible assets understood as network nodes?

RQ2: Is there a relationship between the value creation network, the knowledge network, the resource network, and the task network that constitute the meta-network approach to the organisation?

RQ3: Which nodes have the most influential position in the network?

3.2. Literature background

Network approach

The theoretical context of these studies and research questions is network theory (see Barabási, 2005; Borgatti & Foster, 2003; Borgatti & Halgin, 2011), which creates the foundations for the interpretation of the behaviour of social actors in the organisation and the understanding of interdependencies occurring in the organisational meta-network. According to the assumptions of network theory, the actor's position in the network determines his limitations and opportunities in terms of his/her achievements, behaviours, or beliefs (Borgatti et al., 2018). The value creation, key practices, and processes depend on the individual actions of social actors of organisations, groups, and networks of people. Here, activities will constitute deliberate interactions between actors (social actors), value creation, knowledge, resources, and tasks, which are also the essence of the meta-network approach to the organisation (see Ujwary-Gil, 2020). The resource-based view complements this theoretical context in which resources (intangible assets) are perceived in relation to the activities of social actors who can use them productively to create value in an organisation.

Therefore, organisation management can be characterised, *inter alia*, as the science of managing relationships in networks to achieve organisational goals such as high performance and value creation or leading to the network strategy (cf. Barczak et al., 2021; Canestrino & Forouharfar, 2021; Miller et al., 2021). The network approach allows looking at the organisation from a multimodal perspective, including social actors (employees), and their knowledge and skills, resources (assets), and tasks. We can assume that the organisation is based on at least these four interdependent elements and their operation. The meta-network approach to the functioning of an organisation is one of the most interesting approaches in connection with the network paradigm that is developing in management sciences. This paradigm distinguishes the research approach used, including collecting and managing network data, network data features, level of analysis, and network variables obtained from the data (see Borgatti & Foster, 2003). The central premise for undertaking this research is to understand the complexity of the functioning of an organisation understood as a set of interdependent networks of relations. The meta-network allows for the simultaneous analysis of many interrelated elements in the organisation. Using a multimodal network perspective and network measures (here, mainly centrality), we can measure the position of social actors in the organisational network and optimise planned activities. It is impossible to measure the complex network of interactions between social actors, information flows, knowledge, skills, resources used, and tasks performed using traditional organisational charts.

For the purposes of this chapter, in the network approach, we list: social actors (employees); their knowledge and skills; resources, including intangible assets, understood as structural capital, software, and also the communication and IT infrastructure, which becomes a platform for flows and relations, creating the relational capital of a given organisation (Nuryakin, 2021); in addition, tasks and activities that are inherently related to actors and resources (intangible assets). Finally, value creation results from the interactions between actors, knowledge, resources, and tasks.

Value creation and intangible assets

The logic of the functioning of modern enterprises, oriented towards achieving a competitive advantage, requires close interaction of tangible resources and intangible assets in value creation. Nowadays, creating value in an enterprise is perceived not through the prism of the amount of profit achieved but from the generated added value, which is then redistributed among stakeholders related to the enterprise. As early as 1944, Knight wrote about intangible assets as immeasurable capital, a hidden factor of production that grows faster than the possibility of compensating for the declining income generated by measurable capital.

One of the domains of strategic management, apart from strategy formulation and implementation, is value creation and the company's competitive advantage. A widely recognised approach in strategic management is also the resource approach, the sources of which go back to the works of Amit and Schoemaker (1993), Barney (1991), Peteraf (1993), Rumelt (1984), and Wernerfelt (1984). The complexity of value creation cannot be explained on the basis of a resource approach alone, as resources themselves do not carry value. Value creation is possible due to their use or transactions (DaSilva & Trkman, 2014), emphasises the resources used in action by accumulating, allocating resources, their integration, or applications. The sustainable ability of organisational value creation resides in the ownership and protection of tangible and intangible assets that guarantee an ongoing competitive advantage. It requires understanding and managing how to continuously develop, deploy, operate, and combine these organisational assets to update, renew, and build organisational skills. Of course, it is not just about asset gathering, but how resources are transformed into a process, product, reputation, and brand that creates value that is transformed into a financial return for stakeholders (Confente & Kucharska, 2021). Especially that value is incorporated in products/services due to the development of organisational knowledge resources. The way in which value is created is determined by such factors as the key logic of the company's operation (business model), cultural assumptions, cognitive environment influencing managerial decisions, and competences that legitimise the creation of value from resources. These factors and their interaction lead to value creation.

Value is not only relative but also ambiguous and subjective. Value means a set of features characteristic of a given person or thing, which constitutes its values that are valuable to people and can satisfy their needs (Ujwary-Gil, 2017b). Money can be a measure of tangible and intangible values, because value determines how much something is materially worth. Value understood in this way is an attribute of the products and services offered. Products and services are the subjects of a relationship (exchange) between the company and the buyer (customer). From the point of view of the offered products and services, value for the customer is essential, that is, the benefits that the company offers in the form of products and services to ensure customer loyalty and satisfaction in target market segments (Kaplan & Norton, 1992). Value for the customer is, therefore, the ratio of benefits contained in products and services offered to costs associated with their purchase, including the financial and non-financial burdens borne by the customer. Thus, the value of products or services is usually (cf. Hossain et al., 2021): 1) technical level of products, 2) total costs incurred by the user, 3) convenience of the ordering procedure and payment deadline, 4) installation assistance, use of the product, and solving any problems that may arise, and 5) additional benefits, affecting the customer's attachment and loyalty to the company. Value lies at the heart of Porter's value chain, which saw the company as a system of delivering value to the customer (cf. Isabelle et al., 2020). Value creation takes place with the help of basic functions (i.e., supply and distribution logistics, trade and sales, services and production) and auxiliary functions (i.e., human resources management, technology development, procurement, related to infrastructure, structural capital of the enterprise). In order for the enterprise to create value effectively, the organisational infrastructure cannot be static but should constantly adapt to new conditions, both market and internal. In terms of the network, intangible and tangible assets are closely related, such as a computer (software) with an employee, and measuring these two elements independently is pointless. The computer can analytically combine information into new models, but it cannot integrate them into something wholly new and interpret the processed data on its own. To better understand the essence of value creation, it is reasonable to define a business model on the basis of which the company will determine future development opportunities in the digital economy.

An enterprise owns intangible assets in coded form (e.g., software and databases) that may be a source of benefits (value) in the future (Corrado et al., 2017). Similarly, in accounting, assets are defined as assets controlled by an entity (enterprise) with a reliably determined value, arising from past events, which will result in an inflow of economic benefits in the future (Andrikopoulos, 2010). Assets understood in this way, including intangible assets, may be controlled by an enterprise instead of human capital (employees' knowledge), which is not owned by it. While in the theory and practice of human resources, man is perceived as a priority and is at the same time the most important source of the company's success, in the well-known concept of intellectual capital (e.g., Kucharska, 2021), the so-called soft factors and tangible resources are complementary to each other. In this complementarity, we should look for the sources of added value or the competitive advantage of the enterprise. The concept of intangible assets from the network perspective takes on a different meaning. Valuable, rare, inimitable, and non-substitutable (VRIN) are those resources that arise in an organisational and inter-organisational network configuration that are difficult to replicate by competitors (van Rijnsoever & Eveleens, 2021).

If we consider value creation from the process point of view, value understood in this way will be constantly created and re-transformed into a new form, thanks to the dynamic interaction (behaviour) taking place between people, information, knowledge, and resources. Value creation is, therefore, a process in continuous construction. As in the case of creating innovations (new knowledge), this process is integrated and networked, containing numerous interactions and feedback. Value should be considered in the context of measurement or calculation and understanding the essence of its creation and development based on the existing networks of connections between specific elements. Value creation is certainly relational. It is most often analysed in the context of business models and intellectual capital that perform identical functions oriented towards creating value as a result of interactions between their components (Beattie & Smith, 2013; Ujwary-Gil, 2017a). Osterwalder and Pigneur (2010) similarly treat resources and activities as components of the business model influencing the value proposition, the realisation of which is possible due to interactions between key resources, activities, customer groups, distribution channels, relationships with customers, partners, sources of income and costs. Organisational intangible resources are a significant contribution to value creation and are static until they are activated (identifying relationships and links with other resources used in creating value or results for the organisation).

3.3. Methodological approach

Network research, compared to other social studies, distinguishes the acquisition and management of network data (data confidentiality, no anonymity, ethics of network research), features of network data (interdependence), the level of analysis (the entire network, dyad, single node), and network variables taking the form of a matrix. The network data was obtained in the first quarter of 2017 in an IT sector company employing at that time 47 employees (social actors) based on an online survey questionnaire. The selection of the case for the research was deliberate, based on the criterion related to the importance of knowledge and strategic maturity of the organisation, which increases the probability of noticing the sought-after resources and intangible assets and their relationship with value creation and strategy. An additional criterion for purposeful selection was the availability criterion (Creswell & Poth, 2017).

The basis for the development of the research questionnaire was an interview with the Director of the Implementation Department, which concerned (along with many other issues) the identification and analysis of elements of the company's business processes, broken down into knowledge, resources (intangible assets), and tasks. A total of 45 employees (A) took part in the study, which constitutes 98% of the population, thus eliminating the problem of missing data (nodes), which are quite problematic in network research. The average number of years of total professional experience was 10.20 and standard deviation (SD) 7.14, where the minimum value is 1 year and the maximum value is 35 years. The average experience in the examined company is 4.28 (SD 3.46, min. = 1, max. = 13); 14% were women and 85% were men. The average age of the employees is 32.91 (SD 7.49, min. = 23, max. = 62).

The types of relations (variables) that form the following matrices have been identified and will form the basis centrality measure, that is, prominent (influential) nodes in the networks mentioned:

- AKij (actor/task)—knowledge use j by actor i;
- ARij (actor/resource)—resource use j by actor i;

- ATij (actor/task)—task j performed by actor i;
- AVij (actor/value)—value creation j by actor i.

In matrices, strong relationships (on the Likert scale 4 and 5) constitute the relationship between row nodes and column nodes. In the AVij matrix, actor i is associated with value creation j due to the duties performed in a given job. The remaining matrices are the respondents' answers (A) regarding the knowledge they use (AKij), resources (ARij), and tasks performed (ATij) from the available list (see Table 3.1), which was created on the basis of the

Table 3.1 Meta-network approach to an enterprise—network nodes

Actors (A)	A01; A02; A03; A04; A05; A06; A07; A08; A09; A10; A11; A12; A13; A14; A15; A16; A17; A18; A19; A20 A21; A22; A23; A24; A25; A26; A27; A28; A29; A30; A31; A32; A33; A34; A35; A36; A37; A38; A39; A40; A41; A42; A43; A44; A45.
Knowledge and skills (K)	K01. Analytical thinking; K02. Assertiveness (being able to make one's case); K03. Copywriting; K04. Organisational activities; K05. Creatively solving complex problems; K06. Accounting; K07. Mathematical thinking; K08. Personnel and legal services; K09. General knowledge on the product group; K10. Organisational structure; K11. Detailed knowledge on products; K12. Verbal (communication) skills; K13. Negotiation skills; K14. Implementation progress reporting skills; K15. Product targeting (matching products to customers and their business processes); K16. Knowledge on BI (Business Intelligence); K17. Knowledge on the IT industry; K18. Knowledge on the customer's industry (e.g., construction); K19. Knowledge on partner's Comarch Optima; K20. Knowledge on partner's Comarch XL; K21. Knowledge on DMS (Data Management System); K22. Knowledge on CRM (Customer Relationship Management); K23. Knowledge on the company's operations; K24. Knowledge on hardware infrastructure; K25. Knowledge on customers (their size, organisational structure, business processes, etc.); K26. Knowledge on document flows; K27. Knowledge on customers' business processes; K28. Knowledge on competitors' products; K29. Knowledge on past customer implementations (what has been implemented); K30. Knowledge on project management; K31. Knowledge on current licenses; K32. Technical (IT) knowledge; K33. Subject matter knowledge (logistics); K34. Subject matter knowledge (production); K35. Debt collection; K36. Organisational document management; K37. Mail management; K38. Insurance and lease document management; K39. Object-oriented programming; K40. Knowledge on SQL databases; K41. Knowledge of customers' technical parameters (e.g., servers, platforms, login processes, IP addresses); K42. Knowledge of implementation methods; K43. Knowing people involved in the project; K44. Knowledge of references; K45. Knowledge on Web portal construction; K46. Knowledge on company operation; K47. Knowledge of SEO principles.

(*Continued*)

Table 3.1 (Continued)

Actors (A)	A01; A02; A03; A04; A05; A06; A07; A08; A09; A10; A11; A12; A13; A14; A15; A16; A17; A18; A19; A20 A21; A22; A23; A24; A25; A26; A27; A28; A29; A30; A31; A32; A33; A34; A35; A36; A37; A38; A39; A40; A41; A42; A43; A44; A45.
Resources and assets (R)	R01. Programming libraries; R02. Crystal Reports; R03. Google Adwords; R04. Help desk; R05. Microsoft SQL; R06. MS Office; R07. Website traffic tracking software; R08. E-mail; R09. Projector; R10. Conference room; R11. Car; R12. "Płatnik"—the social security document submission system; R13. The Data Management System; R14. The financial and accounting system; R15. Team Viewer; R16. Phone; R17. Visual Studio; R18. Computer.
Tasks (T)	T01. (Re)negotiating contract terms; T02. Customer needs analysis; T03. Delegating tasks; T04. Initiating processes, for example, development; T05. Installing software; T06. Matching contracts to billing documents; T07. Company brand image building; T08. Monitoring competitors' activity; T09. Negotiating sales terms; T10. Customer service for the accounting company; T11. Employee payroll services; T12. Customer service (customer retention); T13. Network maintenance (servers, domains); T14. Hardware maintenance; T15. Developing pre-implementation documents; T16. Developing specialised portals; T17. Preparing presentation points; T18. Drawing up contracts; T19. Handling customer requests; T20. Search engine optimisation for the company website; T21. Handling the company blogs; T22. Renewing contracts; T23. Providing references; T24. Referring interested customers to the sales division; T25. Providing trainings in the implementation process; T26. Developing prospective customer databases; T27. Preparing an offer; T28. Reporting; T29. Fulfilling service requests (repairs); T30. Customer billing; T31. Software development; T32. Communication with customers (remote/personal); T33. Adjusting the system to the customer's needs (e.g., configuration and/or reconfiguration); T34. Recording specifications; T35. Regulatory reporting; T36. Selling customer warranties/assistance; T37. Selling the service; T38. Technical services for company events (e.g., trainings and conferences); T39. Contacting customers by phone; T40. Software testing; T41. Writing source code; T42. Customer system maintenance; T43. Visiting customers; T44. Recording and/or finding customers in the database; T45. Preliminary customer classification by product; T46. Delivering presentations for customers; T47. Issuing invoices; T48. Closing service requests.
Value (V)	V01. Satisfying a wide range of customers' IT and IT-related needs; V02. Long-lasting customer attachment through the professional character of services; V03. Competing on quality, not price; V04. Long-lasting cooperation with customers; V05. Handling customers' issues that they need not be burdened with.

IT company's business processes identified in the interview (more on this in Ujwary-Gil, 2020, 2017a). In total, 47 K nodes (knowledge and skills), 18 R nodes (resources and intangible assets), 48 T nodes (tasks and activities), and 5 V nodes (value) were identified. Then, the two-mode matrices (AK, AR, AT, AV) were folded into one-mode matrices, which were correlated to investigate statistically significant relationships between the value creation network, the knowledge network, the resource network, and the task network.

ORA-PRO (Organizational Risk Analyzer), version 3.0.9.9.87 (Altman et al., 2020), was used to measure the network centrality out-degree and centrality in-degree. Additionally, UCINET 6 (Windows version 6.730) (Borgatti et al., 2002) was used to visualise four networks. In addition to basic quantitative statistics such as standard deviation, mean, minimum and maximum values, the quadratic assignment procedure (QAP) was used. QAP is a non-parametric test that measures the relationship between two variables of the same dimension using the Pearson correlation coefficient. The QAP test is a procedure in which the matrix data is stretched into an observation vector on which ordinary multiple regression is performed, producing the traditional beta coefficient estimated for each independent variable. The problem, however, is that traditional estimates of standard errors of these coefficients are very sensitive to autocorrelation in the data; therefore, they do not constitute the basis for significance tests of these coefficients (Dekker et al., 2007). The distribution is made by randomly permuting the matrix multiple times (5,000 in our case), each time recalculating the correlation coefficients for each variable (Hinds et al., 2000). The *p*-value is estimated from the relative frequency of statistical values in the reference distribution obtained by permutation that is greater than or equal to the empirically observed value (Dekker et al., 2007).

3.4. Results and discussion

As a result of the interview, a list of nodes was created on the basis of a glossary of own terms of an organisation operating in the IT sector. The identification of the nodes was possible based on the definition of the company's basic business processes (i.e., the commercial process (including advertising, telemarketing, and sales), the implementation process, the customer retention (service) process, the production process, and the administrative process), which was analysed in terms of the required knowledge (skills), resources (assets), and tasks. Then, the value creation area was identified as part of the company's business model. All nodes are listed in Table 3.1. Detailed identification of actors or employees (A) of the enterprise is not possible due to the nature and ethics of network research (see Borgatti & Molina, 2005). The identity of respondents remains protected.

On the basis of the identified nodes, four two-mode networks were created: AKij (actor/knowledge)—knowledge use j by the actor i (Figure 3.1); ARij (actor/resource)—resource use j by the actor i (Figure 3.2); ATij (actor/task)—task performed j by an actor i (Figure 3.3); AVij (actor/value)—creating value j by an actor i (Figure 3.4). Figures show a visualisation of the networks mentioned.

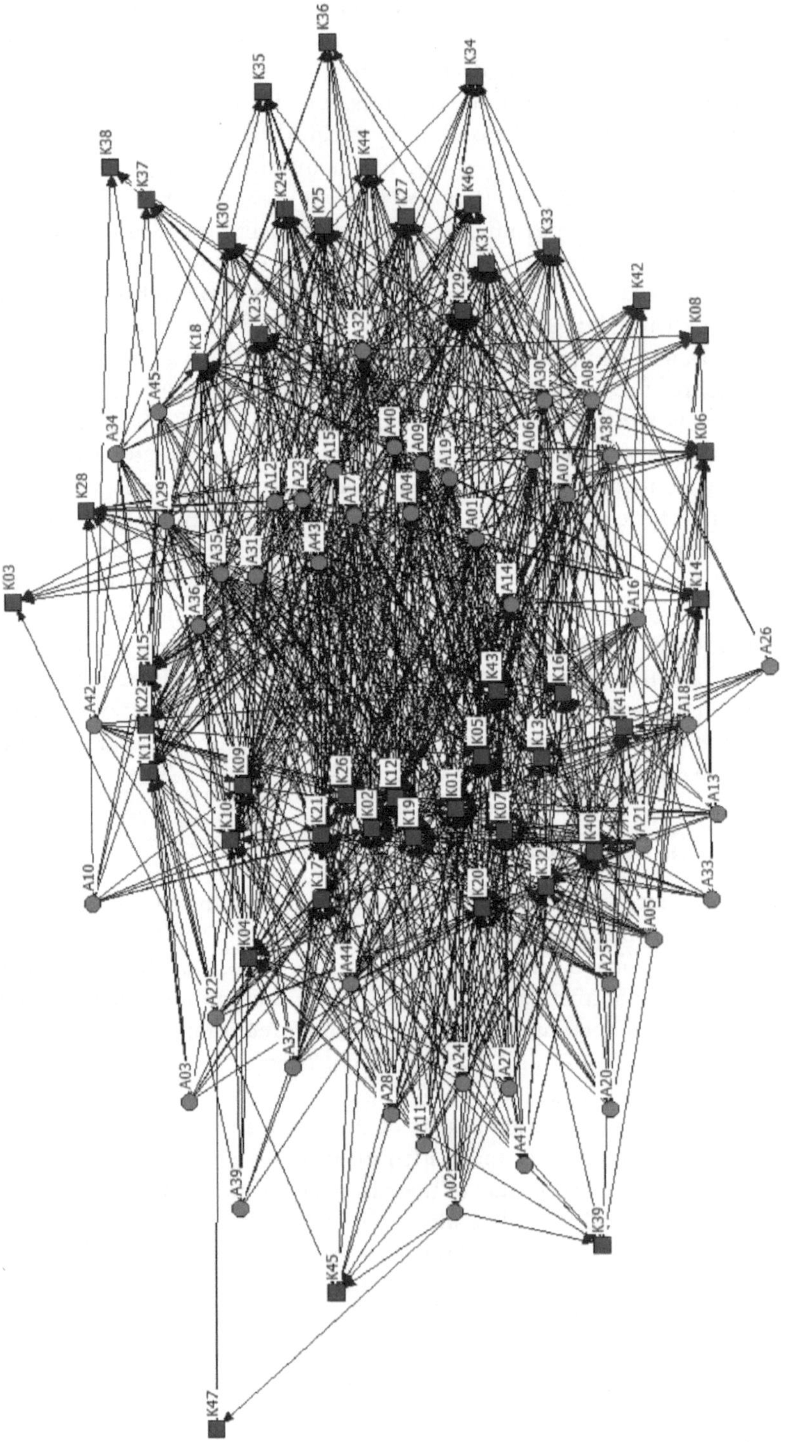

Figure 3.1 AK_{ij} (actor/knowledge)—knowledge use *j* by actor *i*

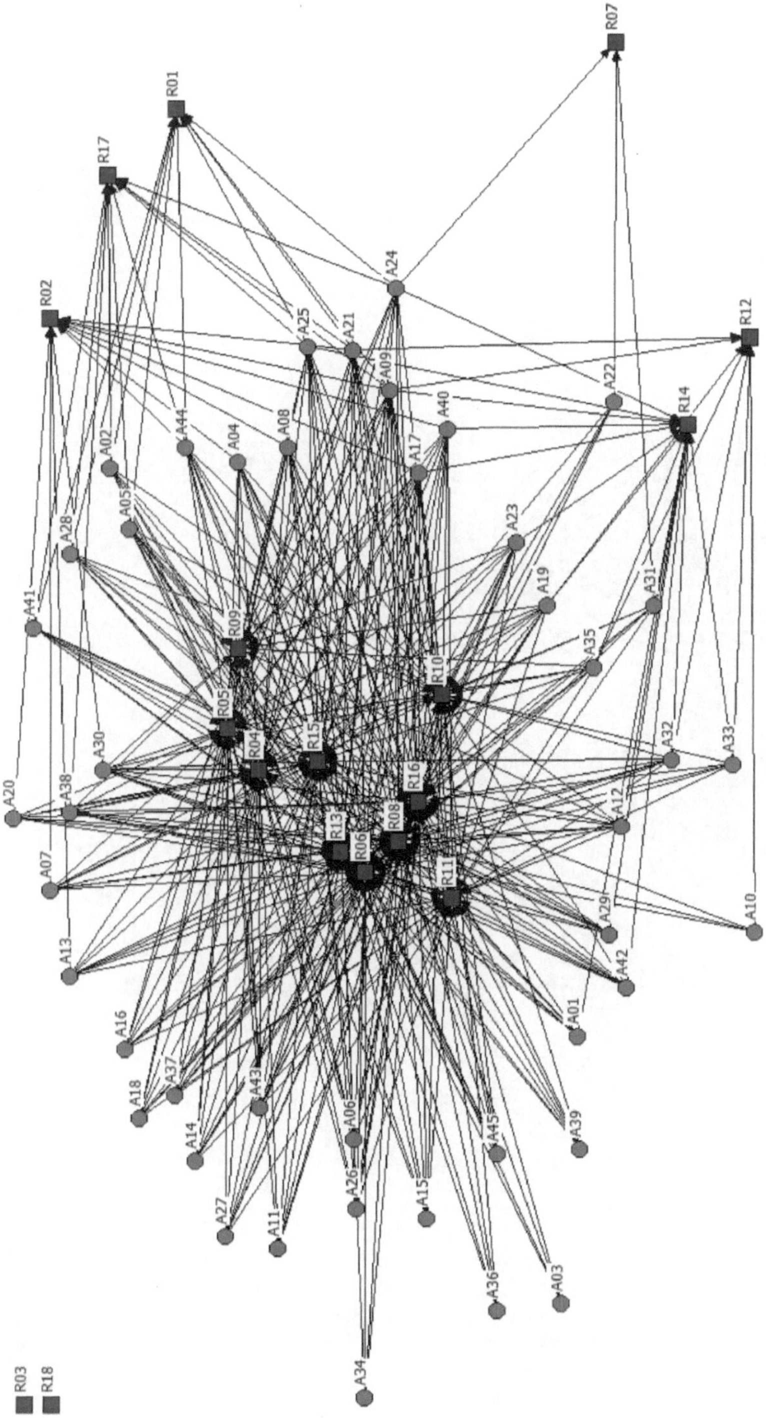

Figure 3.2 AR_{ij} (actor/resource)—resource use *j* by actor *i*

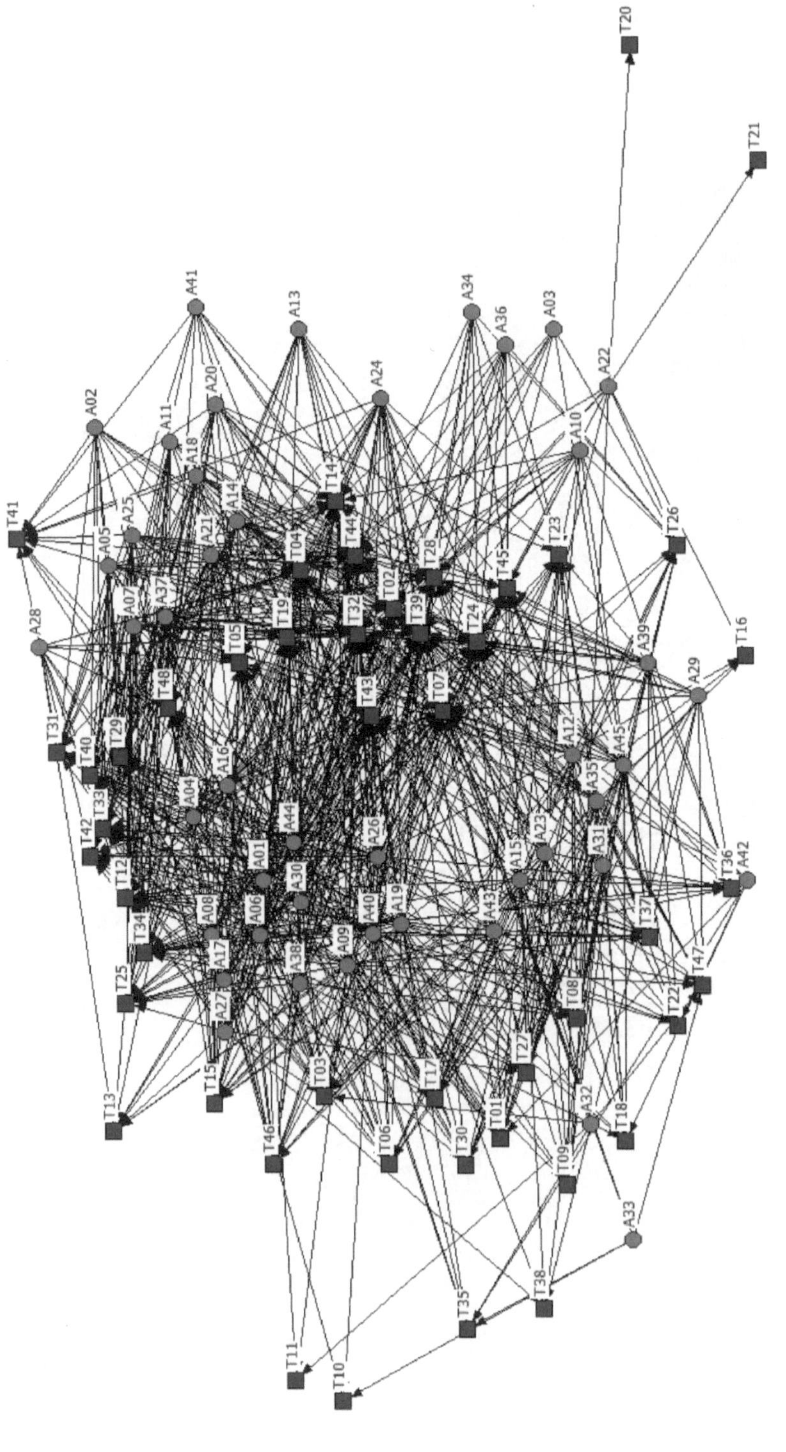

Figure 3.3 AT_{ij} (actor/task)—task performing *j* by actor *i*

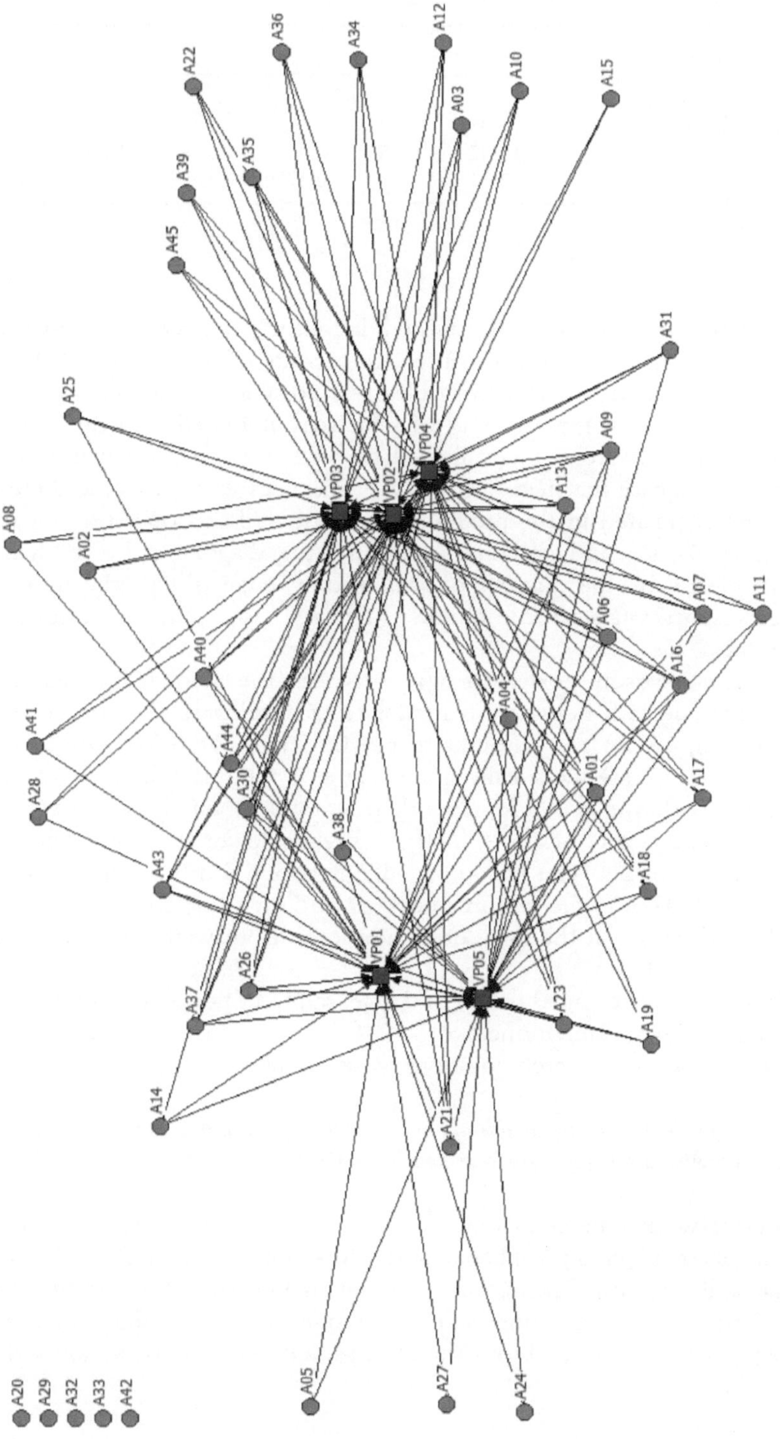

Figure 3.4 AV_{ij} (actor/value)—value creation *j* by actor *i*

Table 3.2 The results of the correlation of the knowledge network (skills), the network of resources (assets), the network of tasks, and the network of values

Networks	*M*	*SD*	*1*	*2*	*3*	*4*
1. Knowledge (skills) network	11.87	5.87	1.00			
2. Resource (assets) network	6.95	2.07	0.60*	1.00		
3. Task network	10.92	6.45	0.57*	0.70*	1.00	
4. Value creation network	3.11	1.16	0.37*	0.39*	0.60*	1.00

Note: N = 1980 relationships; *p < .001.

In order to correlate and indicate the relationships between the networks mentioned, the QAP method was used, the results of which are as follows (Table 3.2). Correlating matrix variables was possible due to the so-called folding operation, the functionality of which is integrated into the ORA-PRO network software, which allowed to reduce rectangular matrices to unimodal and square matrices (AAij). Only matrices with the same dimension can be correlated in the program. As a result of this operation, at the intersection of rows and columns (excluding the diagonal), the following appear, respectively: the number of shared knowledge (skills); the number of shared resources (assets); the number of shared tasks; and the number of shared values.

The linear Pearson correlation (r) between the knowledge network and resource and task networks is moderate (according to Guilford's notation (Guilford, 1977)) and amounts to $r = 0.60$ and $r = 0.57$, respectively. These relationships are statistically significant at $p < 0.001$. Likewise, for the resource network and the task network ($r = 0.70$), then the task network and value creation network ($r = 0.60$). A slightly lower level was recorded for the correlation between the knowledge network and the value creation network ($r = 0.37$) and the resource network and the value creation network ($r = 0.39$), which are at the low correlation level. Both were statistically significant, $p < 0.001$.

Table 3.3 presents detailed results of the centrality of nodes (the most influential) in the networks mentioned.

The answers to the research questions are as follows:

RQ1: What is the meta-network approach to the organisation, value creation, and its intangible assets understood as network nodes?

The meta-network approach to the presented organisation consists of at least four elements of organisational behaviour: actors or employees (A), the knowledge and skills they use (K), resources and intangible assets (R), and the tasks they perform (T). Value creation (V) is a consequence of interactions and interdependencies occurring between the above-mentioned network nodes that

Table 3.3 Centralities of all presented nodes (actors, knowledge, resources, tasks, values)*

Rnk	A	VS	UVS	K	VS	UVS	A	VS	UVS	R	VS	UVS	A	VS	UVS	T	VS	UVS	A	VS	UVS	V	VS	UVS
1	**A09**	**0.872**	**41**	**K12**	**0.956**	**43**	**A09**	**0.833**	**15**	**R08**	**1**	**45**	**A09**	**0.792**	**38**	**T39**	**0.978**	**44**	A01	1	5	**V02**	**0.778**	**35**
2	**A04**	**0.787**	**37**	**K01**	**0.911**	**41**	**A21**	**0.722**	**13**	**R16**	**1**	**45**	**A19**	**0.792**	**38**	**T32**	**0.844**	**38**	A04	1	5	V03	0.756	34
3	**A40**	**0.787**	**37**	**K05**	**0.889**	**40**	**A17**	**0.667**	**12**	**R13**	**0.956**	**43**	**A40**	**0.792**	**38**	**T07**	**0.822**	**37**	A06	1	5	V04	0.689	31
4	**A23**	**0.723**	**34**	**K02**	**0.778**	**35**	**A19**	**0.667**	**12**	**R06**	**0.933**	**42**	**A26**	**0.688**	**33**	**T02**	**0.756**	**34**	A07	1	5	V01	0.644	29
5	**A17**	**0.660**	**31**	**K19**	**0.756**	**34**	**A24**	**0.667**	**12**	R15	0.822	37	**A44**	**0.667**	**32**	**T44**	**0.733**	**33**	A09	1	5	V05	0.556	25
6	**A19**	**0.660**	**31**	**K07**	**0.733**	**33**	**A25**	**0.667**	**12**	R04	0.756	34	**A01**	**0.625**	**30**	**T28**	**0.711**	**32**	A13	1	5			
7	**A43**	**0.660**	**31**	**K21**	**0.733**	**33**	**A40**	**0.667**	**12**	R05	0.711	32	**A15**	**0.604**	**29**	**T19**	**0.689**	**31**	A16	1	5			
8	**A15**	**0.638**	**30**	K09	0.667	30	**A44**	**0.667**	**12**	R10	0.689	31	A23	0.583	28	**T05**	**0.667**	**30**	A17	1	5			
9	A44	0.596	28	K26	0.667	30	A04	0.611	11	R11	0.644	29	A17	0.542	26	**T24**	**0.667**	**30**	A18	1	5			
10	A12	0.574	27	K20	0.644	29	A05	0.611	11	R09	0.533	24	A04	0.521	25	**T48**	**0.667**	**30**	A21	1	5			
11	A14	0.574	27	K43	0.644	29	A08	0.611	11	R14	0.333	15	A06	0.521	25	T43	0.644	29	A23	1	5			
12	A31	0.574	27	K32	0.578	26	A23	0.611	11	R02	0.244	11	A16	0.521	25	T04	0.578	26	A26	1	5			
13	A06	0.553	26	K13	0.556	25	A30	0.611	11	R17	0.222	10	A30	0.521	25	T29	0.578	26	A30	1	5			
14	A35	0.553	26	K29	0.556	25	A35	0.611	11	R01	0.200	9	A12	0.500	24	T03	0.533	24	A37	1	5			
15	A01	0.511	24	K40	0.556	25	A06	0.556	10	R12	0.156	7	A08	0.479	23	T12	0.533	24	A38	1	5			
16	A07	0.511	24	K41	0.556	25	A28	0.556	10	R07	0.067	3	A37	0.479	23	T14	0.533	24	A40	1	5			
17	A08	0.511	24	K16	0.533	24	A38	0.556	10	R03	0	0	A21	0.458	22	T33	0.511	23	A43	1	5			
18	A32	0.511	24	K17	0.533	24	A43	0.556	10	R18	0	0	A31	0.458	22	T34	0.489	22	A44	1	5			
19	A21	0.489	23	K31	0.511	23	A01	0.500	9				A35	0.458	22	T40	0.489	22	A11	0.800	4			
20	A30	0.489	23	K10	0.489	22	A02	0.500	9				A14	0.438	21	T42	0.489	22	A19	0.800	4			
21	A36	0.489	23	K15	0.489	22	A07	0.500	9				A18	0.438	21	T45	0.467	21	A31	0.800	4			
22	A29	0.447	21	K04	0.467	21	A12	0.500	9				A24	0.438	21	T25	0.444	20	A02	0.600	3			
23	A16	0.426	20	K22	0.467	21	A13	0.500	9				A38	0.438	21	T15	0.422	19	A03	0.600	3			
24	A22	0.426	20	K11	0.444	20	A14	0.500	9				A45	0.438	21	T17	0.422	19	A08	0.600	3			
25	A24	0.426	20	K23	0.444	20	A16	0.500	9				A07	0.417	20	T23	0.400	18	A10	0.600	3			
26	A25	0.426	20	K27	0.444	20	A18	0.500	9				A27	0.417	20	T06	0.378	17	A12	0.600	3			
27	A28	0.426	20	K18	0.422	19	A26	0.500	9				A05	0.396	19	T01	0.356	16	A14	0.600	3			

(*Continued*)

Table 3.3 (Continued)

Rnk	*A*	*VS*	*UVS*	*K*	*VS*	*UVS*	*A*	*VS*	*UVS*	*R*	*VS*	*UVS*	*A*	*VS*	*UVS*	*T*	*VS*	*UVS*	*A*	*VS*	*UVS*	*V*	*VS*	*UVS*
28	*A38*	*0.426*	*20*	*K25*	*0.422*	*19*	*A31*	*0.500*	*9*				*A25*	*0.396*	*19*	*T08*	*0.356*	*16*	*A22*	*0.600*	*3*			
29	*A05*	*0.404*	*19*	*K33*	*0.422*	*19*	*A32*	*0.500*	*9*				*A20*	*0.375*	*18*	*T27*	*0.356*	*16*	*A25*	*0.600*	*3*			
30	*A18*	*0.362*	*17*	*K46*	*0.422*	*19*	*A37*	*0.500*	*9*				*A43*	*0.375*	*18*	*T31*	*0.356*	*16*	*A28*	*0.600*	*3*			
31	*A27*	*0.362*	*17*	*K14*	*0.356*	*16*	*A41*	*0.500*	*9*				*A11*	*0.354*	*17*	*T37*	*0.356*	*16*	*A34*	*0.600*	*3*			
32	*A37*	*0.362*	*17*	*K24*	*0.333*	*15*	*A42*	*0.500*	*9*				*A39*	*0.354*	*17*	*T46*	*0.356*	*16*	*A35*	*0.600*	*3*			
33	*A45*	*0.362*	*17*	*K44*	*0.333*	*15*	*A11*	*0.444*	*8*				*A28*	*0.313*	*15*	*T26*	*0.289*	*13*	*A36*	*0.600*	*3*			
34	*A11*	*0.340*	*16*	*K42*	*0.311*	*14*	*A15*	*0.444*	*8*				*A10*	*0.292*	*14*	*T30*	*0.289*	*13*	*A39*	*0.600*	*3*			
35	*A02*	*0.298*	*14*	*K06*	*0.289*	*13*	*A20*	*0.444*	*8*				*A13*	*0.271*	*13*	*T41*	*0.267*	*12*	*A41*	*0.600*	*3*			
36	*A34*	*0.298*	*14*	*K30*	*0.289*	*13*	*A27*	*0.444*	*8*				A02	0.250	12	*T22*	*0.244*	*11*	*A05*	*0.400*	*2*			
37	*A42*	*0.298*	*14*	*K28*	*0.267*	*12*	*A29*	*0.444*	*8*				A22	0.229	11	*T47*	*0.244*	*11*	*A15*	*0.400*	*2*			
38	A41	0.277	13	K34	0.222	10	*A45*	*0.444*	*8*				A29	0.229	11	*T09*	*0.222*	*10*	*A24*	*0.400*	*2*			
39	A13	0.255	12	K35	0.200	9	*A33*	*0.389*	*7*				A32	0.208	10	*T18*	*0.222*	*10*	*A27*	*0.400*	*2*			
40	A20	0.234	11	K08	0.178	8	*A39*	*0.389*	*7*				A36	0.208	10	*T36*	*0.222*	*10*	*A45*	*0.400*	*2*			
41	A03	0.213	10	K36	0.178	8	A22	0.333	6				A41	0.208	10	*T13*	*0.200*	*9*	A20	0	0			
42	A33	0.213	10	K39	0.178	8	A36	0.278	5				A34	0.188	9	T35	0.156	7	A29	0	0			
43	A10	0.191	9	K45	0.178	8	A03	0.222	4				A42	0.167	8	T38	0.133	6	A32	0	0			
44	A26	0.149	7	K37	0.156	7	A10	0.222	4				A03	0.146	7	T16	0.111	5	A33	0	0			
45	A39	0.149	7	K03	0.111	5	A34	0.222	4				A33	0.104	5	T10	0.067	3	A42	0	0			
46				K38	0.089	4										T11	0.067	3						
47				K47	0.044	2										T20	0.022	1						
48																T21	0.022	1						
	Min	0.149	7	**Min**	0.044	2	**Min**	0.222	4	**Min**	0	0	**Min**	0.104	5	**Min**	0.022	1	**Min**	0	0	**Min**	0.556	25
	Max	0.876	14	**Max**	0.956	43	**Max**	0.833	15	**Max**	1	45	**Max**	0.752	38	**Max**	0.987	44	**Max**	1	5	**Max**	0.778	35
	M	0.455	21.40	**M**	0.455	20.49	**M**	0.515	9.267	**M**	0.515	23.17	**M**	0.424	20.36	**M**	0.424	19.09	**M**	0.684	3.42	**M**	0.684	30.80
	SD	0.173	8.136	**SD**	0.222	10.01	**SD**	0.130	2.332	**SD**	0.352	15.84	**SD**	0.171	8.212	**SD**	0.228	10.26	**SD**	0.322	1.61	**SD**	0.080	3.60

Note: *If the node of interest has a higher than normal value (greater than 1 standard deviation(s) above the mean), the row is **bold**. The row is *italic* if the node is within 1 standard deviation of the mean. Finally, the row is normal font if the node has a lower than normal value (less than 1 standard deviation(s) below the mean).

Rank—rank; A—actor; VS—value statistics; UVS—unvalued statistics; K—knowledge; R—resource; T—tasks; V—value; M—mean; SD—standard deviation.

create two-mode relationship networks (AKij, ARij, ATij, AVij). In detail, each node is listed in Table 3.1.

RQ2: Is there a relationship between the value creation network, the knowledge network, the resource network, and the task network that constitute the meta-network approach to the organisation?

There is a moderate and low correlation between the networks listed (see Table 3.2). Interpreting the strength of a relationship is less important than whether or not a relationship is statistically significant. All correlations are statistically significant at the significance level $p < 0.001$, with some being stronger and others weaker. We can assume that according to the adopted significance level, the obtained value is the result of the desired relationship, which does not exclude the influence of other variables that have not been specified here.

RQ3: Which nodes have the most influential position in the network?

The study used two measures of centrality (out-degree and in-degree) for two-mode knowledge network (AK), resource network (AR), task network (AR), and value creation network (AV) (see Table 3.3). In the AK network, actor A09 has a dominant position (the scaled value is 0.872), and the dominant knowledge of K is K12 (with a scaled score of 0.956). In the AR network, also the A09 actor occupies a prominent position (0.833), along with the resources R08 and R16 (scaled value 1). Subsequently, in the task network (AT), the A09 actor occupies the most influential position (0.792) *ex aequo* with the A19 and A40 actors. The dominant task is T39 (0.978). The last one, value creation network, has a slightly different distribution due to the small number of V nodes. Eighteen employees are involved in value creation (V01–V05), including the value of V02 (0.778), which is dominant in this network.

The results show that it is possible to identify actors, knowledge components, resources, tasks, and their direct and indirect possibilities of influencing value creation understood as a network of relationships. Therefore, value creation in the context of this research depends on intra-organisational relationships and the management of intangible assets in conjunction with actors (employees). Central nodes indicate the most influential in the context of organisational activities conditioned by business processes. Failure to understand where value can be created in an organisation leads to an inefficient allocation of resources.

3.5. Conclusion

This research investigates the relationships between the network and relational approach to organisational value creation and intangible assets. The primary determinant is actors (employees), their knowledge (skills), resources, and tasks closely related to the central business processes. The identified nodes explained which knowledge, resources (including intangible assets), or tasks can lead to value creation in the organisation. This research takes a theoretical perspective of network theory, which treats an organisation as a system of interconnected nodes and interdependencies. The data was analysed using the quadratic assignment procedure and centrality measures. These obtained results broaden the knowledge of the interdependencies between the network nodes, the boundary determined by the analysed organisation, and the value creation is relational. The findings also suggest that value creation from intangible assets is conditioned by a network of relationships between specific nodes.

Theoretical and practical implications

The current literature recognises the potential of the network to study and understand the complexities of value creation and intangible assets, and the interactions and interdependencies of their elements, which can be analysed in the context of a network approach. It has been shown how to identify interdependencies between network nodes. The theoretical background of value creation presented in the chapter from the resource and network approach perspective enriches the literature with a dynamic approach to creating a network of relationships understood as interpenetrating networks (nodes). The resource approach considers a set of resources (both tangible and intangible), which are the essential components that determine value creation. The network approach defines value creation as a network of interrelated elements that interact in unilateral or reciprocal relationships. The theoretical implications can be linked to the methods used to assess value creation and the network analysis itself. Value creation nowadays requires an interdisciplinary approach to the analysis of the company's business opportunities, expressed in the use of methods that, in a complementary way, would allow to create a real image of the business venture being carried out.

The research results using network analysis presented in this chapter provide information to analysts and managers responsible for value creation for the company. The network and resource approach is useful in assessing a company's business opportunities, designing new ventures, and monitoring resilience to change in value creation. By identifying the components that are key to creating value, we can identify the nodes and their attributes needed to perform network analysis. The practical implications of the network approach are expressed in the benefits of using network analysis as a tool complementing traditional methods of economic analysis of the enterprise, by obtaining information about the interdependence of resources, their real value, usefulness, impact on other resources (components), or the dynamics of changes over time. By discovering the most influential (central) nodes of the network, it becomes possible to determine the rank of individual actors, knowledge, resources (intangible assets), and tasks in creating value in connection with the least central nodes.

Directions for future research and limitations

In general, network analysis, especially a dynamic approach to it, allows to regulate the behaviour of the network by adding or removing nodes and/or relationships. The change in the relation and the strength of its intensity can also be simulated. The basic processes influencing the change of a node in the network are the addition or removal of tasks, resources, change in technology, etc. In most organisations, due to missing capital and investment outlays, changing tasks and resources is more difficult than changing people and knowledge, at least in the short term. Many organisations recognise the importance of knowledge or resources when they are no longer available. In order to simulate the loss of data in the network, it is possible to calculate the change in the size of selected network measures after the loss of a given node, indicating changes in the structure of the entire network or individual nodes. Removal of nodes can be deliberate or random over any number of repetitions, allowing you to assess whether the removed node or nodes contribute to value creation. The selection of the appropriate network intervention depends on many factors, including the type and nature of available network data, the type of behaviour change, and the environmental or situational context. These efforts can bring considerable scientific insight into organisational value creation, maintenance, development, and flexibility in social engineering systems. These behaviours affect the effectiveness of the entire organisational network and individual nodes, which can be understood from the perspective of, *inter alia*, network density; its fragmentary nature (isolation of nodes); network centralisation (prominence of nodes in the network); distribution of knowledge and resources; or redundancy of knowledge, resources, and tasks in the organisational network. The organisation and employees in the relationship network and the network efficiency are quantified by network analysis based on graph theory (e.g., Wilson, 2012). It allows measuring the position of organisations and employees in the network or the entire network structure and their graphic visualisation. The effectiveness of the network can be assessed, *inter alia*, through the prism of possible fragmentation (unconnected nodes in the network) or redundancy (redundancy) of nodes and relationships.

Further research should focus on identifying constructive relationships between the organisation and the people employed in it, in connection with the effectiveness of business processes on the basis of which the basic nodes of the intra-organisational network have been identified. Since the identified intangible assets are based on business processes, it would be an added benefit to investigate how, within the chosen business process, knowledge, tasks, and resources are related and which of them have the greatest impact on value creation.

The research allows to assess the prominence (influence, importance) of individual human and non-human actors. But does it allow to evaluate whether a given resource (its properties) is equally unique in other organisations? The results obtained on the basis of a selected case study (IT sector company) cannot be considered in the context of other organisations, as a single case study does not qualify for this. In typical network studies, each variable takes the form of a matrix and is measured by applying the relationship question within one network (see Ibarra, 1995). It is important to note that the unit of analysis in the study assumes a relationship between pairs of subjects, so all variables are dyadic. The data is cross-sectional, which means that all the variables were collected at the same point in time, which makes it impossible to infer cause–effect relationships. In order to deepen the relationships in the network of interest to us, further analysis (including longitudinal) of employees (actors) should be carried out to control or take into account the effects of other potential variables (e.g., age, gender, work experience, and even the position held or the specificity of the tasks performed), to exclude other possible explanations.

References

Alberti, F. G., & Belfanti, F. (2021). Do clusters create shared value? A social network analysis of the motor valley case. *Competitiveness Review, 31*(2), 326–350.

Altman, N., Carley, K. M., & Reminga, J. (2020). *ORA user's guide 2020*. Carnegie Mellon University, School of Computer Science, Institute for Software Research, Pittsburgh, Pennsylvania, Technical Report CMU-ISR-20-110.

Amit, R., & Schoemaker, P. J. (1993). Strategic assets and organizational rent. *Strategic Management Journal, 14*(1), 33–46.

Andrikopoulos, A. (2010). Accounting for intellectual capital: On the elusive path from theory to practice. *Knowledge and Process Management, 17*(4), 180–187.

Barabási, A. L. (2005). Network theory–the emergence of the creative enterprise. *Science, 308*(5722), 639–641.

Barczak, T., Kafel, T., & Magliocca, P. (2021). Network approaches and strategic management: Exploration opportunities and new trends. *Journal of Entrepreneurship, Management and Innovation, 17*(3), 7–35. https://doi.org/10.7341/20211731

Barney, J. (1991). Firm resources and sustained competitive advantage. *Journal of Management, 17*(1), 99–120.

Beattie, V., & Smith, S. J. (2013). Value creation and business models: Refocusing the intellectual capital debate. *The British Accounting Review, 45*(4), 243–254.

Bertani, F., Ponta, L., Raberto, M., Teglio, A., & Cincotti, S. (2021). The complexity of the intangible digital economy: An agent-based model. *Journal of Business Research, 129*, 527–540.

Borgatti, E., & Freeman, L. C. (2002). *Ucinet 6 for windows: Software for social network analysis*. Analytic Technologies.

Borgatti, S. P., Everett, M. G., & Johnson, J. C. (2018). *Analyzing social networks*. Sage Publications.

Borgatti, S. P., & Foster, P. C. (2003). The network paradigm in organizational research: A review and typology. *Journal of Management, 29*(6), 991–1013.

Borgatti, S. P., & Halgin, D. S. (2011). On network theory. *Organization Science, 22*(5), 1168–1181.

Borgatti, S. P., & Molina, J.-L. (2005). Toward ethical guidelines for network research in organizations. *Social Networks, 27*(2), 107–117.

Buskens, V. (2020). Spreading information and developing trust in social networks to accelerate diffusion of innovations. *Trends in Food Science and Technology, 106*, 485–488.

Canestrino, R., & Forouharfar, A. (2021). Networks and network strategies: New theorization based upon a systematic literature review. *Journal of Entrepreneurship, Management and Innovation, 17*(3), 37–66. https://doi.org/10.7341/20211732

Carley, K. M. (1999). Learning within and among organizations. *Advances in Strategic Management, 16*, 33–56.

Chen, G. (2020). Research on the development of network economy under the background of big data. *Journal of Physics: Conference Series, 1624*(3), 1–5.

Confente, I., & Kucharska, W. (2021). Company versus consumer performance: Does brand community identification foster brand loyalty and the consumer's personal brand? *Journal of Brand Management, 28*(1), 8–31.

Corrado, C., Haskel, J., & Jona-Lasinio, C. (2017). Knowledge spillovers, ICT and productivity growth. *Oxford Bulletin of Economics and Statistics, 79*(4), 592–618.

Creswell, J. W., & Poth, C. N. (2017). *Qualitative inquiry and research design: Choosing among five approaches*. Sage Publications.

DaSilva, C. M., & Trkman, P. (2014). Business model: What it is and what it is not. *Long Range Planning, 47*(6), 379–389.

Dekker, D., Krackhardt, D., & Snijders, T. A. (2007). Sensitivity of MRQAP tests to collinearity and autocorrelation conditions. *Psychometrika, 72*(4), 563–581.

Florek-Paszkowska, A., Ujwary-Gil, A., & Godlewska-Dzioboń, B. (2021). Business innovation and critical success factors in the era of digital transformation and turbulent times. *Journal of Entrepreneurship, Management, and Innovation, 17*(4), 7–28. https://doi.org/10.7341/20211741

Gajdzik, B., Grabowska, S., & Saniuk, S. (2021). Key socio-economic megatrends and trends in the context of the industry 4.0 framework. *Forum Scientiae Oeconomia, 9*(3), 5–22. https://doi.org/10.23762/FSO_VOL9_NO3_1

Giza, W., & Wilk, B. (2021). Revolution 4.0 and its implications for consumer behaviour. *Entrepreneurial Business and Economics Review, 9*(4), 195–206. https://doi.org/10.15678/EBER.2021.090412

Guilford, J. P. (1977). *Fundamental statistics in psychology and education* (6th ed.). McGraw-Hill College.

Han, S. H., Yoon, S. W., & Chae, C. (2020). Building social capital and learning relationships through knowledge sharing: A social network approach of management students' cases. *Journal of Knowledge Management, 24*(4), 921–939.

Hinds, P. J., Carley, K. M., Krackhardt, D., & Wholey, D. (2000). Choosing work group members: Balancing similarity, competence, and familiarity. *Organizational Behavior and Human Decision Processes, 81*(2), 226–251.

Hossain, M. A., Akter, S., & Yanamandram, V. (2021). Why doesn't our value creation payoff: Unpacking customer analytics-driven value creation capability to sustain competitive advantage. *Journal of Business Research, 131*, 287–296.

Ibarra, H. (1995). Race, opportunity, and diversity of social circles in managerial networks. *Academy of Management Journal, 38*(3), 673–703.

Isabelle, D., Horak, K., McKinnon, S., & Palumbo, C. (2020). Is Porter's five forces framework still relevant? A study of the capital/labour intensity continuum via mining and IT industries. *Technology Innovation Management Review, 10*(6), 28–41.

Jabłoński, M., Timmers, P., & Sarkis, J. (2020). Sustainability in business models in the network economy. *Electronic Markets, 30*(4), 675–678.

Kaplan, R. S., & Norton, D. P. (1992). The balanced scorecard—measures that drive performance. *Harvard Business Review, 70*(1), 71–79.

Knight, F. H. (1944). Diminishing returns from investment. *Journal of Political Economy, 52*(1), 26–47.

Křenková, E., Rieser, K., & Sato, A. (2021). How software robots can facilitate the procurement process? A case study of Siemens in the Czech Republic. *Entrepreneurial Business and Economics Review, 9*(3), 191–203. https://doi.org/10.15678/EBER.2021.090312

Kubsch, M., Touitou, I., Nordine, J., Fortus, D., Neumann, K., & Krajcik, J. (2020). Transferring knowledge in a knowledge-in-use task—investigating the role of knowledge organization. *Education Sciences*, *10*(1), 1–16.

Kucharska, W. (2021). Leadership, culture, intellectual capital and knowledge processes for organizational innovativeness across industries: The case of Poland. *Journal of Intellectual Capital*, *22*(7), 121–141. https://doi.org/10.1108/JIC-02-2021-0047

Kurbanov, R. A., Belyalova, A. M., Gurbanov, R. A., Ibragimova, Y. E., Balanyuk, L. L., Matvienko, V. V., Kulkova, M. A., & Vagapov, B. R. (2019). Social networks ecology: Socio-psychological phenomena and new means in communication system. *EurAsian Journal of BioSciences*, *13*(2), 1583–1587.

Miao, Z. (2021). Digital economy value chain: Concept, model structure, and mechanism. *Applied Economics*. https://doi.org/10.1080/00036846.2021.1899121

Miller, N. J., Engel-Enright, C., & Brown, D. A. (2021). Direct and moderation effects on U.S. apparel manufacturers' engagement in network ties. *Journal of Entrepreneurship, Management and Innovation*, *17*(3), 67–113. https://doi.org/10.7341/20211733

Moon, Y., Um, H., & Kim, M. S. (2019). Social network analysis to explore the organizational knowledge transfer patterns—from a social capital perspective. *Asia Life Sciences, Supplement*, *20*(1), 117–126.

Nuryakin, N. (2021). Mediating effect of relational capabilities in the relationship between entrepreneurial orientation and SMEs performance. *Journal of Entrepreneurship, Management and Innovation*, *17*(1), 129–146.

Osterwalder, A., & Pigneur, Y. (2010). *Business model generation: A handbook for visionaries, game changers, and challengers*. John Wiley and Sons.

Peteraf, M. A. (1993). The cornerstones of competitive advantage: A resource-based view. *Strategic Management Journal*, *14*(3), 179–191.

Rakhimova, S., Goncharenko, L., Sybachin, S., Kunanbayeva, K., & Fatkullina, A. (2020). Organizational and economic mechanisms for designing the development of the digital economy in developing countries. In *E3S web of conferences* (Vol. 210, p. 10006). EDP Sciences. https://doi.org/10.1051/e3sconf/202021010006

Rumelt, R. P. (1984). Towards a strategic theory of the firm. *Competitive Strategic Management*, *26*, 556–570.

Rymarczyk, J. (2021). The impact of industrial revolution 4.0 on international trade. *Entrepreneurial Business and Economics Review*, *9*(1), 105–117. https://doi.org/10.15678/EBER.2021.090107

Skvarciany, V., & Jurevičienė, D. (2021). An approach to the measurement of the digital economy. *Forum Scientiae Oeconomia*, *9*(3), 89–102. https://doi.org/10.23762/FSO_VOL9_NO3_6

Sorescu, A., & Schreier, M. (2021). Innovation in the digital economy: A broader view of its scope, antecedents, and consequences. *Journal of the Academy of Marketing Science*, *49*(4), 627–631.

Su, C. (2021). To share or hide? A social network approach to understanding knowledge sharing and hiding in organizational work teams. *Management Communication Quarterly*, *35*(2), 281–314.

Tamburis, O., & Bonacci, I. (2019). Clusters and communities: Raising the bar towards open innovation 2.0 paradigms. *International Journal of Pharmaceutical and Healthcare Marketing*, *13*(3), 288–305.

Tsuda, N., & Tsugawa, S. (2021). Effects of community structure in social networks on speed of information diffusion. *Studies in Computational Intelligence*, *943*, 51–61.

Ujwary-Gil, A. (2017a). Intra-organizational two-mode networks analysis of a public organization. *Economics & Sociology*, *10*(3), 192–205.

Ujwary-Gil, A. (2017b). The business model and intellectual capital in the value creation of firms: A literature review. *Baltic Journal of Management*, *12*(3), 368–386.

Ujwary-Gil, A. (2019). Organizational network analysis: A study of a university library from a network efficiency perspective. *Library & Information Science Research*, *41*(1), 48–57.

Ujwary-Gil, A. (2020). *Organizational network analysis: Auditing intangible resources*. Routledge.

Ujwary-Gil, A., & Potoczek, N. R. (2020). A dynamic, network and resource-based approach to the sustainable business model. *Electronic Markets*, *30*(4), 717–733.

Valente, T. W. (2010). *Social networks and health*. Oxford University Press.

van Rijnsoever, F. J., & Eveleens, C. P. (2021). Money don't matter? How incubation experience affects start-up entrepreneurs' resource valuation. *Technovation*, *106*. https://doi.org/10.1016/j.technovation.2021.102294

Wernerfelt, B. (1984). A resource-based view of the firm. *Strategic Management Journal*, *5*(2), 171–180.

Wilson, R. J. (2012). *Introduction to graph theory* (5th ed.). Pearson.

Ya, S., Yue, L., & Man, Z. S. (2021). Analysis of value creation process of platform-driven scientific and technological innovation value chain: The perspective of informationization. In *E3S web of conferences* (Vol. 257, p. 02014). EDP Sciences. https://doi.org/10.1051/e3sconf/202125702014

4 Explaining the TECH brand value with economic-financial and stock market information

The booming digital economy

María Ángeles Alcaide González, Elena De La Poza Plaza, and Natividad Guadalajara Olmeda

1.1. Introduction

The technology (TECH) sector has suddenly burst into the world's economy, and more forcibly, since the 1990s, especially since the start of the present century, and has constantly grown in terms of both number of firms and turnover (Alcaide et al., 2019a; Asikainen & Mangiarotti, 2016; Cid-López et al., 2015; Li-Ting & Dong-Shang, 2020). Such growth is the result of not only technological progress but also of new technologies being integrated into the set of society's sectors (Teodorescu & Korchagina, 2021), which have allowed them to name this era the 4th Industrial Revolution (Schwab, 2017). Not even such a marked recession of all economies as that witnessed today, caused by the COVID-19 health pandemic, has significantly and negatively affected this sector (Alcaide et al., 2021), which is instead being reinforced. This is because today's pandemic has promoted rapid progress towards digital transformation, which both individuals and companies have been forced to undertake. Following this line, the European Union has launched a digital programme with 7.5 billion euros to accelerate recovery and to drive Europe's digital transformation (European Commission, 2020).

This technological revolution affects not only markets but also technology-based companies' brands (Ray & Sharma, 2020), because these firms possess more of the brands that occupy the top posts of international brand value rankings for more consecutive years. All of this evidences both the strong impact of TechBrands on economies worldwide and the need for companies and investors to know the economic value of these very valuable intangible assets. In fact, estimating brand values is a complicated task because their market is poorly concurrent and quite opaque. In addition, knowing how these assets acquire their values, what internal or external company factors affect brand values, and which methods allow suitable valuations to be made will all help firms to create stronger and more valuable brands, and to manage them as if they were a company's strategic assets.

Nowadays, despite the importance of brands as firms' strategic assets, there is a legal gap in the valuation method because no standard exists that

DOI: 10.4324/9781003184638-5

specifies how to value such assets. Nevertheless, the following three international standards include methodologies to value intangible assets in general: IAS (International Accounting Standard) 38 of International Financial Reporting Standards (IFRS Standards, 2018), IVS (International Valuation Standard) 210 (International Valuation Standards Council, 2019), and VPGA (Valuation Practice Guidance-Application) 6 of the RICS Valuation-Global Standards 2020 (Royal Institution of Chartered Surveyors, 2020). They are all based on economic-financial information, and recognise the three traditional assets valuing approaches: income-based, market-based, and cost-based. The first and unique world-specific brand valuation standard appeared in 2010 by means of ISO 10668:2010 (International Organization for Standardization, 2010). This standard is not compulsory, but grants a higher degree of confidence to those companies following it. Therefore, the only existing standard is ISO 10668:2010, which is why most companies and professionals use it despite it not being compulsory because they need to confer their outcomes objectiveness and trust. ISO 10668:2010 also offers knowledge from multidisciplinary experts, including financial experts, consultants, specialists in market research, or lawyers, whereas all other standards on intangible assets, such as IVS or IAS, are clearly set out from an accounting-financial perspective. Hence, ISO 10668:2010 attempts to compile ideas from a broader perspective about brand valuation for the first time on a world scale. In doing so, it represents progress towards harmonising criteria in one discipline, that of intangible assets valuation, which is extremely complex. It is noteworthy that ISO 10668:2010 indicates that valuations must include not only financial aspects but also other customer performance (brand strength and market research) and legal aspects. Customer performance is determined by surveys conducted to know customer performance, while legal aspects refer to elements like the level of legal protection of the asset being valued or the duration of this protection.

The fact that no specific compulsory European regulation exists on brand valuations has favoured, on the one hand, many valuation methodologies appearing in the literature (Damodaran, 1994; Majerova & Kliestik, 2015; Salinas & Ambler, 2009) and, on the other hand, the appearance of important international brand valuation consultancy companies (IBVCC) that apply their own methodologies following the previously cited standards (ISO 10668, 2010), and includes brand strength-based customer performance. Nevertheless, the methods that these IBVCC employ to determine brand strength are neither objective nor transparent, which is their main drawback. Moreover, these IBVCC only value the most important and well-established brands even though the value of many existing technology brands needs to be known, which poses a major problem for the investors and managers of these brands. Knowing brand values is important for the accountancy of companies, and also for their sales and purchases, mergers, procurements, etc.

The present chapter aims to analyse and model the TECH brand value given by IBVCC to the best 21st-century TechBrands using economic-financial according to IAS, IVS, and RICS, and stock market information. These values of shares can be comparable to the brand strength that ISO 10668:2010 indicates. The market research and legal aspects that ISO 10668:2010 contemplates are not herein taken into account. Finally, using the valuation models herein obtained, this work estimates the brand values of TECH firms, not included by IBVCC, that made the most profits in 2020 which are, in turn, the companies that have recently and abruptly appeared on stock market-financial markets and have recently become very important internationally.

Therefore, this chapter aims to deliver scientific evidence based on quantitative methods on how digital technologies through the best 21st-century technology brands contribute to the growth of today's societies. Their importance lies mainly in the need to obtain a reliable method to value brands, and one that is objective, simple to apply, and more rigorous to consider the financial aspects indicated by standards IAS, IVS, and RICS, as well as the brand's stock market/strong aspects according to ISO 10668:2010. This model will be an excellent contribution to companies, investors, and professionals for the valuation they need for valuing technology brands in the growth phase and are not found in the top 100 of IBVCC.

To do so, the following two hypotheses are studied.

Firstly, the literature (Aaker, 1996; Salinas, 2009; Salinas & Ambler, 2009) shows differences in the methods followed to value brands, which do not focus on analysing the specific case of these very prestigious IBVCC, but are actually theoretical studies. The IBVCC value brands according to the income-based approach by capitalising income at the adjusted discount rate according to each brand's risk and attributes (Alcaide et al., 2020). Yet they all have their own peculiarities and include qualitative elements. This means that the valuations provided by one same company in the same year may differ. Therefore, it is necessary to empirically evidence the variability or difference in these valuations as some other authors have done (Alcaide et al., 2019a; Bagna et al., 2017; Janoskova & Krizanova, 2017). This will allow this gap in the literature to be bridged because other works, like those later indicated, do not model differences (Janoskova & Krizanova, 2017), or do so for a maximum three-year period without focusing on the TECH sector (Bagna et al., 2017; Janoskova & Krizanova, 2017), or relate a brand to other areas like corporate social responsibility (Alcaide et al., 2019a). Our contribution in this chapter is important for understanding today's problems in the brand valuation domain and, consequently, for posing the following hypothesis.

H1. A high degree of variability exists in the scores given by IBVCC in their rankings to the most important TechBrands during the 2000–2020 period.

Secondly, as previously mentioned, IBVCC estimate their brand values by combining quantitative economic-financial information and mainly brand strength; that is, with qualitative information. This economic-financial information that belongs to the companies on the stock exchange can be used to estimate brand value models with a given explanatory power. This explanatory power corresponds to the weight that the economic-financial information would have for the brand values of each IBVCC. The brand value's remaining explanatory power would correspond to qualitative information or brand strength. This brand strength would be related to the expected future earnings made from brands; that is, to the price that shareholders would be willing to pay for shares on stock markets. This means that brand strength could be estimated with quantitative variables and, therefore, with completely objective and quantifiable models that comply with ISO 10668:2010. Thus, we pose the next hypothesis.

H2. It is possible to estimate the value of TechBrands, as published by the most prestigious IBVCC, using only the economic-financial and stock market variables for the 2000–2020 period.

Finally, if the previously obtained models (H2) have a high explanatory power, they will be useful for estimating the value of the brands of the TECH companies that made the most profits in 2020 (El Economista, 2020), but have not yet been included in the Top 100 of the IBVCC rankings. Applying H2 will demonstrate the effectiveness of our proposed approach and will evidence the possibility of applying it to value any technology brand on the stock market.

This chapter is organised as follows. Section 1 introduces the aim of this chapter. Section 2 offers a background about brands valuation and the IBVCC that we refer to herein. Section 3 describes the sample and the employed methodology. Section 4 presents the results. Finally, the conclusions are offered in Section 5 and the discussion in Section 6.

1.2. Background: brand valuation and consultancy companies

On the market (business circles) and in the literature, there is evidence that brands have become the most valued intangible asset for firms. On the market, Barron (2017) stated that brands are the most important asset for firms. The Economist (2014) underlines that brands contribute 30% of the market value of S&P 500 companies. The literature contains many references that confirm their positive relation (Bistrova et al., 2017), and one of the reference works of the theme clearly states: "*brands are one of the most valuable intangible assets that firms have*" (Keller & Lehman, 2006). This is why brands have become a priority for managers, who wish to know their value and what variables affect them to improve their value.

Nonetheless, the fact that brands are intangible assets, and no market or specific compulsory standard exists, mean that their valuation is complex, and even ambiguous (Janoskova & Krizanova, 2017).

Even though many methods appear in the literature that are followed to value brands, they can all be grouped into two main perspectives. The first is based on the consumer point of view, or the "Marketing perspective" (Erdem & Swait, 1998; Kamakura & Russell, 1993; Lambin, 1995). These methods employ qualitative variables by means of the brand's relation to consumers to obtain its value. The second perspective, which is known as "economic-financial," centres on brands' financial performance; that is, on quantitative variables. It uses three traditional valuation approaches (An-Chin, 2013; Juliá-Igual et al., 2017), which we previously mentioned: market-based (Damodaran, 1996; Salinas & Ambler, 2009; Simon & Sullivan, 1993; Virvilaitė & Jucaytė, 2008), cost-based (Abratt & Bick, 2003), and income-based (Srinivasan et al., 2001).

Apart from these three approaches, some studies (Damodaran, 1994; Haigh, 1996) employ a combination of the three to determine a brand's quantitative value. Other studies have even used mixed methods by combining marketing techniques and those from the economic-financial perspective (Majerova & Kliestik, 2015; Salinas & Ambler, 2009), which is what IBVCC do to incorporate standard ISO 10668:2010 into their valuations.

This chapter refers to Interbrand, Brand Finance, and Millward Brown as IBVCC. They annually publish rankings with the Top 100 values of the world's best brands, and have done so since 2006, except for Interbrand that started doing so in 2000.

The three IBVCC comply with standards IAS, IVS, RICS, and ISO 10668:2010. They utilise mixed methods and combine income-based and market-based approaches. This is how Interbrand and Brand Finance obtain their brand values, by updating profits from the earnings made with a brand and expressing it as a rate. This rate is calculated. To do so, each IBVCC employs its own algorithms into which it incorporates brand strength (Interbrand, 2020; The Brand Finance Group, 2021). Millward Brown calculates brand values by multiplying earnings made with a brand by a multiple of the brand, which the IBVCC estimates using information from Bloomberg, and all this is multiplied by the percentage of the brand's contribution according to consumers by means of online and face-to-face research performed worldwide (Kantar Millward Brown, 2021). Brand strength is included in these last two concepts.

These IBVCC are the most prestigious ones in this domain worldwide. Many researchers (Agus & Salas, 2017; Basgoze et al., 2016; De Oliveira et al., 2018; Flisikowski & Kucharska, 2018; Johansson et al., 2012; Kim, 2019) utilise their valuations in their works, although the vast majority only employ valuations of one IBVCC. Only four works have jointly used the valuations of all three IBVCC. Alcaide et al. (2019b) modelled brand values in relation to corporate social responsibility. Bagna et al. (2017) developed models to explain brand value in relation to the income, sales, and sales growth of 71 brands from listed companies for the 2013–2015 period. These authors respectively obtained brand values of 28%, 73%, and 90% for Brand Finance, Interbrand, and Millward Brown. Janoskova and Krizanova (2017) made a pairwise comparison of 12 global well-known brands from different sectors for the 2013–2016 period. They found statistically significant differences among rankings. No regression model was developed in their work. These last two cited works agreed that the Brand Finance method was more prudent than others. More recently, Laghi et al. (2020) also employed the values of IBVCC. Rather than independently analysing them, they estimated the mean brand value. Their objective was to validate a direct method to measure relational capital by estimating brands for both listed and non-listed companies. Models were tested with a sample of non-financial firms for the 2006–2019 period by distinguishing among International Accounting Standards (IAS)/International Financial Reporting Standards (IFRS) and US Generally Accepted Accounting Principles (US GAAP) reporting standards. The results show that the identified set of market and accounting multiples proved to be significant information for estimating the value of brands within the IAS/IFRS framework, while less explanatory power was assessed for the US GAAP firms. They also confirmed that this approach was more accurate for valuating listed firms.

1.3. Method

Sample

The companies in the TECH sector making up the sample are the only ones included from 2000 to 2020 in the Top 100 of at least two of the three analysed world rankings of brand valuations, and for at least three years. Note that all the firms included in these rankings are on the stock exchange. With this selection criterion, the intention is to analyse the best 21st-century TechBrands according to the most reputable valuation consultancies in the world.

Seventeen companies make up the sample (see Table 4.1), and these companies are grouped according to the industry to which they belong in line with the Global Industry Classification Standard (GICS). The brand values in

Table 4.1 Classification of the TECH firms making up the sample per industry

Highest brand value (million $) and year reached	*Company*	*Headquarter*	*Creation date*	*Industry*
352,206 (2021)	Apple	Cupertino (USA)	1977	Consumer Electronics
39,717 (2010)	HP	Palo Alto (USA)	1939	
102,623 (2021)	Samsung	Suwon (South Korea)	1938	
16,409 (2000)	Sony	Tokyo (Japan)	1946	
359,004 (2021)	Adobe	San José (USA)	1982	Software—Infrastructure
326,544 (2021)	Microsoft	Redmond (USA)	1975	
26,295 (2021)	Oracle	Redwood (USA)	1977	
30,489 (2021)	Salesforce	San Francisco (USA)	1999	Software—Application
57,578 (2021)	SAP	Walldorf (Germany)	1972	
415,855 (2021)	Amazon	Seattle (USA)	1994	
162,106 (2018)	Facebook	California (USA)	2004	Internet Content & Information
323,601 (2021)	Google	Mountain View (USA)	1998	
45,889 (2021)	Netflix	Los Gatos (USA)	1997	
41,437 (2021)	Accenture	Dublin (Ireland)	1989	Information Technology Services
115,985 (2011)	IBM	Armonk (USA)	1911	
35,559 (2019)	Cisco	San Jose (USA)	1984	Communication Equipment
43,293 (2018)	Intel	Santa Clara (USA)	1968	Semiconductors

the first column refer to the maximum brand value given by one of the three IBVCC herein included to characterise the importance of these assets.

The sample is made up of 17 TECH firms from seven different industries.

Measures

In order to carry out the study, the following information was collected from secondary sources:

1. Brand valuations (million $):

   They were collected from the websites of Interbrand, Brand Finance, and Millward Brown. The Interbrand data were collected from 2000 to 2020, and from 2006 for the other two IBVCC.

2. Economic-financial and stock market information:

   It was taken from the annual accounts of the companies owning the selected brands from the 2000–2020 period. The collected data were accounts receivables, dividends, financial expenses, net results, number of employees, research and development (R&D), sales, total assets, and total liabilities. Market price was also included, which was obtained from the Yahoo Finance website, where monthly prices can be obtained when the stock market closes. The mean was calculated with them to obtain each company's annual price. All the companies' listings were provided in USD $, except for Samsung, whose listing value was converted from South Korean won (KRW) into USD $, and Sony, which was converted from Japanese yen (JPY) into USD $.

This information was used to calculate a set of eight other variables, which were used as the control variables: earnings per shares (EPS = Net result/No. Shares), price to earning (PER = Listing value/EPS), profitability from dividends (dividend per share/listing value × 100), financial profitability (Return on Equity or ROE = Net result/Total stakeholders' equity × 100), economic profitability (Return on Assets or ROA = Operating income/Total assets × 100), leverage (Total liabilities/Total assets × 100), payout (Dividends/Net result); and margin (Sales/Operation income).

The time variable was also added as a control variable, where t = 1 corresponded to the first analysed year (2000), t = 2 to the second year, and so forth. In the end, ten economic variables and nine control variables form part of this study.

Finally to prove H2, of the 18 TECH firms that made the most profit in 2020 (El Economista, 2020), those that had not appeared in the Top 100 of the rankings each year were selected. Of the eight resulting firms, one was eliminated (Dassault Systèmes) because its annual accounts for 2020 were not published when this work was underway. Another company was added, Baidu, which was in the Top 100 of these rankings, but did not meet the previous criteria to be selected for our sample because it is included in the Top 100 of two IBVCC and for less than three years. This left the following eight firms, which were selected to verify H2: Autodesk, Baidu, Booking Holding, Cognizant, Intuit, ServiceNow, VMware, and Workday. Only the net income for 2020, along with the average for that year, was collected from these companies. The values for Baidu were converted from Chinese Yuan (CNY) into USD $.

Procedure

The methodology followed to examine H1, that is, to know if a high degree of variability existed among the TECH brand values given by IBVCC, was a descriptive statistics analysis (mean and standard deviation) and a dispersion graph analysis for each IBVCC and studied year. If variability existed in the brand values given by each IBVCC with time, this methodology allowed it to be observed in detail.

The methodology followed to analyse H2 was a multivariate linear regression analysis by Ordinary Least Squared (OLS). The following equation was employed:

$$Y = \alpha + \beta_1 X_1 + \ldots + \beta_m X_m + \beta_t T + \varepsilon \qquad (1)$$

where
Y= each company's score provided by Interbrand, Brand Finance, and Millward Brown every year
α = constant term
$\beta_1 \ldots \beta_m, \beta_t$ = coefficients of the explanatory economic-financial and stock market variables (1, 2, . . . m) and time
$X_1 \ldots X_m$ = explanatory economic-financial and stock market variables
T = time variable
ε = random disturbance term

By this methodology, a first analysis was performed using only firms' net income as the explanatory variable (Model 1) to determine what percentage of these brand values was explained by this quantitative and objective information granted by each IBVCC. Then a second analysis was carried out by adding the explanatory variable price (Model 2) to know what additional percentage was explained by the firms' earnings that each IBVCC expected them to make (brand strength). Finally, a third analysis was run using the set of 19 explanatory variables (Model 3).

In order to reinforce H2, three models were obtained for all the companies as a whole where, apart from the previous independent variables, three dummy variables relating to each IBVCC were added: 1 if the ranking scored a company, and 0 otherwise.

Models' goodness of fit was measured by the adjusted R^2 and Student's t. The considered error levels were 1%, 5%, and 10%. Multicollinearity was measured by the condition index (CI) and the variance inflation factor (VIF).

Finally, to estimate the brand values of those firms with the most profits in 2020, the models obtained in the previous analysis were employed (H2). Model 2 was used because it is the simplest model when fulfilling ISO 10668:2010. As verified, its explanatory power was similar to that obtained in Model 3 for each IBVCC. Hence, three brand values were estimated per firm for 2020 following Model 2 obtained by each IBVCC.

1.4. Results

H1: A high degree of variability exists in the scores given by IBVCC in their rankings to the most important TechBrands during the 2000–2020 period

Table 4.2 offers the results obtained by the descriptive statistics. The first column shows the year and the three columns following the values correspond to each IBVCC. For each ranking, the mean value of brands is taken (nominal values in million $). The number of analysed brands (n) and their standard deviation (σ) are shown in brackets. The total number of brands studied in each ranking, and their mean, minimum, maximum values and range, are found at the bottom of Table 4.2.

For the three companies, the mean and standard deviation values undergo a generalised increase with time, particularly Millward Brown, except for the first years for Interbrand.

According to the results shown at the bottom of Table 4.2, we see that the mean brand value obtained by Interbrand is 33,373 million $, 45,549 million $ for Brand Finance, and 59,422 million $ for Millward Brown. This tells us that Interbrand is the IBVCC that gives the most prudent values, conversely to Millward Brown. When we examine the mean data in Table 4.2, we see for the early years, especially from 2006 to 2016, that the two first agencies give similar mean values, while the third one always grants a much higher mean value. The highest value given by this agency during the study period is 415,855 million $ (Amazon in 2021), while the maximum value given by Interbrand is 322,999 million $ (Apple in 2021), and the highest by Brand Finance is 263,375 million $ (Apple in 2021). Thus coincidences appear in the highest valued brand in one same company and in the same year. Conversely, the lowest valued brand is given by Interbrand with 3,130 million $ (Amazon in 2001), 5,494 million $ by Brand Finance (Amazon in 2006), and 5,524 million $ by Millward Brown (Facebook in 2010). In this case, a coincidence appears in the same company, but not in the same year. Apart from Millward Brown being the IBVCC to provide the highest values, it also presents the widest variability; that is, the distance or difference between its maximum and minimum points is longer or bigger, respectively (range=410,331 million $). So we can state that Brand Finance is the agency that offers stable valuations (within a narrower range).

Table 4.2 Descriptive statistics results

Year	*Interbrand*	*Brand Finance*	*Millward Brown*
2020	72,905 (16; 91,378)	92,710 (13;91,308)	132,225 (15; 143,419)
2019	57,179 (17; 64,668)	83,242 (12;70,133)	109,306 (16;117,385)
2018	52,684 (17; 58,130)	78,267 (12; 60,120)	96,051 (16;103,745)
2017	46,683 (17; 49,699)	67,905 (12;52,002)	75,065 (16; 80,668)
2016	48,364 (15; 48,249)	53,695 (12; 37,721)	62,433 (17; 73,069)
2015	45,850 (15; 45,291)	48,150 (13; 40,225)	62,540 (15; 69,515)
2014	40,300 (15; 35,118)	46,720 (12; 35,779)	54,165 (14; 51,629)
2013	37,107 (15; 31,168)	39,740 (13; 30,383)	49,293 (14; 52,774)
2012	32,631 (15; 25,563)	34,009 (12;23,746)	49,262 (14; 52,162)
2011	28,346 (14; 20,385)	30,196 (12;18,516)	46,882 (14; 45,426)
2010	25,119 (14; 19,114)	25,051 (11; 11,847)	39,070 (14; 35,454)
2009	22,502 (14; 17,377)	21,350 (11; 9,654)	35,967 (13; 29,949)
2008	23,472 (13; 17,258)	17,822 (11; 9,168)	33,160 (13; 25,287)
2007	21,745 (13; 17,369)	23,119 (12; 13,670)	24,517 (13; 17,722)
2006	20,439 (13; 17,494)	21,262 (10; 10,452)	21,384 (13; 15,739)
2005	19,754 (13; 18,250)		
2004	20,579 (12; 19,072)		
2003	20,078 (12; 19,654)		
2002	19,442 (12; 19,528)		
2001	21,466 (11; 20,644)		
2000	24,195 (10; 22,731)		
N	293	178	217
Mean	33,373	45,549	59,422
Range	319,869	188,488	410,331
Minimum	3,130	5,494	5,524
Maximum	322,999	263,375	415,855

In order to evaluate the variability among the valuations provided by the three brand rankings, Figures 4.1, 4.2, and 4.3 depict a graphic analysis that points out the best TECH brand and the lowest valued brand in each year. Next to the symbol representing each brand, we see the brand value obtained that year according to each IBVCC.

When we compare the three figures, we see that no coincidences appear for the best and worse values given to the TechBrands by any IBVCC for any year. If we look at the lowest values given by all three IBVCC, we find that those from Brand Finance and Millward Brown, which display a similar trend, are much higher than those from Interbrand. However, when we contemplate the highest brand values, the Interbrand values are higher than those of Brand Finance, especially until 2010, and also from 2015 to the present day. The Millward Brown values are the highest of the three IBVCC. This confirms that Brand Finance is the IBVCC that offers the least variability between the highest and the lowest values given to TECH firms during our study period.

We also see how Interbrand is the IBVCC that appears to give more stable values for TechBrands, particularly for the first eight studied years. According

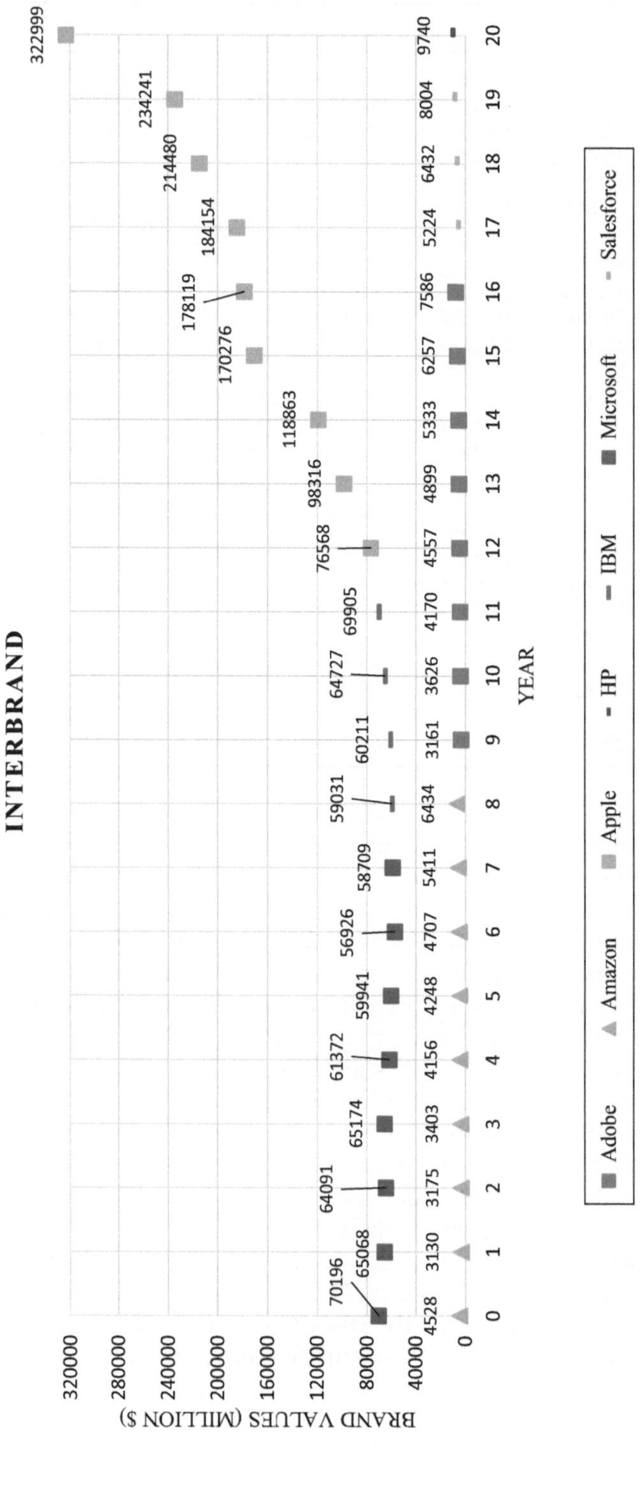

Figure 4.1 The best and worse valued TechBrands according to Interbrand for the 2000–2020 period

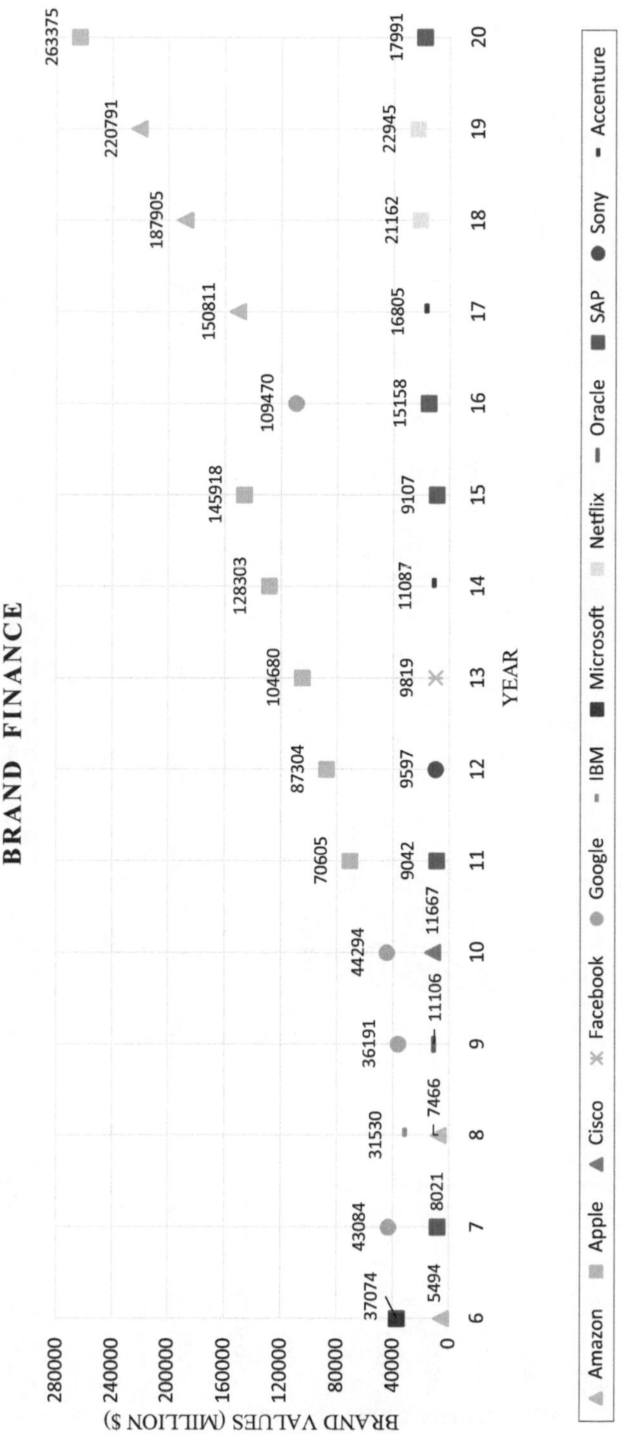

Figure 4.2 The best and worst valued TechBrands according to Brand Finance: 2006–2020

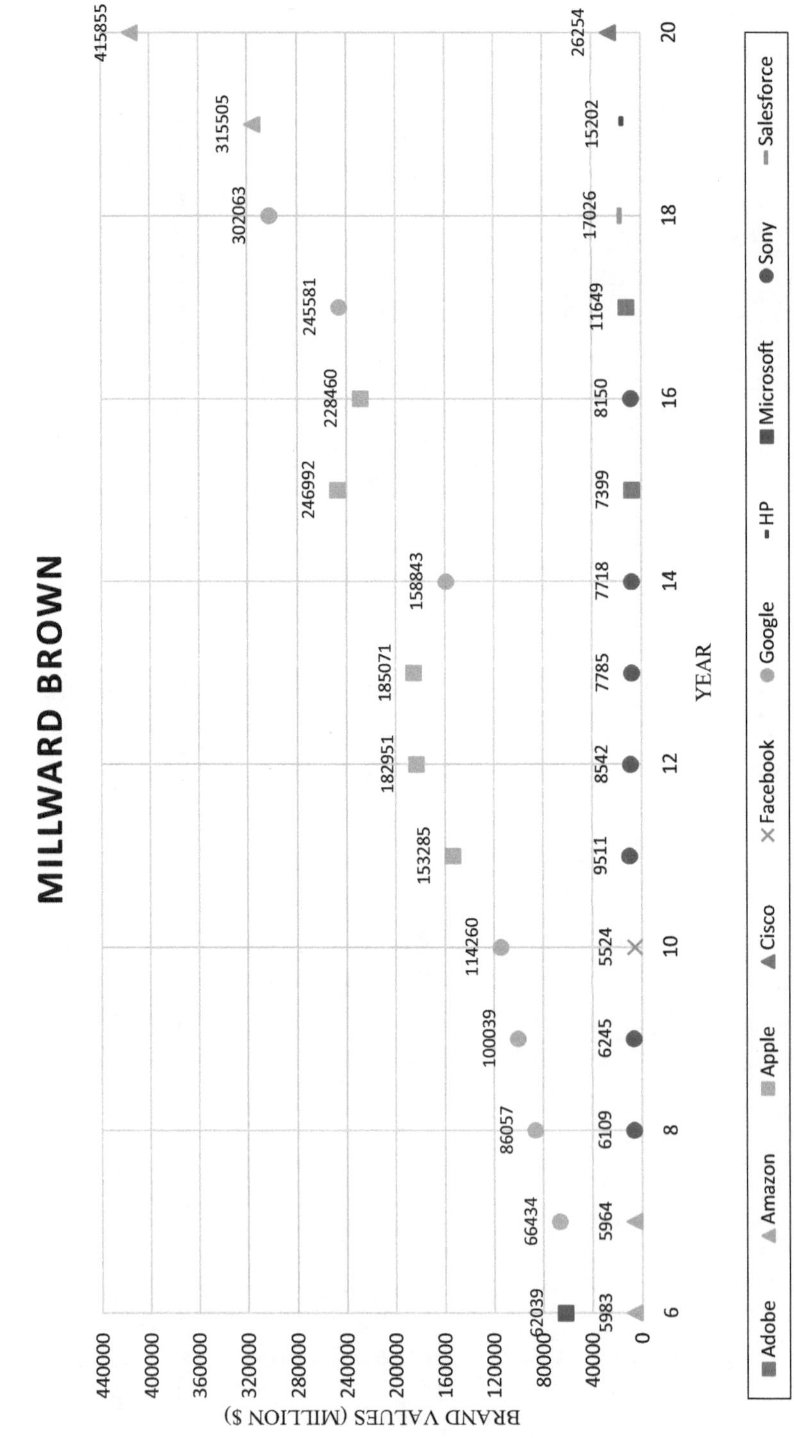

Figure 4.3 The best and worst valued TechBrands according to Millward Brown: 2006–2020

to Figure 4.1, from 2000 to 2008, the worst valued firm of our sample is always Amazon, from 2009 to 2016 it is Adobe, for the next three years it is Salesforce, and in 2020 it changes to HP. The best valued firm in the first eight years is Microsoft. In the second stage (2008–2011), the best valued brand is IBM, and it is Apple from 2012 to the present day. In other words, a trend of repeating positions between the best and the worst valued brands appears. We stress the maximum values given from 2012, which constantly grow, but remain more stable at around 62.5 million $ in earlier years. A more constant trend is seen for the minimum values, about 4.6 million $. However, this trend slightly increases over the last two years.

Figure 4.2 shows that the highest brand values given by Brand Finance for TechBrands practically cover three brands, albeit randomly. In the early years, the highest values basically go to Google, from 2011 to 2015, and they are for Apple in 2020, and for Amazon from 2017 to 2019. These values also remain quite stable and then start continuously growing from 2011 to the present day. No such stable trend appears for minimum values, and the SAP brand more frequently occupies this position.

Figure 4.3 illustrates how Millward Brown also confers certain stability to the TechBrands given from 2006, especially for the best given values. The following brands occupying these positions are stressed: Google, Apple, and, more recently, Amazon. The brand that more often occupies the worst position is Sony.

H2: It is possible to estimate the value of TechBrands, as published by the most prestigious IBVCC, using only economic-financial and stock market variables for the 2000–2020 period

Table 4.3 shows the linear regression models obtained for each IBVCC according to Equation (1). Three models were obtained for each IBVCC, and three others for the set of valuations that these companies made jointly. Thus, in the first model, the company's Net results were the only explanatory variable, while the second was adding the Listing value. The third included all the explanatory variables.

The overall models for all three IBVCC were obtained for the years when data were available for all three companies (2006–2020) using the reference company, namely Interbrand.

The residuals were analysed. It was verified that no multicollinearity existed among the variables for any model. The CI and VIF values were lower and went below the threshold of 30 and 9, respectively (Gujarati, 2003).

In the models that depended only on the variable Net result (Models 1), this variable was capable of explaining between 51.1% (Brand Finance) and 70.4% (Interbrand) of the brand value given by the IBVCC, while the joint model explained 55.9%. This means that the Net result of a company owning a brand defined 51%–70% of the brand value from brand rankings, while the rest was accounted for by the brand's qualitative aspects.

Table 4.3 Linear regression models for the high-value brands of the IT sector

	Interbrand Model 1 (00–20)	*Interbrand Model 2 (00–20)*	*Interbrand Model 3 (00–20)*	*Brand Finance Model 1 (06–20)*	*Brand Finance Model 2 (06–20)*	*Brand Finance Model 3 (06–20)*	*Millward Brown Model 1 (06–20)*	*Millward Brown Model 2 (06–20)*	*Millward Brown Model 3 (06–20)*	*Three rankings jointly Model 1 (06–20)*	*Three rankings jointly Model 2 (06–20)*	*Three rankings jointly Model 3 (06–20)*
Constant	7157.92***	3586.89***	9110.68***	11957.92***	2092.65	959.15	11669.48*	−2431.33	14793.11***	1364.83	−7469.47***	4996.63*
N.Result	3.26***	3.01***	2.72***	2.79***	2.50***	1.50***	4.79***	4.26***	4.03***	3.64***	3.32***	3.17***
L.Value		50.79***	96.20***		85.43***	73.32***		136.68***	135.01***		84.549***	81.58***
T			−1380.26***									
T.Liabil.			0.25***			0.17***			0.68***			0.26***
Sales						0.13***						
ROA						295.79**			545.67***			
Leverage						−190.46***			−457.43***			−79.42***
T.Assets									−0.37***			−0.13***
A.Recei.									0.92***			0.56***
F.Expen.									−7.63***			−3.61***
D.MB										22228.35***	22436.42***	22846.69***
Adj. R^2	70.4%	80.8%	86.8%	51.1%	87.2%	89.4%	52.8%	81.6%	88.2%	55.9%	75.8%	79.1%
N	291	291	192	177	177	129	215	213	178	614	612	517
CI	2.075	2.265	6.314	2.427	2.650	15.169	2.226	2.451	17.308	2.79	2.983	15.170
VIF	1.000	1.039	2.014	1.000	1.015	9.342	1.000	1.022	1.373	1.001	1.021	1.359

***, **, and * are the 1%, 5%, and 10% levels of error, respectively. CI is the condition index which, in all the obtained models, presents a level that is lower than or equal to 17.308. VIF is the inflation factor of variance, with a low level in all the models. Thus, there was no multicollinearity among variables.

When the shares' listing was added (Models 2), explanatory power rose to 80.8%–81.6% (Interbrand and Millward Brown) and 87.2% (Brand Finance) of the brand value given by the IBVCC, while the joint model rose to 75.8%, which is a mean increase of about 15% for Interbrand, 70% for Brand Finance, and 54% for Millward Brown.

In the model generated with all the explanatory variables (Model 3), the explanatory power slightly rose, with about 87% for all the models. The same occurred with the joint model, where its R^2 dropped to 79.1%.

The only two explanatory variables added to Model 3 to affect the Interbrand values were total liabilities and Time (T); four were added to the Brand Finance model: total liabilities, sales, ROA, and leverage; and six to the Millward Brown model: total liabilities, ROA, leverage, total assets, accounts receivables, and financial expenses. The same last six affected the joint model, except for ROA.

In these models, all the variables intervened positively in the three IBVCC models to explain brand values, except the variables leverage, financial expenses, and total assets. For the first two cases, naturally the higher the value of these variables, the lower the brand value. In other words, these variables negatively affect the brand value given by the IBVCC. Total assets indicate that IBVCC penalised the brand value of bigger companies depending on their assets. The Time variable (T) took a negative sign as it was influenced by the lowest brand value in the first years (2000–2009), as Table 4.2 shows. However, it affected only the Interbrand ranking, which is natural because it is the ranking that has been available for the most years (2000–2020). The dummy variable of the Millward Brown ranking took a positive sign. This means that if all the other variables were on an equal basis, Interbrand and Brand Finance would value below Millward Brown, specifically by more than 22,000 million $ below. This was also seen in the simple models, where the coefficient of Net result was higher for Millward Brown and lower for Brand Finance.

Finally, given the high explanatory power of the obtained models (H2) (Table 4.3), their application is proposed to value the TechBrands that made the most profits in 2020 and were not included in the Top 100 of IBVCC. The results obtained by applying Model 2 generated by each IBVCC are provided in Table 4.4. These Models 2 only have two independent variables (net income and price), and their explanatory power is 80%–87%.

Table 4.4 TECH value brands (million $) in 2020 according to the Models 2 of H2

	Interbrand	*Brand Finance*	*Millward Brown*
AUTODESK	18,713.88	24,440.12	33,636.95
BAIDU	19,881.28	21,141.96	28,894.46
BOOKING	91,569.13	149,929.68	234,109.43
COGNIZANT	11,175.79	11,289.82	12,645.53
INTUIT	24,489.37	32,571.27	46,806.80
SERVICENOW	25,462.46	38,584.17	55,982.53
VMWARE	16,847.76	19,123.31	25,351.70
WORKDAY	12,569.17	17,924.90	22,825.28

We observe that the TECH brand valuations made with the Interbrand model were the most prudent ones, while those made with the Millward Brown model were the highest. This coincides with the models obtained according to H2.

1.5. Conclusions

This study analyses the international valuation brand rankings in the TECH sector for the 2000–2020 period. It contributes to the scarce empirical literature about brand valuation modelling in the TECH sector. As previously stated, a consensus about the methodology employed to value brands is lacking, but there is no transparent market for these types of intangible assets. Hence, these factors lead many multinational consulting companies' methodologies to emerge, which aim to assess and rank international brands.

First of all, the obtained results confirm our H1 because a high degree of variability exists between the scores that IBVCC give to the most important TechBrands during our study period (2000–2020). This variability also remains constant throughout the study period, and reveals that the values estimated by Millward Brown are always higher than those given by Brand Finance which, in turn, always exceeds those given by Interbrand, which coincides with Janoskova and Krizanova (2017).

Secondly, this study confirms our H2; that is, it is possible to explain the value of TechBrands given by the most prestigious IBVCC only with economic-financial and stock market variables partly in compliance with standard ISO 10668:2010. So it is possible to account for between 80.8% and 87.2% of the values estimated by IBVCC with only the variables Net income and Price (Model 2). It is even possible to improve this explanatory power with Model 3, which goes from 86.8% to 88.2%. The remaining explanatory power is given by the customer performance obtained with the market studies, and perhaps also by legal aspects. Our results improve the study by Bagna et al. (2017), who explain the brand value, but with three variables (income, sales, and sales growth) and less explanatory power (between 28% and 90%).

Finally, with the brand valuation models based on firms' economic-financial information, the brand value of a sample of TECH firms on the stock exchange that made high profits in 2020 was estimated (El Economista, 2020). Thus, the models developed for TECH firms, whose brands will probably appear shortly in the top ranking of world brands, were applied. In this way, both managers and investors can know the value of such valuable intangible assets like brands. What is more, the developed models are also capable of measuring brand value evolution and positioning it in relation to competitors. The herein obtained models also eliminate subjective and opaque parameters that IBVCC employ to include brand strength. Hence, the present work provides objective, simple, transparent, and reliable valuation models of TechBrands.

This work also empirically evidences that results differ depending on the methodology followed to value brands. In addition, no previous study has shown this for the assessments made by prestigious international consulting firms or for a 20-year period.

Research can also continue by developing models to estimate the brand value of companies that have abruptly emerged during the pandemic as a result of society's digitalisation and its changing habits (i.e., teleworking and online shopping). One such case is Zoom, a TECH brand part of the top 100 brand ranking in 2020. However, it is not considered in our study because it does not follow our research criteria in consistency terms of rankings over time.

1.6. Discussion

These results offered in this chapter contribute to the literature by proposing a quantitative approach to value such a valuable asset as brands in the TECH sector employing only economic-financial and stock market information. This ensures using an objective valuation model that is transparent and easy to obtain, unlike most previous works that have taken a qualitative approach or have done so from the marketing perspective (Kapferer & Thoenig, 1991; Keller, 1993). It also uses and compares the three values given by IBVCC conversely to the majority of research works, which have merely employed those valuations made by one of the IBVCC analysed in this chapter (Kucharska et al., 2018; Ratnatunga & Ewing, 2009; Zahari et al., 2020).

By means of quantitative methods, this work also scientifically evidences the differences in valuations of the technology brands that the more prestigious IBVCC have provided over a 21-year period, which makes the present chapter pioneering in this domain because previous works have not analysed the differences among IBVCC (Janoskova & Krizanova, 2017), but have only contemplated the mean brand value of the three IBVCC (Laghi et al., 2020), obtained models for periods of time less than 5 years and have not centred on the TECH sector (Bagna et al., 2017; Janoskova & Krizanova, 2017).

This study represents a considerable advance and contribution for valuation companies, investors, and professionals due to lack of homogeneity and trust in today's existing methods, and also given the need to obtain a more rigorous method for valuing this very valuable asset, especially for technology companies, and to know the contribution they make to society today. This study also acts as a step towards unifying quantitative criteria by complying with ISO 10668:2010.

Finally, this chapter evidences that it is possible to apply the proposed method to value any technology brand on the stock market.

References

Aaker, D. A. (1996). *Building strong brands*. The Free Press.

Abratt, R., & Bick, G. (2003). Valuing brands and brand equity: Pitfalls and processes. *Journal of Applied Management and Entrepreneurship*, *8*, 21–39.

Agus, M., & Salas, T. (2017). Strategic and institutional sustainability: Corporate social responsibility, brand value, and Interbrand listing. *Journal of Product & Brand Management*, *26*(6), 545–558. https://doi.org/10.1108/JPBM-07-2016-1277

Alcaide, M. A., De la Poza, E., & Guadalajara, M. N. (2019a). Assessing the sustainability of high-value brands in the IT sector. *Sustainability*, *11*(6), 1598. https://doi.org/10.3390/su11061598

Alcaide, M. A., De la Poza, E., & Guadalajara, M. N. (2019b). The impact of corporate social responsibility transparency on the financial performance, brand value, and sustainability level of IT companies. *Corporate Social Responsibility and Environmental Management*, 1–13. https://doi.org/10.1002/csr.1829

Alcaide, M. A., De la Poza, E., & Guadalajara, M. N. (2020). Modelling IT brand values supplied by consultancy service companies: Empirical evidence for differences. *Technological and Economic Development of Economy*, *1*(27), 120–148. https://doi.org/10.3846/tede.2020.13755

Alcaide, M. A., De la Poza, E., & Guadalajara, M. N. (2021). *Winners and losers of the Covid-19: An empirical analysis of the Nasdaq-100* (pp. 39–46). Proceedings of the 20th RSEP International Economics, Finance & Business Conference, BC Publishing.

An-Chin, C. (2013). A fuzzy multiple criteria comparison of technology valuation methods for the new materials development. *Technological and Economic Development of Economy*, *19*(3), 397–408. https://doi.org/10.3846/20294913.2013.821687

Asikainen, A. L., & Mangiarotti, G. (2016). Open innovation and growth in IT sector. *Service Business*, *11*, 45–68. https://doi.org/10.1007/s11628-015-0301-2

Bagna, E., Dicuonzo, G., Perrone, A., & Dell'Atti, V. (2017). The value relevance of brand valuation. *Applied Economics*, *49*(58), 5865–5876. https://doi.org/10.1080/00036846.2017.1352078

Barron, J. (2017). *Bringing "brand" into the boardroom*. Retrieved December 20, 2020, from https://themasb.org/wpcontent/uploads/2017/08/G.-Keynote_Bringing-Brand-into-the-Boardroom-Barron-8.17R.pdf

Basgoze, P., Yildiz, Y., & Camgoz, S. M. (2016). Effect of brand value announcements on stock returns: empirical evidence from Turkey. *Journal of Business Economics and Management*, *17*(6), 1252–1269. https://doi.org/10.1080/00036846.2017.1352078

Bistrova, J., Lace, N., Tamosiuniene, R., & Kozlovskis, K. (2017). Does firm's higher innovation potential lead to its superior financial performance? Case of CEE countries. *Technological and Economic Development of Economy*, *23*(2), 375–391. https://doi.org/10.3846/20294913.2016.1266411

The Brand Finance Group. (2021). Retrieved March 9, 2021, from https://brandirectory.com/methodology

Cid-López, A., Hornos, M. J., Carrasco, R. A., & Herrera-Viedma, E. (2015). A hybrid model for decision-making in the information and communications technology sector. *Technological and Economic Development of Economy*, *21*(5), 720–737. https://doi.org/10.3846/20294913.2015.1056281

Damodaran, A. (1994). *Damodaran on valuation*. John Wiley and Sons.

Damodaran, A. (1996). *Investment valuation*. John Wiley and Sons.

De Oliveira, M. O. R., Stefanan, A. A., & Lobler, M. L. (2018). Brand equity, risk and return in Latin America. *Journal of Product and Brand Management*, *27*(5), 557–572. https://doi.org/10.1108/JPBM-02-2017-1418

The Economist. (2014, August 30). What are brands for? *The Economist*. Retrieved February 3, 2021, from www.economist.com/business/2014/08/30/what-are-brands-for

El Economista. (2020, November 4). La tecnología despegará todavía más en 2021 con un 17% más de ganancias. *El Economista*, p. 18.

Erdem, T., & Swait, J. (1998). Brand equity as a signaling phenomenon. *Journal of Consumer Psychology*, 7, 131–157. https://doi.org/10.1207/s15327663jcp0702_02

European Commission. (2020). Retrieved March 3, 2021, from https://ec.europa.eu/commission/presscorner/detail/en/ip_20_2406

Flisikowski, K., & Kucharska, W. (2018). The condition of economies: Do most valuable global brands matter? *Equilibrium: Quarterly Journal of Economics and Economic Policy*, *13*(2), 251–264. https://doi.org/10.24136/eq.2018.013

Gujarati, D. N. (2003) *Basic econometrics* (4th ed.). McGraw-Hill.

Haigh, D. (1996). *Founder and CEO, brand finance*. Retrieved December 20, 2016, from http://brandfinance.com/who-we-are/our-people/person/david-haigh/

Interbrand. (n.d). Retrieved December 20, 2020, from www.interbrand.com/thinking/best-global-brands-2020-methodology/#:~:text=Interbrand's%20brand%20valuation%20methodology%20seeks,delivering%20even%20further%20growth%20tomorrow

International Financial Reporting Standards, IFRS Standards. (2018). Retrieved April 20, 2019, from www.ifrs.org/news-and-events/2018/03/issued-ifrs-standards-2018-red-book-available-to-order-now/

International Organization for Standardization, ISO 10668. (2010). *Brand valuation—requirements for monetary brand valuation*. Retrieved March 11, 2019, from www.iso.org/standard/46032.html

International Valuation Standards Council. (2019). *International valuation standards*. Retrieved November 2, 2020, from www.ivsc.org/standards/international-valuation-standards

Janoskova, K., & Krizanova, A. (2017). Comparison of selected internationally recognized brand valuation methods. *Oeconomia Copernicana*, *8*(1), 99–110. https://doi.org/10.24136/oc.v8i1.7

Johansson, J. K., Dimofte, C. V., & Mazvancheryl, S. K. (2012). The performance of global brands in the 2008 financial crisis: A test of two brand value measure. *International Journal of Research in Marketing*, *29*, 235–245. https://doi.org/10.1016/j.ijresmar.2012.01.002

Juliá-Igual, J. F., Cervelló-Royo, R., & Berné-Lafuente, I. (2017). Market value analyses of a Chinese e-commerce holding group: A multicriteria approach. *Service Business*, *11*(3), 475–490. https://doi.org/10.1007/s11628-016-0316-3

Kamakura, W. A., & Russell, G. J. (1993). Measuring brand value with scanner data. *International Journal of Research in Marketing*, *10*, 9–22. https://doi.org/10.1016/0167-8116(93)90030-3

Kantar Millward Brown. (2021). Retrieved February 1, 2021, from www.brandz.com/about-us

Kapferer, J. N., & Thoenig, J. C. (1991). *The brand: Engine of competitiveness of the companies and growth of the economies*. McGraw-Hill Editions.

Keller, K. L. (1993). Conceptualizing, measuring and managing customer-based brand equity. *Journal of Marketing*, *57*, 1–22. https://doi.org/10.1177/002224299305700101

Keller, K. L., & Lehmann, D. R. (2006). Brands and branding: Research findings and future priorities. *Marketing Science*, *25*(6), 740–759. https://doi.org/10.1287/mksc.1050.0153

Kim, E. (2019). A study on the Chinese translation methods of multinational brand name. *The Journal of Humanities and Social Science*, *10*(2), 129–140. https://doi.org/10.22143/HSS21.10.2.10

Kucharska, W., Flisikowski, K., & Confente, I. (2018). Do global brands contribute to the economy of their country of origin? A dynamic spatial approach. *Journal of Product & Brand Management*, *27*(7), 768–780. https://doi.org/10.1108/JPBM-10-2017-1641

Laghi, E., Di Marcantoni, M., Cillo, V., & Paoloni, N. (2020). The relational side of intellectual capital: An empirical study on brand value evaluation and financial performance. *Journal of Intellectual Capital*. https://doi.org/10.1108/JIC-05-2020-0167

Lambin, J. (1995). *Strategic marketing*. McGraw-Hill Editions.

Li-Ting, Y., & Dong-Shang, C. (2020). Using categorical DEA to assess the effect of subsidy policies and technological learning on R&D efficiency of IT industry. *Technological and Economic Development of Economy*, *26*(2), 311–330. https://doi.org/10.3846/tede.2019.11411

Majerova, J., & Kliestik, T. (2015). Brand valuation as immanent component of brand value building and managing. *Procedia Economics and Finance*, *26*, 546–552. https://doi.org/10.1016/S2212-5671(15)00953-3

Ratnatunga, J., & Ewing, M. T. (2009). An ex-ante approach to brand capability valuation. *Journal of Business Research*, *62*, 323–331. https://doi.org/10.1016/S0263-2373(03)00076-8

Ray, K., & Sharma, M. (2020). Antecedents and outcomes of brand strength: A study of Asian IT organizations towards brand sustainability. *Corporate Reputation Review*. https://doi.org/10.1057/s41299-020-00097-y

Royal Institution of Chartered Surveyors. (2020). *RICS valuation-global standards*. Retrieved February 2, 2020, from www.rics.org/globalassets/rics-website/media/upholding-professional-standards/sector-standards/valuation/rics-valuation-global-standards-jan.pdf

Salinas, G. (2009). *The international brand valuation manual* (p. 420). John Wiley & Sons Ltd.

Salinas, G., & Ambler, T. (2009). A taxonomy of brand valuation practice: Methodologies and purposes. *Journal of Brand Management*, *17*, 39–61. https://doi.org/10.1057/bm.2009.14

Schwab, K. (2017). *The fourth industrial revolution*. World Economic Forum, Crown Business.

Simon, J., & Sullivan, M. (1993). The measurement and determinants of brad equity: A financial approach. *Journal of Marketing Science*, *1*, 28–52. https://doi.org/10.1287/mksc.12.1.28

Srinivasan, V., Park, C., & Chang, D. (2001). Equitymap: Measurement, analysis, and prediction of brand equity and its sources. *Research Paper Series*, *1685*, 110.

Teodorescu, M., & Korchagina, E. (2021) Applying blockchain in the modern supply chain management: Its implication on open innovation. *Journal of Open Innovation: Technology, Market and Complex*, 7(80). https://doi.org/10.3390/joitmc7010080

Virvilaitė, R., & Jucaytė, I. (2008). Brand valuation: Viewpoint of costumer and company. *Engineering Economics*, *56*, 111–119.

Zahari, A. R., Esa, E., Rajadurai, J., Azizan, N. A., & Muhamad Tamyez, P. F. (2020). The effect of corporate social responsibility practices on brand equity: An examination of Malaysia's top 100 brands. *Journal of Asian Finance, Economics and Business*, 7(2), 271–280. https://doi.org/10.13106/jafeb.2020.vol7.no2.271

5 Exploring the effects of digital business strategies and technology scanning on company performance

Minna Saunila, Juhani Ukko, Mina Nasiri, Tero Rantala, and Sariseelia Sore

5.1. Introduction

In recent decades, companies' operating environments have become increasingly digital, which has resulted in interconnections among services, products, and processes (Bharadwaj et al., 2013; Castelo-Branco et al., 2019; Gürdür et al., 2019). However, the adoption of digital technologies poses significant challenges to companies (Li et al., 2018), particularly when connected operations, services, and products alter traditional businesses and require novel strategies for embracing such technologies (Yoo et al., 2012; Kallinikos et al., 2013). The increasing digitalisation of companies' business environments has produced studies on digital business strategies (Bharadwaj et al., 2013; Grover & Kohli, 2013; Matt et al., 2015). Technology brands are no exception, as fierce competition requires new strategic approaches to digital transformation. However, there is no consensus among researchers regarding how companies' digital transformations should relate to their organisational strategies. For example, Hess et al. (2016) explained that several studies have called for digital business strategies that integrate IT and business strategies and may reveal a company's view regarding forthcoming digital business models. Another position is that a company's IT strategy can progress from a functional to an organisational strategy that uses a company's digital resources to generate added value. Therefore, a digital transformation is a crucial strategic initiative that requires its own strategy that would not be a subcomponent of the organisational or functional strategy (Hess et al., 2016).

Despite researchers' growing interest in digital business strategies, all the strategic approaches presented earlier are empirically under-researched. The role of digital business strategy in technology brands' operations is an especially under-explored topic. In addition, most available research on digital business strategies apply to large companies, whereas the digital orientations of SMEs may be different from those of big companies. Pagani (2013) has called for more empirical studies to better understand how digital business strategies create value in the digital economy. Moreover, digital business strategies have been criticised for not providing specific guidelines regarding digital transformations

DOI: 10.4324/9781003184638-6

(Hess et al., 2016). In general, the mechanisms through which digital business strategies contribute to company performance require further investigation.

Ross et al. (2017) have suggested that a sound digital strategy offers the means for selecting the type of digital strategy: a digitised solutions strategy or a customer engagement strategy. A digitised solutions strategy pursues information-enriched services and products that provide new value to customers, whereas a customer engagement strategy pursues outstanding, personalised experiences that generate customer loyalty. The digital business strategy examined in this chapter is more similar to a digitised solutions strategy than a customer engagement strategy. In this context, technology scanning is an essential step in digital transformation. Technology scanning refers to collecting information via new digital channels and devices and to the related user behaviours (Nylén & Holmström, 2015) as well as a company's initiative and capacity to explore and exploit new digital technologies (Hess et al., 2016). However, previous studies have not considered technology scanning as a mediator between a digital business strategy and company performance.

To address these research gaps, this chapter studies the relations between a digital business strategy, technology scanning, and SME performance. We propose that the successful use of a digital business strategy enables SMEs to develop their technology scanning practices, which, in turn, enhances company performance. The data were collected via a survey administered to SMEs in Finland. We used confirmatory factor analysis and structural equation modelling to test the proposed theoretical model. The chapter shows that digital business strategy alone negatively impacts company performance. However, technology scanning acts as a mediator in the relation between a digital business strategy and company performance. The chapter improves our knowledge of digital transformation by showing that digital business strategy can positively impact company performance via technology scanning.

5.2. Theoretical model and hypotheses

Digital business strategy

The emergence of the digital transformation has led to the introduction of the concept of "digital business strategy," which integrates IT strategies and business strategies (Bharadwaj et al., 2013; El Sawy et al., 2016; Hess et al., 2016). In contrast to traditional IT or business strategies, which respond to technology through isolation (Hess et al., 2016), digital business strategies treat digital technologies as connective tissue (Bharadwaj et al., 2013). According to this position, digital technologies provide several opportunities for the creation of disruptive innovations, which change the existing value propositions by offering novel solutions and understandings of customers' preferences through the interplay between services and products (Porter & Heppelmann, 2014; Saunila et al., 2019; Vial, 2019). In other words, digital business strategies can be considered transfunctional activities that rely heavily on sharing information via digital platforms, both inside and outside of companies (El Sawy et al., 2016). Therefore, the practical definition of a digital business strategy highlights the leveraging of digital resources in value creation by means of an organisational strategy (Bharadwaj et al., 2013).

Technology scanning

Nowadays, companies have entered an era in which businesses are not resistant to the cumulative influences of the digital transformation. As digital technology is the main driver of the digital transformation (Hess et al., 2016; Castelo-Branco et al., 2019; Vial, 2019), companies try to find new technological solutions and strategies for implementing such solutions to improve operational performance; this is known as the "digital transformation" (Hess et al., 2016). According to Hess et al. (2016), there are different approaches to the creation, development, and introduction of new technology solutions in the market. For instance, being a traditional follower of technological innovations does not generate competitive advantages; however, new Internet-based technologies enable opportunities that require quick actions (Hess et al., 2016) and precise planning (Nylén & Holmström, 2015). Because of the fast pace of the digital transformation, companies are required to actively identify dynamic devices. These devices should be smart enough to discover customers' preferences through user behaviour and contextual data (Nylén & Holmström, 2015). The active participation of companies in the identification of new technologies is known as "technology scanning."

Company performance

According to Tangen (2005), performance is an umbrella concept for all the factors that measure a company's success and its operations. More specifically, a well-performing company is one that achieves the goals set by the company's management leaders (Lebas, 1995). In a similar vein, Atkinson (2012) claimed that good performance ensures that a company's stakeholders achieve the desired outputs. In this study, performance refers to a company's operational results. Such results can be realised in various forms—for example, as greater profitability or higher sales. Digital transformation is a means for achieving operational results and is thus an antecedent of company performance.

Research model and hypotheses

This chapter aims to improve our understanding of the interplay between digital business strategies, technology scanning, and company performance in the SME context. We propose that successful use of digital business strategies enables SMEs to develop their technology scanning practices, which, in turn, enhances company performance. The hypothesised connections are shown in the research model (Figure 5.1). We controlled for company size, company

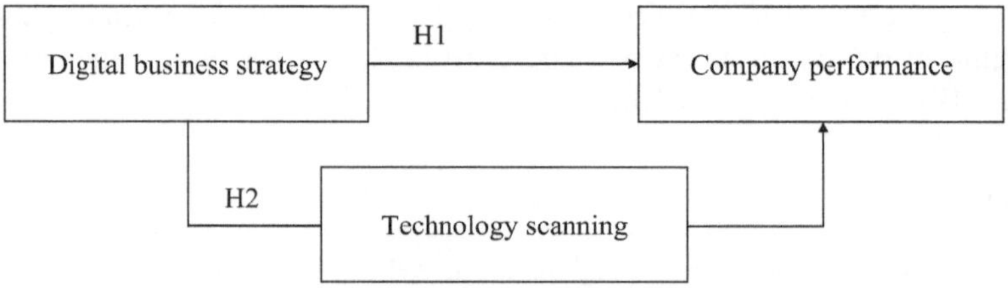

Figure 5.1 The research model

maturity, and the competitive intensity of the markets, as these variables could significantly affect the results of our study.

The definition of a digital business strategy provided by Bharadwaj et al. (2013) highlights the importance of formulating organisational strategies by leveraging companies' digital solutions and resources to create value and improve organisational performance. According to Goerzig and Bauernhansl (2018), a digital business strategy involves decisions related to the adoption of digital technologies to provide value to a company and improve company performance. By using digital business strategies, companies can participate in digital business environments that provide added value and improve performance (Mathrani et al., 2013; Pagani, 2013). Bharadwaj et al. (2013) also argued that digital business strategies have made it possible for companies to democratise the business-related content that they share in digitising business environments and across different digital platforms. Therefore, companies can implement digital business strategies and use digital applications and platforms to expand their businesses and increase sales—for example, companies can give their customers more options to choose the right products and services (Grover & Kohli, 2013). By using such request-for-quote strategies, companies can also become more profitable—for example, by avoiding the offering and storing of unnecessary products. Search tools and request-for-quote strategies can increase companies' performance by integrating distribution and retail operations (Grover & Kohli, 2013). Moreover, according to Bharadwaj et al. (2013), companies that use digital business strategies can fine-tune their operations and personalise their products and/or services based on information on customer preferences. In addition to enabling customers to select and modify their products and services, digital business strategies can also accelerate the speed of product launches (Bharadwaj et al., 2013).

The use of a digital business strategy also allows companies to monitor and scan their operations in real time, which makes it possible to avoid unnecessary work and to fix problems as they appear. Real-time monitoring allows companies to generate more profits. Therefore, due to the low costs of modular and flexible digitisation's building blocks, companies can increase their performance and hence profitability (see Grover & Kohli, 2013). Furthermore, by using digital business strategies, companies can take advantage of the decreasing costs of processing, distributing, and storing information and, subsequently, digitise services and products to achieve higher profitability (Grover & Kohli, 2013; Porter, 2001). Based on the arguments presented earlier, we developed the following hypothesis:

H1: Digital business strategy is positively associated with company performance.

Researchers disagree on whether companies need a digital business strategy or a standalone digital transformation strategy to secure a competitive advantage over other businesses. While a digital business strategy highlights the leveraging of digital resources in value creation by means of an organisational strategy (Bharadwaj et al., 2013), a digital transformation strategy involves insights into how such a digital business strategy should be developed and implemented at the organisational level (Chanias et al., 2019; Hess et al., 2016; Matt et al., 2015). To support the implementation of digital business strategy, Hess et al. (2016) argued that organisations need a standalone strategy for digital transformation that would support and guide the managers through the implementation processes of different digital technologies. This is because, in the contemporary business environment, in which organisations need to balance many different strategies, the digital business strategy does not provide support and guidelines for the digital transformation, even though such a strategy indicates the future business vision of an organisation.

To address the lack of actual transformational steps in digital business strategies, scholars have highlighted the role of technology scanning (Nylén & Holmström, 2015). For example, Hess et al. (2016) claimed that in some organisations, the development of digital technology is forcing organisations to change and update their processes and businesses, whereas, in some cases, it is other business elements that are driving the change, and organisations need to adapt by identifying new technologies. In other words, organisations need to continuously scan the developing digital technologies and identify the most relevant ones either for supporting their existing businesses or developing new services and products. Nylén and Holmström (2015) further suggested that organisations should be aware of the development progress of digital technology and the associated usage patterns. This means that organisations should stay up-to-date on which kinds of solutions, devices, and components are on their way to the business environments in which the organisations are operating. Technology scanning can thus be considered an essential transformational step in the implementation of a digital business strategy for improving company performance. Consequently, we developed the following hypothesis:

H2: Technology scanning mediates the relationship between a digital business strategy and company performance.

5.3. Research methodology

Sample selection and data collection

We collected the data via a web-based questionnaire that assessed company performance in the context of digital business strategies and technology scanning practices among SMEs. The respondents were individuals in management positions, and the analysis unit was the entire company. The respondents worked in SMEs with fewer than 250 employees, which is the maximum number for SMEs designated by the Organisation of Finnish Entrepreneurs. Complete replies were obtained from 98 SMEs situated in the Päijät-Häme area of Finland.

Sixty-seven percent of the responses represented companies with a turnover of less than two million euros, and 33% of the responses represented companies with revenues of at least two million euros. Approximately 30% of the companies surveyed were industrial companies and 70% of the companies were in the service sector. Various industries were represented in the sample, including production, trade, information technology, construction, and real estate.

Measures

All measures were based on the previous literature on the digital transformation. All scales were unidimensional, as verified by means of confirmatory factor analysis regarding model fit indices and content validity (Section 4).

Company performance. Company performance was measured via two subjective indicators. Relative performance measures were used due to the study's multi-company and multi-industry design. The respondents were asked to assess their relative performance, including profitability, and sales compared to their competitors. All company performance items were assessed using a five-point Likert scale that varied from weak (score number 1) to excellent (score number 5).

Digital business strategy. Digital business strategy was evaluated via three items that explored the respondents' perceptions of the introduction of new strategies for transforming what a company is selling (Ross et al., 2017). The construct included the following items: "Our company is strategically aiming at good customer value through its digital product portfolio" (DBS1), "Our company is strategically aiming at good customer value through its digital service portfolio" (DBS2), and "Our company responds to the changing customer needs with digitality" (DBS3). All items pertaining to the digital business strategy were assessed using a five-point Likert scale that varied from totally disagree (score number 1) to totally agree (score number 5).

Technology scanning. Technology scanning was measured via three items that explored the respondents' perceptions of opportunity exploitation for creating aggregated value through digital services and products (Nylén & Holmström, 2015). The construct included the following items: "Our company is actively seeking new technological opportunities" (TSC1), "Our strategic goal is to improve operational performance through digitality" (TSC2), and "Our company is planning to introduce new digital tools" (TSC3). All items pertaining to technology scanning were assessed using a five-point Likert scale that varied from totally disagree (score number 1) to totally agree (score number 5).

Control variables. As company size and company maturity may significantly influence company performance (e.g., Smith & Cooper, 1988), these variables were controlled for. Company size was evaluated via the number of employees working in the respondent's company, while company maturity was evaluated by asking the respondents to indicate the number of years since the company's establishment. Competition in markets can also affect how well a company performs; therefore, it was also considered a control variable (Scott & Christensen, 1995).

Bias

As the data for all constructs were attained using the same questionnaire with self-reported information, there was a possibility of common method bias. This possibility was estimated by employing Harman's single-factor test (Podsakoff & Organ, 1986). An unrotated factor solution involving all items extracted more than a single factor, accounting for 68.20% of the entire variance. The first factor described 48.06% of the variance. As no single factor emerged and no single factor accounted for most of the variance, common method bias was not a significant issue.

5.4. Study results

Assessment of the measurement model

We tested the measurement model using confirmatory factor analysis (CFA) before testing the structural model. Table 5.1 shows the indices that were used to assess the measurement model. The indices included the root mean

Table 5.1 The results of CFA and reliability tests

Constructs	*Item*	*Cronbach's* α	*CR*	*AVE*
Digital business strategy	DBS1	0.863	0.917	0.787
	DBS2			
	DBS3			
Technology scanning	TSC1	0.799	0.882	0.715
	TSC2			
	TSC3			
Company performance	PER1	0.671	0.859	0.753
	PER2			

Note: Goodness-of-fit statistics: RMSEA = 0.053, TLI = 0.979, CFI = 0.986, SRMR = 0.059.

squared error of approximation (RMSEA = 0.053), the Tucker–Lewis index (TLI = 0.979), the comparative fit index (CFI = 0.986), and the standardised root mean squared residual (SRMR = 0.059). These fit indices were acceptable. All constructs were found to be extremely credible because all Cronbach's alpha values were greater than 0.70, as recommended by Fornell and Larcker (1981). Furthermore, the composite reliability (CR) of each construct was between 0.859 and 0.917, above the 0.7 limit suggested by Fornell and Larcker (1981). The average variance extracted (AVE) values ranged between 0.715 and 0.787, above the suggested minimum of 0.50 (Hair et al., 1998). Furthermore, the standardised estimates of the items ranged from 0.70 to 0.93 for digital business strategy, 0.70 to 0.88 for technology scanning, and 0.69 to 0.75 for company performance. Each indicator exhibited significant and substantial loadings on its assumed construct. These measures ensured convergent validity. The desired level of discriminant validity was also met because the square root of the AVE (as shown in Table 5.2) was bigger than the correlations between the factor pairs. Thus, regarding the measurement model, all tests for discriminant and convergent validity, reliability, and overall fit showed acceptable results.

Structural model testing

To estimate the structural relationships, we tested the hypothesised model presented in Section 3. The results of the goodness-of-fit measures demonstrated a good fit: RMSEA = 0.025, TLI = 0.991, CFI = 0.994, and SRMR = 0.080. Figure 5.2 represents the standardised estimates of structural paths. Table 5.3 shows the structural model results described in Figure 5.2. The path between digital business strategy and company performance was significant ($p \leq .05$) and strong (standardised path coefficient = −0.62) but negative. Therefore, making use of a digital business strategy leads to decreased company performance. However, digital business strategy was significantly ($p \leq .001$) and strongly (standardised path coefficient = 0.72) related to technology scanning. Furthermore, technology scanning was significantly ($p \leq .01$) and strongly (standardised path coefficient = 0.92) related to company performance. These findings show that the connection between digital business strategy and company performance is mediated by technology scanning.

Table 5.2 Correlation matrix, descriptive statistics, and discriminant validity

	Mean	*SD*	*1*	*2*	*3*
1 Digital business strategy	3.619	1.053	**0.887**		
2 Technology scanning	3.646	0.978	0.614***	**0.846**	
3 Company performance	2.786	0.547	0.063	0.364***	**0.868**

Note: *** $p \leq .001$; the square root of the average variance extracted is presented in bold diagonal values.

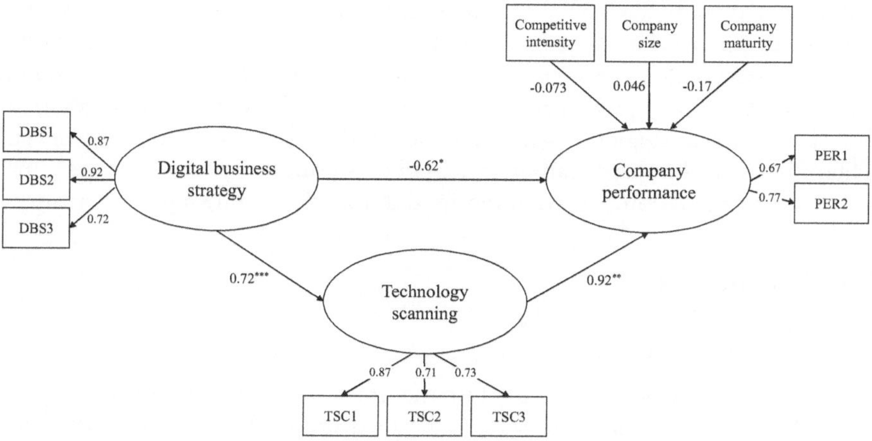

Figure 5.2 Standardised structural path estimates

Table 5.3 Structural model results

Structural paths	*Coefficient*	*SE*	*z-value*
Company performance <- Competitive intensity	−0.027	0.045	−0.61
Company performance <- Company size	0.038	0.110	0.34
Company performance <- Company maturity	−0.134	0.104	−1.28
Company performance <- Digital business strategy	−0.229	0.096	−2.40*
Company performance <- Technology scanning	0.311	0.104	2.99**
Technology scanning <- Digital business strategy	0.788	0.115	6.84***

Note: Goodness-of-fit statistics: RMSEA = 0.025, TLI = 0.991, CFI = 0.994, SRMR = 0.080.
Sign. *** $p \leq .001$, ** $.001 < p \leq .01$, * $.01 < p \leq .05$.

Next, we formulated an alternative model in which technology scanning was treated as an exogenous variable instead of a mediation variable. The model's goodness-of-fit indices were RMSEA = 0.116, TLI = 0.810, CFI = 0.857, and SRMR = 0.220. The model demonstrated a poor fit and thus supported the conception that the structural model with technology scanning as a mediator had higher explanatory power than the competing model.

We also analysed the influence of the control variables, including company size, company maturity, and competitive intensity in the markets, on company performance. However, none of these relationships were targeted by the hypotheses. This analysis revealed that neither company size (standardised path coefficient = 0.046, ns) and company maturity (standardised path coefficient = −0.17, ns) nor competitive intensity in the markets (standardised path coefficient = −0.073, ns) had a statistically significant effect on company performance. Thus, the hypothesised connections were confirmed regardless of company size, company maturity, and competitive intensity in the markets.

In sum, the results demonstrate significant support for the hypothesised connection between digital business strategy and company performance. However, opposite to the hypothesis, the relationship was found to be negative. Also, the findings revealed the significance of technology scanning as a mediator between digital business strategy and company performance. These findings suggest that digital business strategies negatively affect company performance; however, when there is technology scanning, the effect is positive. Company size, company maturity, and competitive intensity did not affect company performance.

5.5. Conclusions

Contribution to theory

The aim of this chapter was to explore the impact of digital business strategies on companies' performance as well as the mediating role of technology scanning in the improvement of company performance in relation to the adoption of digital business strategies. Using a survey distributed to SMEs in Finland, we empirically tested the implications of technology scanning and provided novel contributions to existing theoretical and conceptual studies. Our study contributes to research on digital technologies in operations management in several ways.

First, unlike previous research, our study investigated the relationship between SMEs' digital business strategies and performance. The results clarify the controversial role of digital business strategies in determining company performance among SMEs. The findings demonstrate a negative relation between digital business strategies and company performance. The study contributes to the discussion on digital business strategies by showing that digital business strategy alone does not enhance SME performance. This is the case even if SMEs focus on digitised solutions that target information-enriched services and products (see Ross et al., 2017). The results thus strongly support Hess et al. (2016), who argued that while a digital business strategy may demonstrate a company's vision in terms of forthcoming digital business models, it usually does not describe the concrete steps required to take advantage of the opportunities provided by the company's structures, processes, and products in relation to novel digital technologies.

Second, the study contributes to the debate on digital business strategies in SMEs by showing that technology scanning is an essential mediator and a transformational solution for implementing a digital business strategy in a way that positively affects company performance. This result supports the prior arguments of Nylén and Holmström (2015) and Hess et al. (2016), who highlighted technology scanning as one of the most critical transformational practices for successfully employing a digital business strategy. Thus, the findings do not mean that digital business strategies do not play a role in enhancing SME performance but point to the fact that the influence of digital business strategies on SME performance is mediated by technology scanning.

Contribution to managerial practice

The study offers important insights for SME managers into how to improve companies' performance using both digital business strategies and technology scanning. For instance, SME managers should be aware of the disruptive effects of exclusively relying on digital business strategies for improving companies' performance and should consider digital business strategies along with technology scanning to improve company performance in terms of profitability and sales. Moreover, managers, regardless of company size, maturity, and competitive intensity, should scan the opportunities provided by technical solutions to achieve enhanced performance in the digital economy. In other words, digital transformation creates many opportunities for all types of companies to benefit from technological solutions.

Limitations and future research directions

The study's limitation is that the data were collected in a single country. Therefore, there may be country-specific characteristics influencing the relationships found in this study. Thus, these relationships require further study and better empirical understanding. In future research, it is important to investigate whether SMEs can use a standalone digital transformation strategy instead of a single practice, such as technology scanning. For example, Hess et al. (2016) suggested that companies require a standalone digital transformation strategy that guides management through the change process, beginning with the unification and use of digital technologies. However, this approach has not been empirically tested in the SME context, in which companies often operate with limited resources.

References

Atkinson, M. (2012). Developing and using a performance management framework: A case study. *Measuring Business Excellence*, *16*(3), 47–56.

Bharadwaj, A., El Sawy, O. A., Pavlou, P. A., & Venkatraman, N. (2013). Digital business strategy: Toward a next generation insights. *MIS Quarterly*, *37*(2), 471–482.

Castelo-Branco, I., Cruz-Jesus, F., & Oliveira, T. (2019). Assessing industry 4.0 readiness in manufacturing: Evidence for the European Union. *Computers in Industry*, *107*, 22–32.

Chanias, S., Myers, M. D., & Hess, T. (2019). Digital transformation strategy making in pre-digital organizations: The case of a financial services provider. *The Journal of Strategic Information Systems*, *28*(1), 17–33.

El Sawy, O. A., Kræmmergaard, P., Amsinck, H., & Vinther, A. L. (2016). How LEGO built the foundations and enterprise capabilities for digital leadership. *MIS Quarterly Executive*, *15*(2).

Fornell, C., & Larcker, D. F. (1981). Evaluating structural equation models with unobservable variables and measurement error. *Journal of Marketing Research*, *18*(1), 39–50.

Goerzig, D., & Bauernhansl, T. (2018). Enterprise architectures for the digital transformation in small and medium-sized enterprises. *Procedia CIRP*, *67*, 540–545.

Grover, V., & Kohli, R. (2013). Revealing your hand: Caveats in implementing digital business strategy. *MIS Quarterly*, *37*(2), 655–662.

Gürdür, D., El-khoury, J., & Törngren, M. (2019). Digitalizing Swedish industry: What is next?: Data analytics readiness assessment of Swedish industry, according to survey results. *Computers in Industry*, *105*, 153–163.

Hair, J. F., Black, W. C., Babin, B. J., Anderson, R. E., & Tatham, R. L. (1998). *Multivariate data analysis*. Prentice Hall.

Hess, T., Matt, C., Benlian, A., & Wiesböck, F. (2016). Options for formulating a digital transformation strategy. *MIS Quarterly Executive*, *15*(2).

Kallinikos, J., Aaltonen, A., & Marton, A. (2013). The ambivalent ontology of digital artifacts. *MIS Quarterly*, *37*(2), 357–370.

Lebas, M. J. (1995). Performance measurement and performance management. *International Journal of Production Economics*, *41*(1–3), 23–35.

Li, L., Su, F., Zhang, W., & Mao, J. Y. (2018). Digital transformation by SME entrepreneurs: A capability perspective. *Information Systems Journal*, *28*(6), 1129–1157.

Mathrani, S., Matharani, A., & Viehland, D. (2013). Using enterprise systems to realize digital business strategies. *Journal of Enterprise Information Management*, *26*(4), 363–386.

Matt, C., Hess, T., & Benlian, A. (2015). Digital transformation strategies. *Business & Information Systems Engineering*, *57*(5), 339–343.

Nylén, D., & Holmström, J. (2015). Digital innovation strategy: A framework for diagnosing and improving digital product and service innovation. *Business Horizons*, *58*(1), 57–67.

Pagani, M. (2013). Digital business strategy and value creation: Framing the dynamic cycle of control points. *MIS Quarterly*, *37*(2), 617–632.

Podsakoff, P. M., & Organ, D. W. (1986). Self-reports in organizational research: Problems and prospects. *Journal of Management*, *12*(4), 531–544.

Porter, M. E. (2001). Strategy and the internet. *Harvard Business Review*, *79*(3), 63–78.

Porter, M. E., & Heppelmann, J. E. (2014). How smart, connected products are transforming competition. *Harvard Business Review*, *92*(11), 64–88.

Ross, J. W., Beath, C. M., & Sebastian, I. M. (2017). How to develop a great digital strategy. *MIT Sloan Management Review*, *58*(2), 7.

Saunila, M., Nasiri, M., Ukko, J., & Rantala, T. (2019). Smart technologies and corporate sustainability: The mediation effect of corporate sustainability strategy. *Computers in Industry*, *108*, 178–185.

Scott, W. R., & Christensen, S. (1995). *The institutional construction of organisations: International and longitudinal studies*. Sage.

Smith, C. G., & Cooper, A. C. (1988). Established companies diversifying into young industries: A comparison of firms with different levels of performance. *Strategic Management Journal*, *9*(2), 111–121.

Tangen, S. (2005). Demystifying productivity and performance. *International Journal of Productivity and Performance Management*, *54*(1), 34–46.

Vial, G. (2019). Understanding digital transformation: A review and a research agenda. *The Journal of Strategic Information Systems*, *28*(2), 118–144.

Yoo, Y., Boland Jr, R. J., Lyytinen, K., & Majchrzak, A. (2012). Organizing for innovation in the digitized world. *Organization Science*, *23*(5), 1398–1408.

6 Assessing technology brands with digital media

G. Scott Erickson

6.1. Background

Branding and brand equity

Branding has been seen as a potentially powerful competitive weapon for decades. As customers recognise a branded product and recall good experiences, they are more willing to repurchase. And that repurchase can often be at a higher price point.

A discussion of the theory behind branding often starts with Aaker (1991), who identified the value of brands and the idea that consumer recognition could be associated with higher perceived quality. The obvious question is how to define that value, what came to be called brand equity. Aaker (1996) suggested it was a combination of brand awareness, brand associations, and brand loyalty. Does the customer recognise the brand, what positive/negative experiences are associated with it, and is the customer then more likely to choose the brand over other alternatives? Keller (1993), a similarly well-known branding scholar, suggests a framework based on brand awareness and brand image, with repeated positive interactions and experiences reinforcing the brand's value.

Assessing brand equity or a brand's value can be challenging. Firms survey customers on brand awareness and brand preference routinely, carefully tracking each on an ongoing basis. And how much more individual customers will pay for a branded product can be a good indicator of the added value of the brand (Seggie et al., 2006; Ailawadi et al., 2003). But getting a sense of the full value of a brand to an organisation, the total brand equity, can be challenging.

Numerous approaches exist. Probably the b1st known are proprietary systems for assessing brand equity such as those from consultancy Interbrand and marketing research provider Kantar (BrandZ). Each assesses the value of top global brands on a yearly basis, often agreeing on who is included in the list but not on actual value. In 2020, for example, BrandZ showed Amazon first at $415.9 billion while Interbrand had it second to Apple and valued at $200.667 billion (Interbrand, 2021; Kantar, 2021). Quite a spread.

From a more academic perspective, Kucharska (2016) explored differences in brand valuations based on social media performance, concluding brand equity

DOI: 10.4324/9781003184638-7

is more accurate when assessed by experts than when done by customers. But those metrics were basic social media results such as interest and engagement on the firm's own properties. More in-depth work is possible and can include the full scope of digital media activity across all digital properties. Social media are intended to enhance brand equity (Confente & Kucharska, 2021; Kucharska, 2019; Shivinski & Dabrowski, 2016), so more advanced metrics can better uncover their relationship with brand value.

The difficulty with metrics in this area, of course, is that brand equity is an intangible asset that isn't reported on traditional financial statements. Goodwill is captured on balance sheets when a firm is acquired at a price higher than its market cap (a fairly precise measure of the value of intangibles at a point in time). But that only applies to merger/acquisition events, is only really accurate for that specific moment, and includes all intangibles, not only brand equity. Otherwise, intangible assets such as brand equity aren't part of normal reporting by organisations and so other ways to measure the phenomena are required.

When a compelling metric isn't available, one approach to solving the problem is to look at multiple measurements, often from different perspectives. The commercial brand equity assessments provide a starting point, especially in establishing the value of well-known brands. A second option, from a more academic perspective, comes from the intellectual capital (IC) field. We'll develop the literature behind IC shortly, but one component is relational capital and closely related to customer relationships and brand equity. Further, IC has some established metrics based on objective financial reporting, including Tobin's q looking at the value of a firm versus the tangible assets it holds (Tobin & Brainard, 1977). The difference would be the value of intangible assets, including relational capital. Again, not an exact measurement but readily available and a useful proxy when combined with other options.

Relational capital

Intellectual capital (IC) and the related field of knowledge management (KM) are both predicated on the concept that the knowledge in employees' heads has value and, properly managed, can contribute to an organisation's competitiveness. The idea flows from the resource-based view of the firm suggesting that competitive advantage comes from unique, sustainable resources available to an organisation (Barney, 1991; Wernerfelt, 1984). And a skilled, knowledgeable workforce is something quite unique and quite defensible if the firm can hold onto them. According to the knowledge-based view of the firm, better management of these intangible knowledge assets/resources leads to competitive advantage (Grant, 1996; Teece, 1998).

Better management comes from defining and understanding what these knowledge assets are. Part of that definition and understanding includes characteristics of knowledge, part is measuring the knowledge. Quite a lot of scholarship has gone into identifying types of knowledge as well as the pertinent circumstances in managing them. That's essentially the KM side of the equation. Most important is probably the difference between explicit and tacit knowledge (Nonaka & Takeuchi, 1995) suggesting a difference between easily codified, easily shared knowledge (explicit), and more personal, less easy to share tacit. Importantly, explicit knowledge can often be managed with information technology (IT) solutions while tacit is more of a person-to-person process (Matson et al., 2003; Brown & Duguid, 1991). As the key to effectively managing knowledge is encouraging sharing by employees, KM also gets into worker/employer issues such as trust and culture (Nahapiet & Ghoshal, 1998).

The measuring part is the IC side of things. Intellectual capital is generally seen as having three components: human capital, structural capital, and relational capital (Bontis, 1999; Edvinsson & Malone, 1997). Human capital refers to individuals' knowledge about performing their job, structural capital is more the organisational knowledge that would persist even as individual employees leave, and relational capital is knowledge concerning those outside the organisation. Originally called customer capital, relational capital would be the area including customer knowledge as well as that about other external parties (suppliers, vendors, regulators, investors, etc.) (Roos & Roos, 1997).

Interestingly, while considerable work has gone into defining and measuring these different areas, relational capital is often not featured to the same degree as the others. It is included in well-known firm-specific frameworks such as the Balanced Scorecard (the "customer" portion and metric) or Skandia Navigator ("customer focus") (Kaplan & Norton, 1992; Edvinsson & Malone, 1997). But has been little explored on its own, especially when compared with the voluminous research on human capital. Further, cross-firm studies assessing intellectual capital in multiple organisations often rely on frameworks such as VAIC which contains only human and structural capital (Pulic, 2000).

That seems a mistake, especially when we trace brand equity, which can be a powerful competitive force back to relational capital and customer knowledge. Ongoing relationships with customers have become increasingly important to business, with the steady growth of customer relationship management (CRM) systems and account-based marketing (ABM). Both rely on systems (e.g., Salesforce, Marketo) constantly collecting data concerning customer contact points, allowing marketers to apply what they know about individual customers to develop effective relationships over the customer's lifecycle.

In its connection to brand equity, relational capital has not been totally ignored. There is that recognition that repeated interactions with customers and associated purchases contribute to relational capital (Chang & Tseng, 2005; de Castro et al., 2004). The firm builds knowledge of individual customer needs and wants as well as how to better satisfy them. That knowledge does lead to better performance and, perhaps, competitive advantage. The concept sounds much like brand equity, and the literature does recognise the relationship, even if the perspective differs a bit by field (Sussan, 2012; Stahle & Stahle, 2011). And even with the broader scope of relational capital including non-customer external parties, brand equity clearly makes up a substantial part of the total (Gupta & Bhasin, 2014). Especially in certain industries.

Big data and customers

Beyond measuring intangibles with recognised IC metrics, an additional set of measures is also available in digital media. Most firms with a digital media presence measure their own properties, so they know number of visitors and activities, and can, perhaps, pair up identifiable users with other personal data already collected. From an academic research point of view, such data might be interesting but is also proprietary and somewhat hard to pry away from for-profit firms. But digital media can also be tracked outside of a given firm's platforms, and that adds another avenue as3we try to combine metrics to assess brand equity.

In the years since this three-part IC structure gained some sense of consensus among scholars, the big data and business analytics revolution has arrived, with huge volumes, real-time velocity, and wider varieties of data and information driving performance in a different manner. The trend is particularly clear in certain industries, such as information and communication technology (ICT). ICT providers have both complex operating networks and a multitude of identifiable users (Lechman, 2017). Operations and consumer interactions generate considerable data, including social media (Kaplan & Haenlein, 2010). ICTs can be used to build and manage knowledge assets (Sigala & Chalkiti, 2014; Levy, 2009). This happens internally, as with sharing traditional knowledge management systems (Alberghini et al., 2014) and externally, managing sharing with and between users (Jonassen, 2000).

That capability of ICTs, not only for providers but for firms using them, has also been reflected in the literature. KM and IC were originally seen as higher forms of intangible assets, something more developed and more useful than basic data. This perspective came out of information science theory, largely the DIKW hierarchy credited to Ackoff (1989) among others. That hierarchy suggests a flow from basic data to more organised information to understood-in-context knowledge to insightful wisdom. As noted, knowledge was thought to be more valuable as something a step beyond static data and information. And wisdom was seen as rare, that "eureka" moment associated with creativity and so, while valuable, might be too personal to share widely and manage at a full-firm level.

As data and information have increased in prevalence and in value, understanding the possibilities of the full range of intangibles has become a priority. A more contemporary view, owing much to Kurtz and Snowden's (2003) Cynefin framework sees differences in the intangibles but not a hierarchy. One type of intangible (e.g., data versus knowledge) is not necessarily more valuable than another though firms may see differences in their potential for their specific applications. Further refinements of the framework (Rothberg & Erickson, 2017; Simard, 2014) identify the range of intangible assets as running from data/information through explicit knowledge, then on to tacit knowledge and, eventually, to insight/intelligence. The differences are the degree of personalisation of the asset as well as its amenity to being captured and centralised by the organisation. Data/information, for example, is objective and centrally codified while intelligence is more subjective and more likely to be shared person-to-person on the periphery, if at all, without going through the firm's systems.

What all that adds up to is a range of new possibilities for understanding customer data/information, relational capital, and brand equity. Metrics used to assess intellectual capital can now be more widely understood to assess the full range of intangible assets, especially those like Tobin's q comparing market capitalisation to physical assets. For firms with large customer databases and customer relationship management systems, for example, that are clearly a considerable part of their competitive advantage, both the customer database and the customer knowledge/relational capital drawn from it can be recognised as important and as aspects of brand equity. Further, customer communications, both with the firm and with each other, using ICTs can also be captured in databases and analysed for deeper learnings. Given the tendency of customers to be particularly honest in such settings (Liu et al., 2007; Rovai, 2002), true feelings about firms and brands are more likely to be revealed in social media (Rizun & Kucharska, 2018). As a result, digital media and related sources can provide a different way to examine brand value and brand equity. Moreover, modern tools for gathering digital media data can collect across the entire Internet, not just sites owned by a single firm. Consequently, worldwide reflections on specified brands are available and can be used to assess brand perception and, ultimately, brand value.

In summary, we know brands are valuable but obtaining a consensus brand equity valuation can be challenging. A different perspective on brand equity is relational capital from the intellectual capital field, looking at the knowledge in the firm related to managing customer relationships. That metric also has some questions, especially when trying to compare multiple firms, but does offer more understanding of the concept. In addition, a fuller cast of intangible assets, including digital data and information, can also be accessed. Those metrics on the full intangible assets have greater reliability though the level of intangible customer-related assets can still be hard to determine without more inputs. One of those might be digital media. How can digital media be used to characterise and assess brands, and what would that tell us? What can it add to commercial brand equity estimates and intellectual capital metrics?

6.2. Conceptualisation

This study collects data from digital media concerning several key brands in the information and communication technology area, specifically smartphones. The market is appealing due to its high-tech nature, its close relationship with customers, and the presence of a couple of identifiable global brands. From previous studies using Tobin's q, we know the IT industry has high levels of intellectual capital (Erickson & Rothberg, 2012). Further, from the Interbrand and BrandZ brand equity rankings, we also know that two of the highest value brands have smartphone entries, Apple ($200.667 billion on Interbrand) and

Samsung ($62.289 billion). Consequently, we have a high-tech market with dominant, highly valued brands.

Besides Apple and Samsung, the highest market share brands in 2020 were Xiaomi (actually higher global market share than Apple and noted in the Interbrand Chinese brands rating with an estimated value of $8.342 billion), Oppo, and Vivo. Comparing top ten brand equity firms against other brands in the same product line should provide some insights into the power of tech brands. As a further extension, this study also included an ingredient brand (Erickson et al., 2020), a supplier with a brand meant to attract consumers to other brands on the basis of this quality input. Corning Gorilla Glass is a recognisable brand used as the display component in billions of phones. Including Corning as an ingredient brand provides an additional perspective on brands in this IT market.

Data were collected on worldwide digital media activity surrounding these six brands over five weeks during summer 2021, providing a longitudinal perspective on key indicators (Erickson & Rothberg, 2017). Salesforce Social Studio was used to obtain the data, a web-scraping sentiment program designed to identify any use of selected keywords in any media, including Facebook, Twitter, YouTube, forums, blogs, aggregators, reviews, and other sources. Social Studio reports include volume, top influencers, sentiment, source, country, language, wordclouds, and access to the specific postings (if researchers want the more qualitative text data itself). Further, as noted earlier, this tool collects all mentions of the brand, on any public platform anyway. It's not just accounts owned by the brand itself, but all others with activity surrounding it.

As a matter of isolating pertinent digital media activity, the search was restricted to "Apple iPhone" and "Samsung Galaxy" for those brands. Both have an extensive range of other products beyond smartphones (and Galaxy actually includes tablets as well), and a search on just the parent brand was likely to be both numerically overwhelming and often off-topic compared to the other brands. Apple, of course, would also include results including the fruit, apple pies, and such.

6.3. Results and discussion

Results are presented in Tables 6.1–6.6 (one for each brand/firm). As noted, data were collected over five weeks, starting with the week ending 5 July 2021 and finishing with the week ending 3 August 2021. The influencer metric is based on a Social Studio index (1–100) rating social media postings according to the reach of the contributor. The more followers, likes, retweets, views, etc., depending on the medium, the higher the influencer rating. Closer to 100 has more influence. The results reported here reflect the mean rating of the top ten influencers for each brand.

Volume is the amount of activity mentioning the brand during the week. As seen, this ranges dramatically from 319,000 in one week for Samsung to 4,700 for Oppo and 666 for Corning. Source is the medium of the activity, including Twitter, YouTube, and Facebook. Source also includes aggregators (such as

Table 6.1 Apple iPhone results

Metric		*7/5*	*7/12*	*7/19*	*7/26*	*8/3*
Influencers		98	98	98	98	98
Volume		148K	137K	177K	189K	173K
Source	Twitter	45.2	44.2	50.4	45.7	44.7
	YouTube	28.3	28.2	23.9	28.9	27.9
	Forum Replies	8.9	8.6	8.3	7.7	7.6
	Blogs	8.9	10.0	9.7	9.9	11.1
	Aggregators	3.4	3.4	3.0	3.4	3.5
	Reviews	1.6	1.7	1.3	1.3	1.7
	Forums	2.6	2.5	2.1	2.0	2.1
	Facebook	0.6	0.7	0.7	0.5	--
	Mainstream	--	--	--	--	0.6
	Other	0.5	0.8	0.6	0.6	0.7
Sentiment	Positive	78.1	77.9	78.3	75.7	76.3
	Negative	21.9	22.1	21.7	25.3	23.7
Language	English	58.3	60.3	53.1	55.5	57.8
	Japanese	11.0	10.7	10.8	9.7	9.7
	Spanish	6.4	6.1	5.9	5.7	6.9
	Russian	1.9	2.1	2.9	3.0	2.9
	Thai	--	--	3.6	6.0	2.7
	Portuguese	3.1	2.8	2.6	2.5	2.6
	French	2.4	2.2	8.5	2.4	2.0

Table 6.2 Samsung Galaxy results

Metric		*7/5*	*7/12*	*7/19*	*7/26*	*8/3*
Influencers		98	98	98	98	98
Volume		210K	260K	212K	319K	294K
Source	Twitter	40.6	60.5	45.5	68.3	63.1
	YouTube	45.5	28.7	41.5	23.3	27.4
	Forum Replies	5.0	3.7	4.6	2.8	3.3
	Blogs	3.4	2.7	3.4	2.5	2.6
	Aggregators	2.1	1.6	1.7	1.2	1.4
	Reviews	1.1	0.9	1.2	0.9	1.0
	Forums	1.6	0.9	1.3	0.8	0.9
	Facebook	0.4	0.8	0.7	0.2	0.3
	Mainstream	--	--	--	--	--
	Other	0.3	0.3	0.2	0.1	0.2
Sentiment	Positive	86.2	87.6	88.3	88.7	93.9
	Negative	13.8	12.4	11.7	11.3	6.1
Language	English	58.2	52.6	57.9	49.7	71.0
	Portuguese	5.6	2.5	4.0	2.6	3.3
	Indonesian	3.0	14.0	6.4	--	3.3
	Spanish	5.1	3.7	3.8	--	3.0
	Russian	4.6	2.1	3.2	2.6	3.0
	Korean	--	--	--	7.7	--
	Arabic	--	3.8	2.5	6.8	--
	Malay	--	4.3	1.8	2.9	--

Table 6.3 Xiaomi results

Metric		*7/5*	*7/12*	*7/19*	*7/26*	*8/3*
Influencers		98	98	97	96	97
Volume		115K	131K	84K	60K	61K
Source	Twitter	45.6	61.2	39.5	46.0	44.2
	YouTube	33.6	20.9	33.9	25.0	26.9
	Forum Replies	15.4	13.2	19.4	19.9	18.7
	Blogs	2.0	1.9	2.6	3.5	3.7
	Aggregators	1.1	1.0	1.6	1.9	2.4
	Reviews	0.3	0.2	0.3	0.4	0.9
	Forums	1.7	1.4	2.3	3.0	3.0
	Facebook	0.1	0.1	0.1	--	0.2
	Mainstream	--	--	--	0.1	--
	Other	0.2	0.1	0.2	0.2	0.1
Sentiment	Positive	91.2	83.1	79.6	77.0	76.1
	Negative	8.8	16.9	20.4	23.0	23.9
Language	English	26.9	15.1	21.5	28.0	29.0
	Spanish	6.5	6.1	10.9	14.7	16.4
	Russian	6.1	4.8	6.6	9.4	12.3
	Japanese	28.7	14.3	12.2	9.8	8.8
	Portuguese	3.2	--	4.2	5.3	5.1
	Turkish	2.5	2.2	--	4.2	4.0
	Arabic	6.2	6.9	5.5	--	--
	French	--	--	4.8	3.7	2.0
	Indonesian	2.8	30.6	13.4	--	--

Table 6.4 Vivo results

Metric		*7/5*	*7/12*	*7/19*	*7/26*	*8/3*
Influencers		87	79	80	80	70
Volume		27K	13K	12K	12K	13K
Source	Twitter	36.0	26.7	13.1	11.3	8.1
	YouTube	56.5	57.1	71.1	74.7	78.2
	Forum Replies	0.2	0.7	0.5	0.7	0.7
	Blogs	4.7	11.6	11.4	9.7	9.2
	Aggregators	2.9	2.8	2.9	2.7	2.6
	Reviews	0.1	0.1	0.1	0.3	0.2
	Forums	0.3	0.6	0.6	0.5	0.5
	Facebook	--	--	--	--	--
	Mainstream	0.1	0.2	0.1	0.1	0.4
	Other	0.1	0.2	0.1	0.1	0.1
Sentiment	Positive	95.7	91.1	89.3	79.4	80.8
	Negative	4.3	8.9	10.7	20.6	19.2
Language	English	78.2	75.9	71.8	65.2	70.1
	Portuguese	2.5	3.7	3.6	5.5	5.9
	Hindi/Bengali	7.1	5.4	7.0	11.8	8.8
	Spanish	1.0	1.9	1.9	1.9	1.4
	Indonesian	0.6	1.4	1.5	1.4	1.2
	Russian	--	--	--	--	0.9
	Italian	--	--	--	2.1	--

Table 6.5 Oppo results

Metric		*7/5*	*7/12*	*7/19*	*7/26*	*8/3*
Influencers		92	91	91	91	89
Volume		5.3K	4.7K	9.8K	8.6K	6K
Source	Twitter	32.4	31.1	50.9	58.3	35.4
	YouTube	31.8	26.5	23.8	17.2	32.8
	Forum Replies	15.2	18.2	10.6	10.3	13.6
	Blogs	12.0	14.4	9.3	9.0	11.7
	Aggregators	3.2	4.0	2.8	2.4	2.7
	Reviews	0.6	0.6	0.3	0.2	2.9
	Forums	4.0	3.9	1.8	2.1	0.7
	Facebook	--	--	--	--	--
	Mainstream	0.3	--	0.3	0.4	0.2
	Other	0.4	0.7	0.2	0.1	0.2
Sentiment	Positive	83.6	81.4	93.9	93.4	88.2
	Negative	16.4	18.6	6.1	6.6	11.8
Language	English	39.4	36.9	21.8	25.7	36.3
	Japanese	23.9	27.0	50.1	53.5	29.8
	Italian	5.3	4.4	2.3	2.0	4.0
	Russian	2.0	---	1.7	1.6	3.7
	Spanish	4.9	4.2	3.0	3.1	3.3
	Indonesian	2.7	--	1.6	1.3	2.4
	Chinese	3.5	3.2	1.5	1.5	2.2
	French	3.5	3.3	2.2	2.6	1.7

Table 6.6 Corning results

Metric		*7/5*	*7/12*	*7/19*	*7/26*	*8/3*
Influencers		70	65	75	98	85
Volume		0.85K	0.66K	0.84K	2.8K	1.5K
Source	Twitter	18.0	8.0	18.8	51.5	19.6
	YouTube	29.4	25.1	20.2	10.7	15.9
	Forum Replies	3.4	3.0	1.4	3.4	2.1
	Blogs	30.2	39.3	39.5	18.3	28.4
	Aggregators	11.3	12.9	12.2	12.1	17.7
	Reviews	--	--	--	--	--
	Forums	5.2	6.5	5.0	2.4	4.3
	Facebook	0.7	--	0.5	0.7	1.4
	Mainstream	1.3	3.2	1.5	0.8	0.3
	Other	0.6	1.1	--	0.1	0.3
Sentiment	Positive	93.8	92.0	92.3	84.9	91.9
	Negative	6.2	8.0	7.7	15.1	8.1
Language	English	59.4	60.7	65.6	61.8	58.1
	Spanish	5.4	5.4	3.9	9.7	9.6
	Russian	4.5	4.2	3.7	4.5	6.2
	Turkish	2.6	2.1	1.8	--	4.1
	Indonesian	6.3	4.2	7.7	1.9	3.5
	German	--	4.1	--	2.7	2.5
	Italian	2.5	2.4	1.7	2.8	2.5
	French	--	--	2.5	2.9	1.8

Reddit), various sites with forums and forum replies, various sites with blogs, various sites with reviews, and the mainstream media. Results here include the percentage of overall volume represented by each medium.

Sentiment is based on an assessment by Social Studio of whether each specific piece of content is positive or negative. This is taken from an algorithm built to evaluate positive and negative words, tone, and similar variables. It's not perfect. As the saying goes, the Internet doesn't get sarcasm, but the general results are reasonably reliable. Again, it's a percentage of positive comments versus negative comments.

Language tracks the language used. Country is also available from the system, but that category had a large amount of "undetermined" results, so language seemed the better indicator. That obviously includes some interpretation, including where Portuguese is more spoken (Portugal or Brazil?), but does provide some good information.

In analysing the results, the volume indicator is a good place to start. One would expect the more valuable brands to have more activity, and the metrics don't disagree. Samsung leads the way, ranging between 210K and 319K distinct mentions per week with Apple not far behind with 137K to 189K. Xiaomi also has considerable interest, showing 60K to 131K postings. The lesser recognised brands, Vivo and Oppo, come in at 12K to 27K and 4.7K to 9.8K, respectively. Corning, the ingredient brand, is well behind the consumer brands, ranging from 666 to 2.8K. Clearly differences of substantial magnitude, and as expected.

One result a little less expected is the stability of the volumes. Using the highest week of activity as a base, Samsung (.66) and Apple (.72) both drop by a third or less to their lowest week of activity. The other phone brands show drops of over half with Xiaomi at .46, Vivo at .44, and Oppo at .48, all at similar levels. Corning comes in at a considerably higher magnitude, a drop of over 75% at .24 though from a relatively low base. In short, the brands with higher brand equity appear more stable in the level of social media chatter concerning them, the less-known brands are more variable. Interest in the bran is maintained better over the full observation period.

Influencer totals also have some interesting results. For the big brands, Apple, Samsung, and Xiaomi, the top ten influencers average 98/100, users with a lot of followers. And the average reflects results that don't change much. That pattern changes with the other brands. Oppo and Vivo are noticeably lower in the impact of their top influencers, and the latter has a much greater spread in the results. Corning also shows less connected influencers and little consistency in the metrics.

The source of the activity has similarities across the brands, especially the phone brands proper, but also some differences. Twitter is important to all, over 40% of total activity for the top three (Apple, Samsung, and Xiaomi) and over 30% for Vivo and Oppo. YouTube is also relatively high for all, ranging from very high for Vivo (56%) and high for Samsung (45%) to in and around 30% for the other three brands. Interestingly, all except Apple vary considerably in

YouTube postings. Forums and forum replies rate at about 10% total for the top two brands, Apple and Samsung, but range from much higher for Xiaomi and Oppo to much lower for Vivo. Blogs also come in with double digits for Apple, Vivo, and Oppo, but much less attention for Samsung and Xiaomi. Aggregators have noticeable activity, especially for Apple, Oppo, and Vivo, and less so for Samsung and Xiaomi.

Corning, on the other hand, shows distinctly different patterns. Twitter and YouTube combined are generally only 30–50% except for an outlier (51.6%) on Twitter in one week. Blogs, on the other hand, are noticeably more popular, generally in the high 30% to 50% (again, one lower outlier). Aggregators are also higher, ranging from 11% to 17%, and mainstream media also have some higher readings.

We can discuss in a bit more detail later in the chapter but forums and news sources or aggregators are likely to be oriented more to reporting and opinions on the reporting. Blogs can also be based on more information-based opinions. YouTube is more of a creative outlet while Twitter does have some creative aspects and opinions. And both YouTube and Twitter can have marketing messages. So the heavier attention on Corning in blogs and aggregators isn't that surprising. Meanwhile, YouTube and Twitter users will often signal what kind of smartphone they are using to create content (#appleiphone) as well as have some discussion about brand preference (popping up in forums as well). That can also be true for the lesser known brands like Oppo and Vivo. The simple point, for now, is that different sources of activity are reflected in the different types of brands: consumer versus ingredient and high equity versus lower. Further analysis can help to narrow down more explanation and details by looking more deeply into what Samsung YouTube postings, for example, look like as opposed to Oppo YouTube postings.

Before that, however, let's take a look at sentiment. As noted, postings are sorted into positive and negative categories. One would expect sentiment to be relatively good for a strong brand. It is, in this case, but Apple also has noticeably more negative postings than the other brands. Apple has a positive/negative result around 77/23 for the five weeks while Samsung is more around 88/12, Xiaomi 82/18, Vivo 88/12 (but a high of 95.7), and Oppo also about 88/12. Corning is over 90.

The relatively higher negative results for Apple seem curious but also not entirely unexpected. There are fan bases, as it were, for Apple/iOS and Samsung/Android smartphones and quite a bit of chatter back and forth. If one looks more deeply at the conversations underneath these data, the back-and-forth conversations on which phone/platform is better seem to happen more when Apple is the main point of discussion. So Samsung enthusiasts weigh in on Apple iPhone conversations with negative comments. The feelings are apparently deeply held.

Also, the positives are still much higher, with more than three-quarters of postings. And given the sheer magnitude of the volume, 77% of 170,000 events still show 130,000 positive comments. That would dwarf, say, Oppo's 90% of

7,000 (6,300 positives). So Apple's higher negative sentiments are noticeable and important but also only one part of assessing the power of the brand. Volume and context also matter.

Another, and potentially more important, result in the data is the stability of the sentiments. Much as the high-value brands showed more stable volume, they also have more stable sentiments. Apple's and Samsung's positive sentiment ratings run along a relatively narrow range (75.7–78.3 and 86.2–93.9, respectively). Xiaomi (76.1–91.2), Vivo (79.4–95.7), and Oppo (81.4–93.9) are considerably wider ranges. Corning, the ingredient brand is narrower (84.9–93.8). While sentiments may or may not be reliably higher in the high-value brands, there is evidence that they are noticeably more stable. Once the feelings about the brand are established, they don't vary too much.

Languages are interesting simply as an indicator of where the brands have more activity. These can vary, probably as a result of specific activities taking place in different locations (e.g., sales promotion, product introduction, a deal with a large regional reseller). English is the predominant language for Apple, Samsung, and Vivo, but not so much for Xiaomi and Vivo. Japanese is prevalent for Apple, Xiaomi, and Oppo, but non-existent for Samsung and Vivo (Japan and South Korea have a historically prickly relationship, perhaps explaining the Samsung result). The various European languages are present for all but would include other locations such as South America (Portuguese, Spanish) that could be teased out in more detail by using the country results for analysis as well. One-off results are noticeable such as Samsung's and Xiaomi's (sometimes) strength in Indonesia, and Vivo's unique standing in India. Once again, the higher value brands show some stability but these results are more variable across the board, again because of specific activities that might be occurring.

Finally, looking over the qualitative results, the collection of comments and terms can also help describe the nature of the brands, both with and without high brand equity. Two of the wordclouds for Samsung and Apple are depicted in Figures 6.1 and 6.2. The dominant phrase is the keyword in each case, of course, but other information can also be harvested. Initially, there are references to competitors (and, presumably, comparisons) on both though Samsung is much more prominent in the Apple wordcloud. As noted earlier, Samsung enthusiasts seem to like making their point when Apple is mentioned but not vice versa. Particular features and models, including from competitors, are frequently noted. Interestingly, the digital media platforms are sometimes included (often more so than in these examples), so tweets, videos (YouTube), images (Twitter, others), and other creative outlets can be identified by brand. That information can be helpful in explaining some of the source data discussed earlier.

Further insights can be drawn concerning the languages and countries using the brands, Samsung has more non-English content in this example. Specific references (#jumathepibarengshoppee) and related expressions (bismillah) can be researched further, in this case apparently a popular contest run by an online Indonesian retailer. As noted when discussing the quantitative data earlier, this research method offers deeper qualitative data that can be used to help explain some of the

Figure 6.1 Samsung Galaxy wordcloud (7/12)

Figure 6.2 Apple iPhone wordcloud (7/19)

outlier readings (Samsung, 7/12, lots of Twitter, lots of Indonesian). Other one-offs in the comments include other retailers (Oppo, BicSim) and specific games (Vivo, Garda freefire), details that again provide opportunities to explore deeper levels of brand meaning and associations in specific groups of users.

As noted at the beginning of this chapter, we know brand equity is a complex construct. Using Social Studio or similar methodologies to look more closely to study specific brands provides a perspective difficult to obtain from assessing a single company or multiple firms on more traditional financial measures. Data are rich and plentiful, and when combined with existing brand equity estimates and/or intellectual capital metrics, capable of providing new insights on brands, brand equity, and user relationships. Once we know what patterns are associated with more valuable brands, those can be employed as a dependable indicator for brand equity.

6.4. Conclusions

The concept of a brand is complicated, especially a brand representing a highly technical product that consumers don't necessarily fully understand. We know one brand can be more valuable than another, based on an accumulation of positive customer experiences, and that can raise expectations as well as what customers might pay. But fully defining brand equity and accurately measuring it continues to be somewhat elusive.

Definitions and measures do exist but can be proprietary and opinions vary on what approach might be best. Commercial estimates of brand equity are useful but generally only cover the most valuable brands. From another perspective, intellectual capital and the subcategory of relational capital also offer some guidance (organisational knowledge of external relationships, including those with customers) but again lack wide-scale agreement on a single approach. With the addition of data and information as valuable intangibles, especially high-volume customer data, the nature of relational intangibles widens even further. Those changes do, however, offer some additional possible metrics that might be more objective and more effectively employed. Intangible asset assessments for firms we know have considerable brand equity can be another piece of the puzzle.

An important additional capability in relational capital/intangibles comes from information and communication technologies, enabling constant contact between organisation and customer as well as between customers. These capabilities might also shed further light on the nature of brands and how we might measure them against each other. Investment in data and data holdings, often reflected in the intangible asset estimates just mentioned, can again be helpful.

To further the discussion, this study has looked at yet another metric, longitudinal digital media data on the five largest worldwide smartphone brands and one related ingredient brand. The results show that the more valuable brands (as identified by other metrics) do show more user activity on digital media, generally much more. That is unsurprising, but the data also suggest that the volume levels are less variable, high-impact influencers are less variable, and that sentiment is less likely to change as well. The big brands have consistent high levels of engagement and sentiments seem fairly entrenched.

The data also show variations between brands in terms of what platforms they are more associated with, languages/countries, and general types of user activities. Qualitative data can be examined at a deeper level and can suggest what kinds of contextual circumstances impart the brand metrics (marketing activities, competitors, retail partnerships, and so forth). This initial analysis is only a first step but shows considerable potential for exploring the concept of a brand and its meanings in much more depth using digital media metrics.

Given the difficulties in pinning down brand valuations, multiple metrics can provide a triangulated value that likely gets closer to the true standing of the brand. Repeated use can also help to establish specific indicators of brand value. Digital media metrics such as those employed in this study are uniquely placed to contribute, along with other indicators, to a deeper understanding of how users feel about the brand. Measuring sentiment over time, activity, key influencers, platforms, and keywords provides deep insights, both on an absolute level and in looking at variation over time. Even deeper analysis into the context of user comments allows considerably more depth. This study is just the tip of the iceberg, the possible applications of the techniques are both varied and valuable.

References

Aaker, D. A. (1991). *Managing brand equity*. DIANE Publishing Company.

Aaker, D. A. (1996). *Building strong brands*. The Free Press.

Ackoff, R. (1989). From data to wisdom. *Journal of Applied Systems Analysis, 16*, 3–9.

Ailawadi, K. L., Lehmann, D. R., & Neslin, S. A. (2003, October). Revenue premium as an outcome measure of brand equity. *Journal of Marketing, 67*(4), 1–17.

Alberghini, E., Cricelli, L., & Grimaldi, M. (2014). A methodology to manage and monitor social media inside a company: A case study. *Journal of Knowledge Management, 18*(2), 255–277.

Barney, J. (1991). Firm resources and sustained competitive advantage. *Journal of Management, 17*(1), 99–120.

Bontis, N. (1999). Managing organizational knowledge by diagnosing intellectual capital: Framing and advancing the state of the field. *International Journal of Technology Management, 18*(5–8), 433–462.

Brown, J. S., & Duguid, P. (1991). Organizational learning and communities-of-practice: Toward a unified view of working, learning, and innovation. *Organizational Science, 2*(1), 40–57.

Chang, A., & Tseng, C. N. (2005). Building customer capital through relationship marketing activities: The case of Taiwanese multilevel marketing companies. *Journal of Intellectual Capital, 6*(2), 253–266.

Confente, I., & Kucharska, W. (2021). Company versus consumer performance: Does brand community identification foster brand loyalty and the consumer's personal brand? *Journal of Brand Management, 28*, 8–31. https://doi.org/10.1057/s41262-020-00208-4

de Castro, G. M., Saez, P. L., & Lopez, J. E. N. (2004). The role of corporate reputation in developing relational capital. *Journal of Intellectual Capital, 5*(4), 575–585.

Edvinsson, L., & Malone, M. (1997). *Intellectual capital*. Harper Business.

Erickson, G. S., & Rothberg, H. N. (2012). *Intelligence in action: Strategically managing knowledge assets*. Palgrave Macmillan.

Erickson, G. S., & Rothberg, H. N. (2017). *Digital media and relational capital* (pp. 303–309). Proceedings of the 18th European Conference on Knowledge Management.

Erickson, G. S., Schmidt, J., & Rothberg, H. N. (2020). *Relational capital: Knowledge assets and branding* (pp. 263–269). Proceedings of the 21st European Conference on Knowledge Management.

Grant, R. M. (1996, Winter). Toward a knowledge-based theory of the firm. *Strategic Management Journal, 17*, 109–122.

Gupta, M., & Bhasin, J. (2014). The relationship between intellectual capital and brand equity. *Management and Labour Studies, 39*(3), 329–339.

Interbrand. (2021). Retrieved January 7, 2021, from www.interbrand.com/best-global-brands/

Jonassen, D. (2000). *Theoretical foundations of learning environments*. Lawrence Erlbaum.

Kantar. (2021). Retrieved January 7, 2021, from www.kantar.com/campaigns/brandz/global

Kaplan, A. M., & Haenlein, M. (2010). Users of the world, unite! The challenges and opportunities of social media. *Business Horizons, 53*(1), 59–68.

Kaplan, R. S., & Norton, P. D., (1992). The balanced scorecard—measures that drive performance. *Harvard Business Review, 70*(1), 71–79.

Keller, K. L. (1993). Conceptualizing, measuring, and managing customer-based brand equity. *Journal of Marketing, 57*(1), 1–22.

Kucharska, W. (2016). *Customer assessment of brand valuation and social media* (pp. 134–138). Proceedings of the 3rd European Conference on Social Media.

Kucharska, W. (2019). Online brand communities' contribution to digital business models: Social drivers and mediators. *Journal of Research in Interactive Marketing, 13*(4), 437–463. https://doi.org/10.1108/JRIM-05-2018-0063

Kurtz, C. F., & Snowden, D. J. (2003). The new dynamics of strategy: Sensemaking in a complex-complicated world. *IBM Systems Journal, 42*(3), 462–483.

Lechman, E. (2017). *The diffusion of information and communication technologies*. Routledge.

Levy, M. (2009). Web 2.0 implications on knowledge management. *Journal of Knowledge Management, 13*(1), 120–134.

Liu, X., Magjuka, R. J., Bonk, C. J., & Seung-Jee, L. (2007). Does sense of community matter? An examination of participants' perceptions of building learning communities in online courses. *Quarterly Review of Distance Education, 8*(1), 9–24.

Matson, E., Patiath, P., & Shavers, T. (2003). Stimulating knowledge sharing: Strengthening your organizations' internal knowledge market. *Organizational Dynamics, 32*(3), 275–285.

Nahapiet, J., & Ghoshal, S. (1998). Social capital, intellectual capital, and the organizational advantage. *The Academy of Management Review, 23*(2), 242–266.

Nonaka, I., & Takeuchi, H. (1995). *The knowledge-creating company: How Japanese companies create the dynamics of innovation*. Oxford University Press.

Pulic, A. (2000). VAIC—an accounting tool for IC management. *International Journal of Technology Management, 20*(5–7), 702–714.

Rizun, N., & Kucharska, W. (2018). *Text mining algorithms for extracting brand knowledge: The fashion industry case*. Proceedings of the 31st International Business Information Management Association Conference.

Roos, J., & Roos, G. (1997). Measuring your company's intellectual performance. *Long Range Planning, 30*(3), 45–62.

Rothberg, H. N., & Erickson, G. S. (2017). Big data systems: Knowledge transfer or intelligence insights. *Journal of Knowledge Management*, *21*(1), 92–112.

Rovai, A. P. (2002). Sense of community, perceived cognitive learning, and persistence in asynchronous learning networks. *The Internet and Higher Education*, *5*(4), 319–332.

Seggie, S. H., Kim, D., & Cavusgil, S. T. (2006). Do supply chain IT alignment and supply chain interfirm system integration impact upon brand equity and firm performance? *Journal of Business Research*, *59*(8), 887–895.

Shivinski, B., & Dabrowski, D. (2016). The effect of social media communication on consumer perceptions of brands. *Journal of Marketing Communications*, *22*(2), 189–214.

Sigala, M., & Chalkiti, K. (2014). Investigating the exploitation of web 2.0 for knowledge management in the Greek tourism industry: A utilisation-importance analysis. *Computers in Human Behavior*, *30*, 800–812.

Simard, A. (2014). *Analytics in context: Modeling in a regulatory environment* (pp. 82–92). Proceedings of the International Conference on Analytics Driven Solutions.

Stahle, S., & Stahle, P. (2011). Towards measures of national intellectual capital: An analysis of the CHS model. *Journal of Intellectual Capital*, *13*(2), 164–177.

Sussan, F. (2012). Consumer interaction as intellectual capital. *Journal of Intellectual Capital*, *13*(1), 81–105.

Teece, D. J. (1998). Capturing value from knowledge assets: The new economy, markets for know-how, and intangible assets. *California Management Review*, *40*(3), 55–79.

Tobin, J., & Brainard, W. C. (1977). Asset markets and the cost of capital. In W. Fellner, B. A. Balassa, & R. R. Nelson (Eds.), *Economic progress, private values and public policy, Essays in honor of William Fellner* (pp. 235–262). North-Holland Publishing Company.

Wernerfelt, B. (1984). The resource-based view of the firm. *Strategic Management Journal*, *5*(2), 171–180.

7 Technology brands and the role of GenZ in their co-creation

Case study of Serbia

Tatjana Mamula Nikolić, Sanja Popović-Pantić, and Karolina Perčić

7.1. Introduction

During last decade, exponentially changing digital technology and renewed market landscape have forced businesses to be more innovative and apply a strategy of change with continuous innovations of their brands, approaching consumers by embedding co-creation as a formula for sustainable development. The main role in the process of constant reinvention is played by technology brands that are co-developed and co-created in cooperation with consumers and stakeholders. The definition of technology brands given by Gietl, Baumgarth, Kilian, and Schmidt is "A technology brand arises in the minds of relevant stakeholders through consistent brand management by companies offering technological products and/or services and generating a major portion of their revenue with their own key technologies" (Expert Panel for Technology Brands).

In technology branding, being informed about buyer behaviour requires continuous attention, because the nature of the technology buyer is constantly evolving, with strong significance for branding (DeSantis Breindel, n.d.). Because the Internet and social media permit modern consumers to access to vast amounts of information and content, they feel more qualified to utilise power and are willing to participate substantially in the value-creation processes (García-Haro et al., 2014, 2015). According to some research results, organisations should intensify customer centricity by bringing brands and consumers work together closely (Edelman Trust Barometer, 2021) and advanced companies invest more in intangibles like brands, data, patents, and others (McKinsey, 2021, June). Since the early 2000s, the field has seen a shift from being company-centric to being more customer-oriented (Tronvoll et al., 2011).

Most of company business values originate from intangible assets, that is, the brand which is the most important part of the value of numerous companies, as it has impact on the choice of consumers, clients, and employees, as well as investors and the social community (Mamula, 2012). The two most eminent companies that measure the brand value Millward Brown and Interbrand, as well as Forbes magazine, show in the 2020 report that the most successful

DOI: 10.4324/9781003184638-8

were technology brands. Despite the fact that during the COVID-19 pandemic period many businesses faced bankruptcy, tech giants and major TechBrands are still thriving. Results based on Millward Brown's research (3.8 million consumer interviews and financial data from 17,801 brands across 51 markets) show dominance of the top 20 technology companies in 2020 according to their brand value (Millward Brown, 2021). According to the Forbes "The World's Most Valuable Brands in 2020," companies including Amazon, Netflix, and PayPal show substantial gains in brand value since last year's list, falling in line with trends related to e-commerce, streaming, and digital payments. Their list of the first five brands illustrates technology brands—Apple, Google, Microsoft, Amazon, and Facebook (Forbes, 2021).

Similar results are shown in Interbrand report for 2020 that shows leading cluster consisted of Apple, Amazon, Microsoft, Google, Samsung, Facebook, LinkedIn, and PayPal. All of them have proved their value and sustainability during the COVID-19 pandemic and resilience during turmoil. Spotify, Netflix, and Amazon have shown the biggest growth in ranking during global COVID-19 lockdowns. The many years of dominance of Coca-Cola was broken for the first time in 2012 when Apple overpassed Coca-Cola's brand value. In 2012, the top risers were also Amazon and Samsung. Since 2017, the biggest brands are technology brands such as Amazon, Google, Apple, Microsoft, and Samsung. Chinese technology brands have entered the top ten most valuable world brands (Interbrand, 2021) and thus became the latest example of the significant influence of technology brands on the economic growth of a country (McKinsey Global Institute, 2017). Instagram, YouTube, and Zoom entered Interbrand's ranking list for the first time in 2020 as newcomers.

7.2. Literature background

In the digital world, companies need to create more complex and interrelated ecosystems or relationships network with stakeholders that contribute to brand value progress for customers, constantly. To be different and to swim in a blue ocean (Kim & Mauborgne, 2017), share innovation (von Hippel, 2005), start involving consumers and external stakeholders in the ideation process (Lafley & Charan, 2008), and constantly developing a different point of view (Hamel & Prahalad, 1994) are the crucial keys in offering customers something new and authentic, involving them in the process of co-creation and consequently creating sustainable environment. Including consumers and stakeholders in co-creating values has led to a significant improvement in the organisations' knowledge process. Roser et al. (2013) state that "co-creation blurs the boundaries of the firm by outsourcing innovation and value creation to the customer." Further, by the implementation of co-creation, the customer becomes an active partner of the organisation in developing future values. Thus, all participants discuss, test, experiment, communicate, and re-innovate. Most importantly, engaging in co-creation activities offers consumers opportunities for self-development along with social and hedonic resources that lead them to feel close to a brand (Park & Ha, 2016). Business models of technology brands provide values to their customers by co-creating with them. Management in companies that do not adopt or even disrupt and challenge their models are not in a favourable position.

Co-creation as an innovative way of value creation involves all stakeholders who work together (Ind et al., 2012). Ind & Coates (2013) cite examples of the Linux operating system and Wikipedia as examples of co-creations that are still widely used today. Today, we witness the power of global technological brand Waze that is also active among Serbian drivers. Brand Waze together with application users (drivers) contributes to the most efficient and comfortable driving routes. The value of co-creation could be significant for organisation in many aspects, as co-creation could strengthen resourses, economic efficiency, reduce risks, improve relationship marketing, contribute to better understanding, and inspire experience for many consumers in different ways (Kim et al., 2020; Fernando & Chukai, 2018; Hajli et al., 2017; Raza et al., 2020; Ho & Wang, 2020). Co-creation and system of searching for better solutions for customers' needs via experimenting, researching, questioning, and fine-tuning put marketing in its full operation. In comparison to previous examples of cooperation between customers and companies receiving customers' opinions via interviews and focus groups, today the process of co-creation involves creativity and participation in discovering new ideas and solutions, usually in long-term customer communities. So the marketing itself is in a continuous process of transformation led by the innovative approach of active dialogue between brands and customers, caused by the growing impact of digital media, developed customer centricity by brands as well as customers' high level of responsiveness and participation (Mamula & Popović-Pantić, 2015). Rogers (2016) and De Kroon (2021) describe that digital transformation is more about strategy and people as it is about technology, requiring changes to the human side at all levels of the organisation.

Digital platforms, and above all, social media, offer brands special opportunities to connect and interact with stakeholders, as well as the opportunity to co-create with a new generation of consumers in an innovative and interesting way (Mamula Nikolić, 2021). The cohort of GenZ is constantly online, analysing, searching for options and ideas, and making their experience relevant for sharing with their tribe. They are more open-minded and active, as a result of their constant online presence. Connected to the Internet, social media, and all kinds of websites and platforms, they are reading, checking, comparing, analysing, and evaluating options, information, and ideas in order to ensure that they are making the most out of the whole experience (Dimitriou & AbouElgheit, 2019; Cotet et al., 2020; Perić et al., 2021). For GenZ who live and work in the broad technological avenue (robotics, 3D printers, Internet of Things (IoT), Virtual Reality (VR), Social–Mobile–Analytics–Robots–Transformation (SMART) economics, cloud computing, Social Networks including communication B2P, G2C, C2G, B2B, B2C, E2E), the next disruption is something normal, where they want to participate and contribute. They are creative and passionate, with a strong desire for self-expression. Growing up in the VUCA world (Mamula Nikolić, 2021), they are constantly searching for the next big thing, taking an active part in society and looking for new experiences they tend to connect with brands that demonstrate genuine care for their interests and enable relevant experiences. Being informed and involved, the members of GenZ contribute to brand development on a constant basis improving brand indicators in the area of awareness, image, personality, feelings, and attitudes (Zwass, 2010; Kamboj et al., 2018; Nyangwe & Buhalis, 2018; Zhao et al., 2019), thus creating even stronger brand value as an intangible asset (Keller, 2012).

The world's most-used social platforms in April 2021 were Facebook, YouTube, WhatsApp, and FB messenger (KEPIOS analysis based on data published in company statements and earnings announcement and platform self-service tools, April 2021). In Serbia, results show that 47% digitally native generation, age group 12–19 years old, spend more than six hours online daily (Perić et al., 2021). Because they primarily communicate via technology brands such as Instagram, Snapchat, and TikTok, most GenZ communicate and express themselves visually, not verbally—they express themselves through emoticons, images, and video clips. GenZ consumers value social and environmental issues highly, and during the pandemic COVID-19, their expectations concerning brands only increased. Transparency and trust are imperative for conversations between consumers and brands to be productive. Both parties must learn to listen to each other and establish relationships on daily basis. Consumers today have the opportunity to verify the authenticity of CSR company reports which is important for GenZ. Companies are becoming increasingly aware that this is another way to prepare their stories, conceptualising case studies in order to spread value. GenZ is increasingly involved in the process of brand activism (Kotler & Sarkar, 2018; Mamula Nikolić et al., 2022).

While digitalisation on consumer buying behaviour of Millennials was explored thoroughly in many research studies (Prensky, 2001; Tapscott, 2009; Sweeny, 2006; McGinnis Jonson & Ng, 2015; Pew Research Center, 2019; Mamula et al., 2019, 2020; Perić et al., 2019; Paunović et al., 2020), there is a lack of the research studies on the impact of GenZ especially in the context of the emerging digitalisation which is transforming rapidly businesses and their common operations as well as their traditional brands. Digital transformation (DT) enforces development of totally new brands related to the digital markets or adjustments of the traditional, existing brands to digital market. The adoption of new technologies by consumers has accelerated, and the processes of innovation and digital transformation have significantly accelerated in general, thus empowering resources and business climate for the operation of Serbian companies in the future new normal (Mamula et al., 2022).

The purpose of this chapter is to identify the scope of GenZ's participation in the process of co-creation brands in Serbia and to study their potential for co-creation in the future. Co-creation allows Generation Z to demonstrate its values (creativity, flexibility, knowledge) and personalities (innovation) as well as to meet its needs (interactivity and engagement, collaboration and shared learning) and its purpose (because success is measured by how much contributed to society). Unlike previous generations, GenZ members have always had and will have instant access to a wealth of information on a variety of topics. As a result of the availability of information and following up of omnichannel media presence and consumption, GenZ is looking for something specific and unique in all forms of life. Thus, companies and brands should offer some values and experiences that are congruent and in line with GenZ's needs and lifestyle. Implicitly, digital transformation (DT) can be considered as a new, additional innovation-enabling factor. However, some research studies indicate that DT process mainly covered activities that do not provide direct benefit to consumers or are invisible to them, which did not lead to significant changes in their satisfaction level (Popović-Pantić et al., 2019). It could cause the drop in demand in the long run and derogate the sustainability of the companies. Therefore, companies should shift their focus to consumers, that is, to a more productive use of digital technologies, which will be in the function of modernising relations with consumers and generating an optimal digital experience for consumers (Popović-Pantić et al., 2020). In that respect, the concept of co-creation has become relevant especially for the new generations as emerging cohort of purchasing power and trendsetters in consumption. Thus, shift is needed from marketing to consumers, from brand-centric to consumer-centric.

Findings of the previous research studies indicate that the significance of the technology brands will be part of an increasing trend in the forthcoming period, because of the three reasons, at least. First, young people of age 18–30 are increasingly using mobile phones, which eases their access to technology brands. Furthermore, the purpose of using mobile phones is diversified and they prefer them compared to the use of computers (Perčić & Vukadinović, 2019a; Perčić & Vukadinović, 2019b). Second, young people of age 15–24 use Facebook and Instagram frequently to follow the activities of the companies posted on their social media profiles and digital platforms (Perčić et al., 2019; Perčić & Perić, 2021) representing the main precondition to involvement in the co-creation process of technology brands. Last but not least, the pandemic affected the growth of technology brands (Perčić & Mamula Nikolić, 2020) like Netflix, TikTok, Wolt, Glovo, and Yandex which led to an increase in the number of their users in Serbia.

7.3. Methodology and methods

The extent to which technology brands are shaped and influenced by the opinions, needs, attitudes, and intentions of GenZ members (born from 1995 to 2010) was examined by online survey (prepared for the needs of this research and pilot-tested), in the period from 19 January to 21 February 2021, on the territory of the Republic of Serbia. It is an empirical, quantitative research. The sample is intentional and consists of 303 respondents (students of primary and secondary schools). A link to the online questionnaire was sent to primary and secondary school professors who further distributed it to their students. The statistical error of the sample is 5.6%.

SPSS was used for data processing and analysis, as well as for the interpretation of the obtained research results. The following quantitative statistical methods were used: descriptive statistics (frequency distribution, arithmetic mean, and standard deviation) and comparative statistics (t-test, ANOVA test, regression, and correlation). Some questions in the questionnaire are formulated in the form of a five-point Likert scale. t-Test and ANOVA test were applied to find out if there are statistically significant differences in the responses of the respondents in relation to the observed variables, and regression and correlation to find out if there is a significant influence of a certain independent variable on the dependent variable and what kind is the relationship between these two variables. The variables are the subject of the research and their relationships are described in more detail in the research hypotheses.

The sample structure:

- Male respondents make up 40% of the sample and female respondents 60%;
- Respondents aged 10–14 make up 20% of the sample, respondents aged 15–19 make up 25%, and respondents aged 20–26 make up 55% of the sample;
- Over 50% are unemployed and do not look for a job, which automatically means that a large part of this generation is supported by parents who ultimately make the final decision on their purchase.

Based on the results of desktop research (García-Haro et al., 2014, 2015; Kamboj et al., 2018; Lafley & Charan, 2008; Ind et al., 2012; Ind & Coates, 2013; Mamula Nikolić, 2021; Popović-Pantić et al., 2019; Nyangwe & Buhalis, 2018; Perčić et al., 2019; Perčić & Perić, 2021; Perić et al., 2021; Perčić & Mamula Nikolić, 2020; Roser et al., 2013; Zhao et al., 2019; Zwass, 2010) and the authors' assumptions, the following research hypotheses were defined to be tested:

Research hypothesis H_1: Technology brands are frequently used by GenZ members.

Research hypothesis H_2: There is a statistically significant difference in the responses of the respondents of different age categories within GenZ in relation to the frequency of usage of certain technology brands.

Research hypothesis H_3: There is a statistically significant positive correlation between the frequency of use of technology brands and the degree of impact of cooperation of organisations with their consumers regarding brand perception.

Research hypothesis H_4: There is a statistically significant positive correlation between the frequency of use of technology brands and the degree of intention of respondents to participate in the co-creation process (participation in brand, product, or marketing campaign improvement).

7.4. Results and discussion

Understanding the impact of awareness, usage, and general behaviour is crucial for extending the knowledge on how technology brands can successfully contribute to customer satisfaction and their loyalty and consequently technology brands' sustainability. Understanding the connection and correlation between consumer attitudes, awareness, and behaviour towards technology brands is very important for brand managers to properly design co-creation process.

Technology brand awareness

When it comes to asking spontaneously about being familiar with the technology brands among respondents, more than half have heard about the technology brand before. When they hear the term *technology brand* (Graph 7.1), they think of YouTube (55%), Instagram (55%), Netflix (48%), Amazon (33%), and TikTok (22%).

Considering research findings, one could realise that GenZ is the generation that is watching, thinking, and operating in the digital framework. Just because of that, more and more brands move their marketing strategy into the digital framework or they decide to digitalise their business operations. More than 80% of the Generation Z respondents confirmed that they understand very well the concept of "technology brand." YouTube and Instagram are ranked at the leading positions, while Netflix and Amazon as well as TikTok are following them, as the most popular technology brands among younger population.

The frequency of using technology brands

Most of the GenZ members (36%) are spending more than three hours on average on social networks. According to t-test ($p = 0.004 < 0.05$), there is a statistically significant difference in the responses based on the gender of respondents according to the time spent on the social networks, meaning that female respondents spend more time there, on average.

According to ANOVA test ($p = 0.002 < 0.05$), there is a statistically significant difference in the responses according to the age categories, meaning that respondents aged 15–19 in the largest number (44%) spend more than three hours per day on the social networks, followed by 38% of respondents of 20–26 age range, while respondents of 10–14 age range spend maximum two hours on social media per day (37%).

According to the research findings, technology brands are the focus of GenZ. Namely, 60% of GenZ respondents are following the activities of digital companies on social platforms; 53% like the posts of digital companies/brands;

6% make comments; 19% share the posts of the companies on the social network profiles, while 31% of respondents share their experience on the social networks after using certain product/service.

ANOVA test ($p = 0.00 < 0.05$) indicates that there is a statistically significant difference in the responses among respondents according to the age categories in relation to the frequency of sharing the posts of companies on their profiles. The most frequent sharing of the companies' posts is provided by the age group of 10–14 years (50% of them). This activity is much less common among older generations (17% for the age category of 15–19 and 18% for the age group of 20–26).

The most used technology brands by GenZ members in Serbia are YouTube (81%), Instagram (80%), and WhatsApp (57%). This claim is confirmed by the average values (mean) for mentioned technology brands (YouTube 4.38; Instagram 4.23; WhatsApp 3.64), shown in Table 6.1.

According to t-test, there is a statistically significant difference in the responses based on the gender of respondents according to the frequency of usage of the following:

- YouTube ($p = 0.003 < 0.05$), that is, male respondents use it more frequently;
- Instagram ($p = 0.00 < 0.05$), that is, female respondents use this technology brand more frequently;
- TikTok ($p = 0.00 < 0.05$), that is, female respondents use it somewhat more frequently;

Table 7.1 Descriptive statistics related to frequency of use of selected technology brands

Question: Indicate the frequency of use of the listed technology brands from 1 to 5, where 1 means never, 2 rarely, 3 sometimes, 4 often, and 5 almost always	*N*	*Mean*	*Std. deviation*
I use Instagram.	296	4.23*	1.247
I use YouTube.	295	4.38*	1.023
I use WhatsApp.	290	3.64*	1.537
I use Viber.	288	3.28	1.361
I use TikTok.	286	2.44	1.59
I use Facebook.	285	2.34	1.273
I use Pinterest.	285	2.58	1.556
I use Netflix.	284	2.77	1.563
I use Spotify.	283	2.05	1.511
I use Amazon.	282	1.32	0.713
I use Twitter.	282	1.9	1.322
I use Alibaba.	276	1.21	0.649

* *The asterisks indicate the highest mean values (the highest frequency of use).*
Source: *Authors of the paper*

- WhatsApp ($p = 0.00 < 0.05$), that is, female respondents use this technology brand somewhat more frequently;
- Pinterest ($p = 0.00 < 0.05$), that is, female respondents use it somewhat more frequently;
- Netflix ($p = 0.002 < 0.05$), that is, female respondents use it more frequently; and
- Alibaba ($p = 0.00 < 0.05$), that is, male respondents use this brand somewhat more frequently.

On the other hand, male and female GenZ members use technology brands rather equally, as follows: Facebook, Viber, Spotify, and Amazon.

According to ANOVA test, there is a statistically significant difference in responses based on the age categories of the respondents and the frequency of use of technology brands:

- The respondents aged 15–19 (69% of them) use YouTube most frequently; for a shade more than the respondents aged 20–26 (68%) and those of 10–14 years of age (51%) who almost always use this technology brand ($p = 0.00 < 0.05$);
- The respondents aged 15–19 (70% of them) use Instagram most frequently; then respondents of 20–26 follow (63%) and 51% of respondents of 10–14 age range use Instagram most frequently ($p = 0.001 < 0.05$);
- Respondents of 10–14 age range use Facebook less commonly; then respondents of 15–19 age range follow, and those respondents aged 20–26 use this social network most frequently compared to the other two ($p = 0.00 < 0.05$);
- Respondents of 15–19 age range use most frequently WhatsApp (55%); then respondents of 20–26 age follow (52%), and 21% of respondents of 10–14 age range use WhatsApp most frequently. It is interesting that also the largest percentage of respondents who never use WhatsApp are those aged 15–19 (21% of them) ($p = 0.00 < 0.05$); and
- Respondents of 10–14 age range almost always use TikTok (29%), most frequently in the relation to the respondents of other age categories; after them respondents aged 15–19 follow (21% of those who almost always use this social network) and 12% of respondents of 20–26 age range use this technology brand most frequently ($p = 0.00 < 0.05$).

It has been determined that the age of the respondents influences the frequency of use of the following social networks:

- TikTok (regression, $R^2 = 0.107$, $p = 0.00 < 0.05$; 10.7% of the variability of the dependent variable—the frequency of using TikTok is determined by the independent variable—the age of respondents), as well as the correlation between the variables, that is, age of respondents and the mentioned frequency of use (Spearman's rank correlation coefficient = −0.352, $p = 0.00 < 0.05$, for a confidence interval of 99% and a risk of error of 1%), where the correlation is negative and moderate, which means that the older the respondents are, the lower is the frequency of use of TikTok;

- Facebook (regression, $R^2 = 0.200$, $p = 0.00 < 0.05$; 20% of the variability of the dependent variable—the frequency of Facebook use is determined by the influence of the independent variable—the age), as well as the correlation between the variables, that is, the age of the respondents and the mentioned frequency of use (Spearman's rank correlation coefficient = 0.458, $p = 0.00 < 0.05$, for a confidence interval of 99% and a risk of error of 1%), where the correlation is positive and moderate, which means that the older the GenZ members are, the higher is the frequency of use of Facebook.

The purpose of using technology brands

Even 80% of respondents use technology brands for entertainment and 53% for learning and business (Graph 7.2). Regarding the way these brands are consumed, young people claim that they use technology brands for absolutely everything—from learning to entertainment. This imposes new communication goals to the brands: to educate, entertain, and interact with the other side, because the entire analysis shows a strong interest of young people for mentioned digital services.

According to ANOVA test ($p = 0.019 < 0.05$), there is a statistically significant difference in the responses of the respondents according to age categories, that is, respondents aged 15–19 most often use technology brands for entertainment (58%); they are followed by respondents aged 20–26 (52%), and 47% of respondents aged 10–14 use technology brands for the mentioned purpose.

It has been found that there is an influence of age of respondents on the frequency of use of technology brands for learning and work (regression, $R^2 = 0.138$, $p = 0.00 < 0.05$; 13.8% of the variability of a dependent variable—the frequency of use of technology brands is determined by the influence of the independent variable—the age), as well as the correlation between these variables (Spearman's rank correlation coefficient = 0.371, $p = 0.00 < 0.05$, for a confidence interval of 99% and a risk of error of 1%), where the correlation is positive and moderate, which means that the older the members of GenZ are, the higher is the frequency of using technology brands for learning and work.

According to ANOVA test ($p = 0.00 < 0.05$), there is a statistically significant difference in the responses of the respondents according to the age categories, that is, respondents aged 20–26 most often use technology brands for learning and work (33%); they are followed by respondents aged 15–19 (23%), and 11% of respondents aged 10–14 use technology brands for this purpose.

Testing the research hypotheses

The research hypothesis H_1 is confirmed. It has been set out that technology brands are frequently used by GenZ members. As many as 65% of respondents are ready to use technology brands, and in the last two years, 57% of GenZ frequently use some of the technology brands in Serbia (such as KupujemProdajem, Top Shop, Donesi, and CarGo).

According to the research results, it has been confirmed that there is a statistically significant difference in the responses of respondents of different age groups within GenZ in relation to the frequency of use of certain technology brands, and thus **hypothesis H_2 is confirmed.** It has been found that respondents aged 15–19 use YouTube, Instagram, and WhatsApp most frequently, and that respondents aged 10–14 use Facebook the least, and TikTok most frequently, compared to respondents of other age categories of GenZ. It has also been established that the older the respondents, the lower the frequency of use of TikTok; and that the older the members of GenZ, the higher the frequency of using Facebook.

Based on the results of the research presented in Table 7.2, there is no statistically significant correlation between the frequency of use of examined technology brands and the degree of influence of cooperation of the organisations with their consumers (co-creation) on the brand perception. Therefore, **hypothesis H_3 isn't confirmed**.

Based on the results of the research presented in Table 7.3, there is no statistically significant correlation between the frequency of use of examined

Table 7.2 Examining the correlation between the frequency of use of technology brands and the degree of co-creation to brand perception

Frequency of use of	*N*	*Risk of error*	*Spearman's rank correlation coefficient*	*p*
Instagram	255	-	0.04	0.53
YouTube	254	-	0.054	0.39
WhatsApp	249	-	0.071	0.266
Viber	248	-	−0.108	0.09
Netflix	247	-	−0.006	0.919
Facebook	247	-	0.101	0.114
TikTok	246	-	0.051	0.427
Twitter	246	0.05	0.157	0.014*
Pinterest	245	-	0.01	0.874
Amazon	244	-	−0.102	0.113
Spotify	244	-	−0.036	0.578
Alibaba	239	-	−0.009	0.895

* *An asterisk indicates the existence of statistically important significance ($p < 0.05$), but there is a weak correlation (the coefficient is less than 0.30, so we cannot talk about a statistically significant correlation).*

Source: *Authors of the paper*

Table 7.3 Examination of the correlation between the frequency of use of technology brands and the degree of intention of the respondents to participate in co-creation

Frequency of use of	*N*	*Risk of error*	*Spearman's rank correlation coefficient*	*p*
YouTube	288	-	−0.045	0.451
Instagram	289	0.01	0.26	0.00*
WhatsApp	283	0.05	0.124	0.037*
Viber	281	-	0.153	0.01
TikTok	279	-	0.014	0.82
Facebook	278	-	0.107	0.076
Pinterest	278	0.05	0.133	0.026*
Netflix	277	-	0.103	0.088
Spotify	276	-	−0.004	0.943
Amazon	275	-	−0.023	0.699
Twitter	275	-	−0.033	0.588
Alibaba	269	-	0.017	0.785

* *An asterisk indicates the existence of statistically important significance ($p < 0.05$), but there is a weak correlation (the coefficient is less than 0.30, so we cannot talk about a statistically significant correlation).*
Source: *Authors of the paper*

technology brands and the degree of intention of respondents to participate in the co-creation process. Therefore, **hypothesis H_4 isn't confirmed.**

However, from the view of the brand managers, the technology brands are valued according to the frequency of their usage by their target groups and consequently, brand managers search for those technology brands which are used most frequently by their consumers to place their digital strategies. Not surprisingly, the best positioned technology brands among communication channels where GenZ notices the promotional activities are Instagram and YouTube (Graph 7.4).

Based on the findings of our research, there is no statistically significant correlation between the frequency of technology brands usage and the degree of intentions of GenZ members to participate in the process of the brands' co-creation. A statistically significant correlation between the frequency of use of examined technology brands and the degree of influence of organisations' cooperation with their consumers (i.e., co-creation) on the opinion about technology brands has not been confirmed, also. So, it can be concluded that the frequency of use of technology brands is not crucial for the intention of brand managers in Serbia to engage GenZ to join co-creation, and that co-creation as a process has not yet been perceived by brand managers and GenZ as the relevant factor which could enhance the use of technology brands. These findings could open the range of marketing strategies and activities aimed to attract GenZ to use more technology brands, especially those which are not exploited enough, through a well-designed co-creation process. This empowers new communication goals to the brands: to educate, entertain, and interact with GenZ, establishing long-term sustainable bonds with them. As many as 65% of respondents are ready to use technology brands (Graph 7.3), and in the last two years, 57% of the GenZ frequently use some of the technology brands (even regional such as KupujemProdajem, Donesi, Top Shop, and CarGo).

The role of GenZ in the ongoing wave of increased use of technology brands is significant. GenZ quickly shares its opinion with all its virtual friends, not only about the experience with brands but also with companies as well. Our research has also shown that GenZ members in Serbia use technology brands frequently (65%) and more than half of respondents (57%) have used frequently some of the well-known Serbian technology brands including KupujemProdajem and Top Shop (online shopping platforms), Donesi (express food delivery), and CarGo (app for a taxi). There is a statistically significant difference in the responses of the respondents of the different age categories among GenZ members related to the frequency of using certain technology brands. It is established that the respondents of 10–14 age range use YouTube, Instagram, and WhatsApp most frequently, and compared to the respondents of other age categories within GenZ, they use Facebook least commonly and TikTok most frequently. It is also proved that the frequency of use of TikTok is less as the respondents are elderly, and that frequency of Facebook use is higher as GenZ members are elderly.

7.5. Conclusion

This research's results indicate that there will be an increasing trend for technology brands in the forthcoming period due to the ongoing digitalisation process and emerging economic force of GenZ. Therefore, we explored the frequency of use of the technology brands by GenZ and their attitudes about technology brands concluding that more than 80% of them understand the meaning of the "technology brand." They are "digital natives" using technology brands and platforms frequently who will become financially independent in the following years and, consequently, their impact on the developing technology brands will be even stronger. Even 70% of respondents aged 15–19 years used some technology brands in the last two years; as well as 61% of respondents aged 20–26 years and 33% of respondents aged 10–14 years. Most technology brands, including Apple, Amazon, Microsoft, Google, Samsung, Facebook, LinkedIn, and PayPal, have proved their value and resilience during the turmoil of COVID-19 pandemic. Spotify, Netflix, and Amazon have shown the biggest growth in ranking during global COVID-19 lockdowns. GenZ uses more frequently technology brands such as Instagram and Youtube in Serbia while Netflix, TikTok, Wolt, Glovo, and Yandex have increased their business significantly during COVID-19 pandemic.

Co-creation allows Generation Z to demonstrate its values (creativity, flexibility, knowledge) and personalities (innovation) as well as to meet its needs (interactivity and engagement, collaboration and shared learning) and its purpose (because success is measured by its contribution to the society). According to the Serbian research findings, the co-creation process is not substantially recognised and developed among the target group GenZ by marketing and brand managers as an ecosystem for empowering technology brands and their values as future profit generators. This finding gives companies a space for stronger cooperation with young consumers in building stronger brands as well as sustainability. This imposes new communication goals to the brands, such as to educate, to entertain, and to interact with GenZ, because the entire analysis shows a strong interest of young people for regional and international technology brands. In spite of the fact that some companies have recognised the power of technology brands and digital transformation for newcomers (GenZ), there is plenty of space for intensifying this process in the Serbian economy.

We may consider that the limitation of the study is a limited resource of other similar worldwide researches to be compared with. Since the technology brands are emerging and new brands are blooming rapidly (like TikTok and others), our goal is to analyse the results of the papers with similar topic in different resources, as well as to bring integrative findings and conduct follow-up researches during the next period.

References

Cotet, G. B., Carutasu, N. L., & Chiscop, F. (2020). Industry 4.0 diagnosis from an iMillennial educational perspective. *Education Sciences*, *10*, 21. https://doi.org/10.3390/educsci10010021

De Kroon, D. (2021). *The partner leading McKinsey's digital capability centers in Europe*. www.mckinsey.com/about-us/new-at-mckinsey-blog/new-center-in-italy-prepares-businesses-for-digital-renaissance

DeSantis Breindel. (n.d.). *DeSantis Breindel technology branding building long-term value in a system update world*. www.desantisbreindel.com/wp-content/uploads/Technology-Branding-Chapter.pdf

Dimitriou, C. K., & AbouElgheit, E. (2019). Understanding GenZ's social decision-making in travel. *Tourism and Hospitality Management*, *25*(2), 311–334.

Edelman Trust Barometer. (2021). www.edelman.com/trust/2021-trust-barometer

Fernando, Y., & Chukai, C. (2018). Value co-creation, goods and service tax (GST) impacts on sustainable logistic performance. *Research in Transportation Business and Management*, *28*, 92–102.

Forbes. (2021). www.forbes.com/the-worlds-most-valuable-brands/#401f0235119c

García-Haro, M. Á., Martínez-Ruiz, M. P., & Martínez-Cañas, R. (2014). The effects of the value co-creation process on the consumer and the company. *Expert Journal of Marketing*, *2*(2), 68–81.

García-Haro, M. Á., Martínez-Ruiz, M. P., & Martínez-Cañas, R. (2015). The influence of value co-creation on consumer satisfaction: A mediating role of consumer motivation. *International Journal of Online Marketing (IJOM)*, *5*(4), 60–83. http://doi.org/10.4018/IJOM.2015100104

Gietl, J., Baumgarth, C., Kilian, K., & Schmidt, H. (n.d.). *Brand experts, expert panel for technology brands*. www.brand-trust.de/en/glossary/technology-brands.php

Hajli, N., Shanmugam, M., Papagiannidis, S., Zahay, D., & Richard, M. O. (2017). Branding co-creation with members of online brand communities. *Journal of Business Research*, *70*, 136–144.

Hamel, G., & Prahalad, C. K. (1994). *Competing for the future*. Harvard Business School Press.

Ho, C. W., & Wang, Y. B. (2020). Does social media marketing and brand community play the role in building a sustainable digital business strategy? *Sustainability, 12*, 6417. https://doi.org/10.3390/su12166417

Ind, N., & Coates, N. (2013). The meanings of co-creation. *European Business Review, 25*(1), 86–95. https://doi.org/10.1108/0955534131128775

Ind, N., Fuller, C., & Trevail, C. (2012). *Brand together: How co-creation generates innovation and re-energizes.* Kogan Page. ISBN 978-0-7494-6325-0; ISBN 978-0-7494-6326-7.

Interbrand. (2021). www.interbrand.com/

Kamboj, S., Sharmah, B., Gupta, S., & Dwivedi, J. K. (2018, April). Examining branding co-creation in brand communities on social media: Applying paradigm of stimulus-organism-response. *International Journal of Information Management, 39*, 169–185. https://doi.org/10.1016/j.ijinfomgt.2017.12.001

Keller, K. L. (2012). Brand strategy. In V. Shankar & G. Carpenter (Eds.), *Handbook of marketing strategy* (pp. 289–305). Edward Elgar.

KEPIOS. (2021). https://kepios.com/; https://datareportal.com/reports/digital-2021-global-overview-report

Kim, D. W., Trimi, S., Hong, S. G., & Lim, S. (2020). Effects of co-creation on organizational performance of small and medium manufacturers. *Journal of Business Research, 109*, 574–584.

Kim, W. C., & Mauborgne, R. (2017). The W. Chan Kim and Renée Mauborgne blue ocean strategy. Harvard Business Review Press. http://17imc.ir/uploads/uploads/W_Chan_Kim_Rene%CC%81e_A_Mauborgne_The_Blue_Ocean_Strategy_Reader_The.pdf

Kotler, P., & Sarkar, C. (2018). *Brand activism: From purpose to action.* Idea Bite Press.

Lafley, A. G., & Charan, R. (2008). *The game-changer: How you can drive revenue and profit growth with innovation.* Crown Business.

Mamula Nikolić, T., Perčić, K., & Nećak, M. (2022). MSMEs need to change the game in challenging times such as COVID-19 crisis: Changes in consumer behavior habits. *Teme. Vol. XLVI, No 1*, 2022 Print ISSN: 0353-7919 Online ISSN: 1820-7804

Mamula Nikolić, T., Paunović, I., Milovanović, M., Lozović, N., & Đurović, M. (2022). Examining Generation Z's Attitudes, Behavior and Awareness Regarding Eco-Products: A Bayesian Approach to Confirmatory Factor Analysis. *Sustainability* 2022, February DOI: 10.3390/su14052727

Mamula Nikolić, T. (2021). *New generation consumers and leaders behavior in the VUCA world.* Metropolitan University and iLearn. ISBN: 978-86-89755-20-6, COBISS 36603145.

Mamula Nikolić, T., Popović-Pantić, S., & Muller, I. (2020). The impact of ICT and digitalization on consumer purchase behaviour of millennials as emerging economic and social force—the case of Serbia. In E. Lechman & M. Popowska (Eds.), *Society and technology, opportunities and challenges, ICT and social development, conceptual considerations* (pp. 124–150). Society and Technology, Routledge. https://doi.org/10.4324/9780429278945.

Mamula T., Perić, N., & Vujić, N. (2019). The contribution of innovative leadership style as an answer to global and business changes. *Calitatea, 20*(170), 9–14. Access to Success QAS, p-ISSN 1582–2559; e-ISSN 2668–4861; ISSN-L 2668–4861.

Mamula, T., & Popović-Pantić, S. (2015). Relationship between innovativeness and strategic planning—empirical research. *Industrija, 43*(4), JEL, L100. https://doi.org/10.5937/industrija43–8718 UDC: 005.342:005.51 Original Scientific Paper.

Mamula, T. (2012). The role of marketing metrics in strategic brand management. *Marketing Magazine*, pp. 49–61, 43. ISSN 0354–3471, COBISS.SR-ID 749828.

McGinnis Jonson, J., & Ng, E. S. W. (2015). Money talks or millennials walk. *Review of Public Personnel Administration*, 1–23.

McKinsey Global Institute. (2017). *China's digital economy a leading global force*. www.mckinsey.com/~/media/mckinsey/featured%20insights/China/Chinas%20digital%20economy%20A%20leading%20global%20force/MGI-Chinas-digital-economy-A-leading-global-force.ashx

McKinsey Global Institute. (2021, June). *Getting tangible about intangibles: The future of growth and productivity?* Discussion Paper. McKinsey Global Institute.

Millward Brown. (2021). www.visualcapitalist.com/the-worlds-tech-giants-ranked/

Milovanović, M., Đurović, M., & Mamula Nikolić, T. (2021, April). *GenZ' attitudes on circular economy: The case of Republic of Serbia and Republic of Srpska*. International Conference on "Circular and Bieconomy" 2021, Engineering Management Society of Serbia.

Nyangwe, S., & Buhalis, D. (2018). Branding transformation through social media and co-creation: Lessons from Marriott international. In B. Stangl & J. Pesonen (Eds.), *Information and communication technologies in tourism 2018*. Springer. https://doi.org/10.1007/978-3-319-72923-7_20

Park, J., & Ha, S. (2016). Co-creation of service recovery: Utilitarian and hedonic value and post-recovery responses. *Journal of Retailing and Consumer Services*, *28*, 310–316.

Paunović, I., Dressler, M., Mamula Nikolić, T., & Popović Pantić, S. (2020). Developing a competitive and sustainable destination of the future: Clusters and predictors of successful national-level destination governance across destination life-cycle. *Sustainability*, *12*, 4066. https://doi.org/10.3390/su12104066

Perčić, K., & Mamula Nikolić, T. (2020). Innovation in the Working environment as a Way to Overcome the Crisis and Create New Consumer Habits. In: Karabašević, D., Vukotić, S., Popović, G. MEFKON20 – Innovation as an Initiator of the Development, „Innovations in the Function of Development", International Thematic Monograph – Thematic Proceedings, Digital Edition, University Business Academy in Novi Sad, Faculty of Applied Management, Economics and Finance Belgrade, Belgrade, 3rd December 2020, pp. 71-92, ISBN 978-86-84531-50-8

Perčić, K., & Perić, N. (2021). The effectiveness of direct marketing media regarding attitudes of different target groups of consumers in Serbia. *Periodica Polytechnica—Social and Management Sciences*, *29*(1), 21–32. https://doi.org/10.3311/PPso.13616

Perčić, K., Perić, N., & Kutlača, Đ. (2019). The adoption of internet media as marketing innovations in Serbia. *Management: Journal of Sustainable Business and Management Solutions in Emerging Economies*, *24*(2), 63–72. https://doi.org/10.7595/management.fon.2018.0032

Perčić, K., & Vukadinović, L. (2019a). Innovative written expression of youth in Serbia. *Zbornik Matice srpske za društvene nauke*, *LXX*(172), 517–535. https://doi.org/10.2298/ZMSDN1972517P

Perčić, K., & Vukadinović, L. (2019b). Reading habits amongst university students in the Republic of Serbia. *TEME—Journal for Social Sciences*, *XLIII*(2), 413–435. https://doi.org/10.22190/TEME181107026P

Perić, N., Mamula Nikolić, T., & Slijepčević, M. (2019). Clothes consumption in Republic of Serbia: Customer behaviour overview. *Tekstilec*, *62*(2), 137–147. https://doi.org/0.14502/Tekstilec2019.62.137-147

Perić, N., Mamula Nikolić, T., & Delić, T. (2021). Analysis of attitudes of GenZ toward media and consumption: The region of Balkans. *Marketing*, *3*(51), 210–218. https://doi.org/10.5937/markt2003210P

Pew Research Center. (2019). *Defining generations: Where millennials end and GenZ begins.* www.pewresearch.org/fact-tank/2019/01/17/where-millennials-end-and-generation-z-begins/

Popović-Pantić, S., Semenčenko, D., & Vasilić, N. (2019). The influence of digital transformation on business performance: Evidence of the women-owned companies, *Ekonomika preduzeća, Serbian Association of Economists Journal of Business Economics and Management*, 397–414. UDK: 005.591.6 658:007:004 005.7–055.2. https://doi.org/10.5937/EKOPRE1908397P

Popović-Pantić, S., Semenčenko, D., & Vasilić, N. (2020, January–March). Digital technology and the financial performance of female SMEs in Serbia: The mediating role of innovation. *Ekonomski anali, Economic Annals, LXV*(224), 53–81. UDC: 3.33 ISSN: 0013–326. https://doi.org/10.2298/EKA2024053

Prensky, M. (2001). Digital natives, digital immigrants. *On the Horizon, 9*(5), 1–6.

Raza, A., Saeed, A., Iqbal, M. K., Saeed, U., Sadiq, I., & Faraz, N. A. (2020). Linking corporate social responsibility to customer loyalty through co-creation and customer company identification: Exploring sequential mediation mechanism. *Sustainability, 12*, 2525.

Rogers, L. D. (2016). *Digital transformation playbook: Your business for the digital age.* Columbia Business School Publishing. https://doi.org/10.7312/roge17544

Roser, T., DeFillippi, R., & Samson, A. (2013). Managing your co-creation mix: Co-creation ventures in distinctive contexts. *The European Business Review, 25*(1), 20–41.

Sweeny, R. (2006). *Millennial behaviors & demographics.* http://unbtls.ca/teachingtips/pdfs/sew/Millennial-Behaviors.pdf

Tapscott, D. (2009). *Grown up digital: How the net generation is changing your world.* McGraw-Hill.

Tronvoll, B., Brown, S. W., Gremler, D. D., & Edvardsson, B. (2011). Paradigms in service research. *Journal of Service Management, 22*(5), 560–585. https://doi.org/10.1108/09564231111174951

Von Hippel, E. (2005). *Democratizing innovation.* The MIT Press.

www.youtube.com/watch?v=fQZVUs2h0Tw

www.youtube.com/watch?v=sFEZvgHW4II

Zhao, Y., Chen, Y., Zhou, R., & Ci, Y. (2019). Factors influencing customers' willingness to participate in virtual brand community's value co-creation: The moderating effect of customer involvement. *Online Information Review, 43*(3), 440–461. https://doi.org/10.1108/OIR-08-2017-0232

Zwass, V. (2010). Co-creation: Toward a taxonomy and an integrated research perspective. *International Journal of Electronic Commerce, 15*(1), 11–48. Published online 2014. https://doi.org/10.2753/JEC1086-4415150101

Appendix

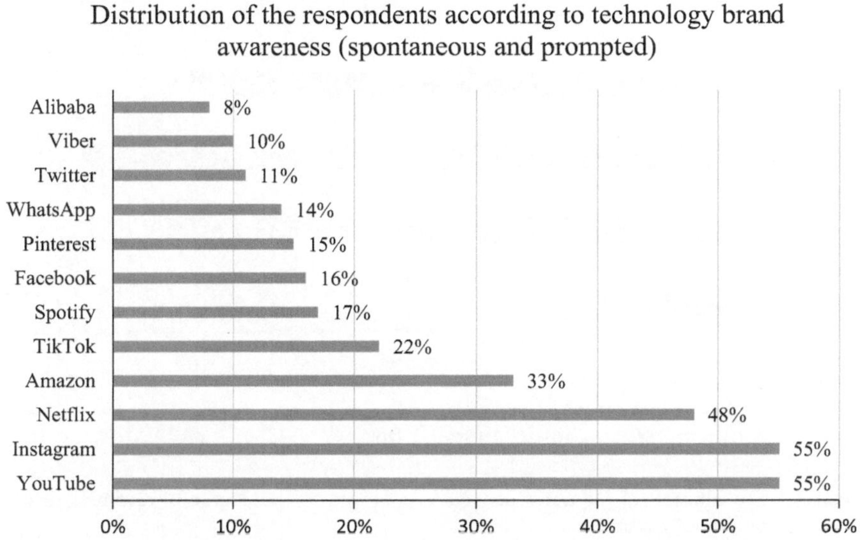

Graph 7.1 Distribution of GenZ in Serbia according to technology brand awareness (spontaneous and prompted)

* *It was a multiple-choice question.*

Source: *Authors of the paper*

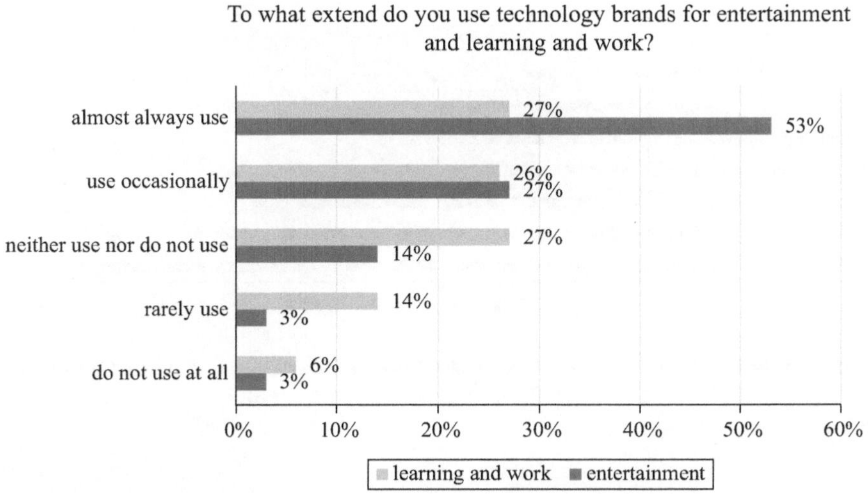

Graph 7.2 Distribution of members of GenZ according to the degree and purpose of using technology brands

Source: *Authors of the paper*

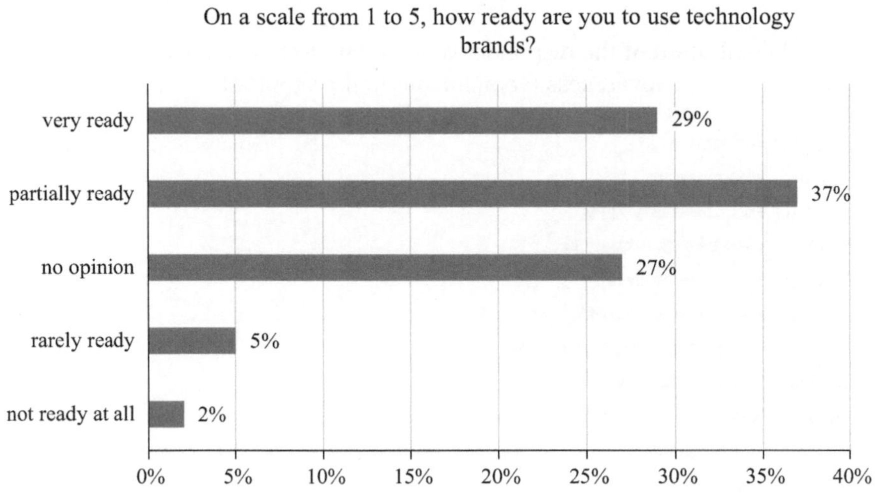

Graph 7.3 Distribution of members of GenZ according to the degree of readiness to use technology brands

Source: *Authors of the paper*

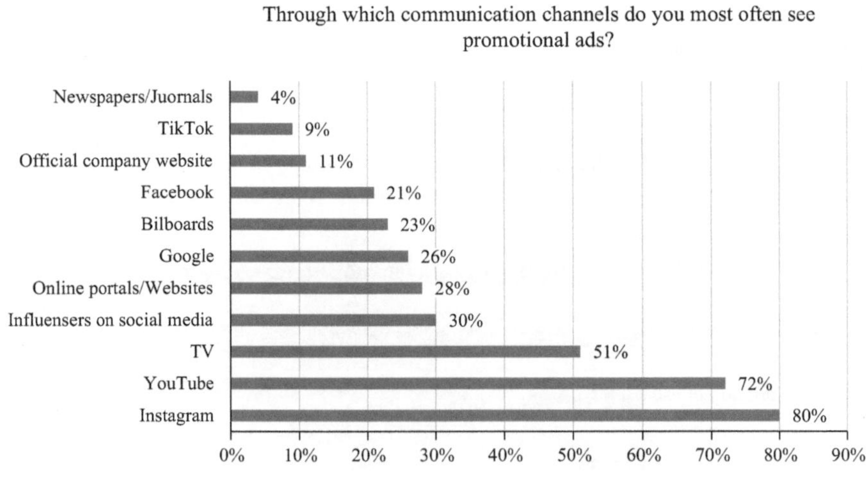

Graph 7.4 Distribution of GenZ in Serbia according to communication channels through which they see promotional ads

Source: *Authors of the paper*

8 Place branding and social media in the sharing economy

A literature review

Abdullah M. Alahmari, Bruno Schivinski, and Xiufang (Leah) Li

8.1. Introduction

A city with business and economic opportunities attracts people from different regions to settle in and pursue their endeavours (Kavaratzis, 2017). City administrators are aware that their city brand is associated with merits that make them build strong brands (Braun et al., 2018). Place branding has emerged as one of the common practices that cities engage in to guarantee that there are enough opportunities to attract other people from different regions to seek accommodation and shelter in branded cities (Braun et al., 2018). The economic performance of a region is dependent on various factors, such as its location and other available opportunities for economic activities (Cleave et al., 2016). However, the concept of place branding is one of the essential considerations since the brand of a city is likely to influence the rate at which people want to associate with such regions (Eugenio-Vela et al., 2020).

The dynamics of a city encourage sharing economy. Sharing economy occurs when individuals enjoy, occupy, and consume something with other people (Schor & Fitzmaurice, 2015). This form of sharing is crucial since it establishes social relations among people from different regions and backgrounds (Schivinski et al., 2020). The current model of sharing economy allows individuals from diverse origins to exchange goods and services, as opposed to only people from the same community (Schor & Fitzmaurice, 2015). Having people interact from various regions creates an all-inclusive environment that expands the economic flow of cities and regions. The various practices involved in sharing economy include renting, gifting, lending, sharing, selling, and swapping (Laurell & Sandström, 2017). Sharing economy is grounded on the need to manage finite resources in an effort to enhance sustainability (Light & Miskelly, 2019). The concept of sharing economy encourages collective action, social cohesion, mindful consumption, as well as fairer societies (Eckhardt et al., 2019). In other words, sharing economy has become an important aspect of modern cities and a tool for branding.

Social media emerged as a useful tool that promotes interaction and sharing of ideas among different people (Eckhardt et al., 2019). Digital platforms,

DOI: 10.4324/9781003184638-9

including social media, are used to mediate sharing economy of cities by facilitating the exchange between providers and users (Light & Miskelly, 2019). The scholarly literature has acknowledged how the digital economy is becoming more necessary owing to the increase in urbanisation, which creates a greater demand for resources (Palm et al., 2019). Social media platforms can be used to connect people from different parts of the city as well as the nation at large (Light & Miskelly, 2019). The individual's engagement with cities on social media may be on various topics, including entertainment and opportunities present in the different regions (Acuti et al., 2019). Therefore, digital platforms, precisely social media, play an integral role in sharing economy (Schivinski et al., 2020), which in turn helps to brand the city as functional.

Furthermore, the literature has acknowledged stakeholder engagement as a key aspect of sharing economy and place branding (Acuti et al., 2019). The stakeholder groups of the governments, investors, visitors, and residents are the essential players in the city branding. Therefore, this study focuses on the governments and residents in the sharing economy through social media (Acuti et al., 2019). Governments and residents play a significant central role to engage investors and visitors in city branding (Goulart Sztejnberg & Giovanardi, 2017; Kavaratzis, 2017). The government comes in as a brand manager, whereas the residents are classified as consumers. In this case, residents' engagement in social media is meant to seek access to the available opportunities in the city either for lease, rent, borrowing, or any other existing offers (Schivinski et al., 2020). However, the government may get involved in sharing economy through social media by acting in the best interest of the city's brand. In this case, the objective is to promote friendly interactions among people to create an environment that facilitates economic growth in the city (Palm et al., 2019).

Drawing on the extensive scholarly literature, the objective of this chapter and its theoretical contribution rests on incorporating three key aspects of place branding on social media into a single framework in relation to the sharing economy. The first aspect describes the literature link across city branding and social media. The second aspect involves the way stakeholders (i.e., government and residents) use social media to foster city branding. The third aspect describes the ways sharing economy fosters city branding. Finally, this chapter concludes with theoretical and practical implications derived from the literature review.

8.2. The role of social media on city branding

City branding

Regional authorities use city branding strategies for cities' advancement because of intense competition in developing the cities economically (Kavaratzis, 2017). Thus, city branding is a procedure of arranging and planning urban areas to fulfil the requirements of city consumers (Ashworth et al., 2015). The local authorities across the globe have been captured by the imagination of creating and upholding a successful brand of a city (Ntounis & Kavaratzis, 2017). The concept of place branding can be understood from diverse perspectives. Drawing upon the three-dimensional essence of a nation's brand, the process of branding a city can be centred around enhancing key aspects of a city's brand, including physical attributes, functional attributes, and personality traits (Li, 2017; Li & Feng, 2021a). Further, the literature has indicated that some scholars consider place branding as a place marketing instrument, whereas others perceive place marketing as a place branding instrument (Boisen et al., 2018). In fact, the various goals of branding a nation, which is one form of a place, are determined by the three research strands termed the "technical-economic, political, and cultural approaches" (Li & Feng, 2021a, p. 4). When the research is rooted in the discipline of marketing, management, and tourism, the technical-economic approach is often recommended (Li & Feng, 2021a).

In response to the use of the instrumental research strand, approaching place branding as a branding tool may entail the pursuit to establish different brands of a place to enhance its competitive advantage among the diverse target populations (Insch & Walters, 2018). The growing research on place branding has been occasioned by the existing competition between places for tourists, exports, and foreign direct investment (Foroudi et al., 2016). Strong brands leverage economies of countries of origin (Kucharska et al., 2018) and are important positioning elements of national brands (Ferilli et al., 2016). Famous and reputable cities, such as, Barcelona, Dubai, Amsterdam, Rio de Janeiro, Sydney, and New York, are good examples of cities actively contributing to countries positioning (Richelieu, 2018). Therefore, supporting that place branding strategies are an essential part of the longstanding growth plan of developed countries through the cities (Braun, 2012; Fan, 2014). However, other city administrators need to develop a clear understanding of city branding fundamentals by concentrating more on long-term goals, such as nurturing the attention of foreign direct investment (Weber, 2010). Globally, cities are pursuing to improve their image to increase the inflow of investments, business activities, exports, and tourism (Ashworth et al., 2015; Shirvani-Dastgerdi & De-Luca, 2019). This, in turn, suggests that city branding is a long-term strategy that should mirror the improvement and growth of the city (Fan, 2014).

The literature of city branding is also informed using political and cultural research streams. For instance, one of the challenges facing place branding is the identity of a region (Kavaratzis & Kalandides, 2015). City branding needs to aim to leverage and to position cities with a unique identity in stakeholders' minds (Casidy et al., 2019), by incorporating change, continuity, and heterogeneity (Kavaratzis, 2017; Kavaratzis & Hatch, 2013). For instance, the contemporary policy agendas have focused on the branding and marketing of regions, cities, nations, and places, positioning city branding as a form of urban policy (Lucarelli, 2018). This indicates that place branding is adopted as a political instrument for urban policy characterised by a precise political typology (Lucarelli, 2018). Using the political and cultural research approach expands the instrumental research scope on city branding, which has a heavy focus on growing attractions and places images to attract visitors, investors, tourists, and events (Foroudi et al., 2016).

In addition, the scholarly literature demonstrates the emergence of utilising the PR (public relations)-driven relationship-building approach in city branding, featuring the role of stakeholder engagement in branding a place (Li & Feng, 2021b). First, the cognitive and emotional associations that individuals establish with brands are dependent on what the brand is made of and its significance (Kavaratzis & Kalandides, 2015; Schivinski et al., 2015). A brand is a multidimensional construct that consists of emotional, functional, strategic, and relational elements that, when combined, generate a unique relationship with the public mind (Keller, 2003). The contemporary understanding of place branding is linked to the associations that residents make with the branding object (Wassler et al., 2019). This idea implies that associations may be considered as the raw material that stakeholders leverage to create place brands in their thoughts (Gupta et al., 2017; Hudak, 2019).

Second, the entire concept of place branding is related to the general activities carried out within a territory, such as economic practices and other events that can either attract or repel people from associating with a specific region and activities therein (Jonas et al., 2018). This view suggests that place branding can proceed as a participatory process initiated by a legitimate body (Hankinson, 2015; Kavaratzis & Kalandides, 2015). It highlights the role of stakeholders in the entire process of city branding (Sevin, 2016). The stakeholders as individuals or groups affected by or can affect the attainment of the organisation's goals (de Oliveira & Rabechini Jr, 2019). For instance, consultants play an active role in starting this participatory process by offering crucial conceptual insights that are thought-provoking in the implementation and design of city branding (Goulart Sztejnberg & Giovanardi, 2017). Further, the involvement of people from different backgrounds in co-creating brand meaning and motivating citizens to participate in place branding programmes is based on a participatory approach (Li & Feng, 2021b). From this perspective, stakeholders' engagement in place branding is a fundamental practice that can secure not only an effective but also a stable brand for a city (Acuti et al., 2019). Owing to the role of the main stakeholder groups of the government and the residents in branding a place, stakeholder engagement is further identified as how the government engages multiple stakeholders in participating and influencing decision-making about the brand of a place (Li & Feng, 2021b).

In summary, informed by the technical-economic approach, the scholarly literature demonstrates that city branding is a complex process of arranging and developing urban areas to meet the needs of city customers. Consequently, city branding involves the development of various strategies that allow achieving a city's progress and expansion. Furthermore, the literature is concise in that a city's brand is composed of three key aspects, including physical attributes,[1] functional attributes,[2] and personality traits[3] (Li, 2017; Li & Feng, 2021a). These aspects ensure to create and maintain a city's brand identity. However, the success of that is dependent on the use of a stakeholder engagement approach to allow various stakeholder groups, especially the citizens, to participate in and influence decision-making about the three aspects of a city's brand.

Social media in city branding

The expansion in networks regarding information and communication technology has enabled people, places, and objects to connect in more diverse ways and ultimately shaping the reality of urban development (Kolotouchkina & Seisdedos, 2018). Information communication technology, such as social media, is a critical element that allows for increased resource involvement in market operations (Lechman, 2016). Therefore, several places in the world have embraced and transitioned to the smart city format despite the uneven distribution of digital urban innovations globally (Kolotouchkina & Seisdedos, 2018). For effective place branding, a strategic and coherent approach must be initiated (Hanna & Rowley, 2015). The approach taken for place branding should embrace digital branding and be multichannel (Hanna & Rowley, 2015). Technology and society are closely tied; therefore, technology-supported networks significantly contribute to economic growth today (Lechman, 2018). Social media that enhance fostering social networks has been widely used as a communication tool under digital technology to enhance place branding and marketing, especially at the municipal level (Cleave et al., 2017; Paniagua & Korzynski, 2017), aggregating economic values to the city (Cleave et al., 2017).

Social media has enabled communities that were once geographically detached to be linked (Scholz & Smith, 2019). It has provided a platform for the dense networking of these once-remote communities, therefore, making their impact on place branding more substantial and direct (Scholz & Smith, 2019). The literature also supports that technologically enabled socio-economic platforms generated by social media enable sharing economy by allowing processes such as momentary access of material, economic worth transfer, and platform arbitration together with an extended consumer role that ultimately affect the branding of a particular location (Eckhardt et al., 2019). As such, the amalgamation of different communities through social media has amplified place branding through sharing of the economy (Eckhardt et al., 2019).

The effective implementation of social media in the place of branding creates an impact on attracting tourists, investors, visitors, and traders and ultimately enhances the city or country's image and brand (Foroudi et al., 2016). Through enabling word-of-mouth in engagements and interactions for a more personalised experience, social media is on the verge of replacing mainstream media as the perfect alternative for place branding (Govers, 2015; Lund et al., 2018). This form of media allows enhancing commoditisation of virtual brand values, such as innovation, modernity, and openness during place branding (Govers, 2015; Lund et al., 2018). As such, social media enables meaningful, relevant, distinctive, and authentic brand values through symbolic and substance actions for relevance and sustainability (Govers, 2015; Lund et al., 2018; Schivinski et al., 2019).

In summary, the scholarly literature points out that using social media as a communication tool is a critical branding approach for cities to drive economic growth. The literature is consistent in the sense that the interaction of social media helps to integrate different communities in the cities. In contrast, the amalgamation of diverse communities through social media has amplified city branding through shared economy. As a result, there is a scholarly agreement that social media is a suitable option to shape the brand of a place, including a city.

8.3. Stakeholder's engagement in place branding

Government engagement through social media

The literature indicates two core methods to engage stakeholders in city branding (Goulart Sztejnberg & Giovanardi, 2017). The first method is through stakeholder workshops, whereas the second is via internal brand engagement plans (Goulart Sztejnberg & Giovanardi, 2017). Within the context of place branding, the identification of stakeholders needs to be situated within the context of a given country or that of a particular branding initiative (Li & Feng, 2021b). This broadly involves the four different types of stakeholders, including government, public sector organisations, private sector organisations, and citizens (Li & Feng, 2021b). From this aspect, the meaning of a place's brand is negotiated through the government's engagement with the remaining stakeholder groups, which throws light on communication tactics in response to the trend of co-creating a place branding in social media.

Stakeholder engagement promotes the collaboration of governmental organisations, politicians, local businesses, marketing agencies, academic organisations, and the media (Jonas et al., 2018). The simultaneous influence that public and private stakeholders have and the tight association between consumers and producers make places emerge as co-created products with multiple forms of alliances and corporations (Goulart Sztejnberg & Giovanardi, 2017). Consequently, governments around the world utilise social media in attempts to brand their cities (Sevin, 2016). The literature also supports that making brand-related content available on social media creates the potential to content be changed, recreated, and shared with specific audiences (Kucharska, 2019; Schivinski, 2019; Schivinski et al., 2021), which is useful for branding a city (Sevin, 2016). By evaluating the social media presence of its residents, governments can drive city brand campaigns based on media ecology and target-audience communication (Ripoll Gonzalez & Lester, 2018). The residents and governments providing oversight on social media usage in place branding policy influences how the city or area will be able to attract and retain business (Cleave et al., 2016).

Another important aspect of the literature points out that social media has been effectively utilised by governments to revive economies by repairing badly tainted images of a place to attract tourists (Avraham, 2015). For instance, this strategy was successfully employed by the Egyptian military government after the Arab Spring in 2011 to restore sanity to the capital's tourism sector, which was negatively impacted by the violence that attracted massive coverage, ultimately impacting the region's tourism (Avraham, 2015). Stakeholders, including the government, in particular, prefer social media as a communication method, as it effectually bypasses the traditional foreign media to distribute crisis communication (Avraham, 2015, 2016). Also, social media is useful for altering a place image and building a quality brand in an attempt to enable quality interaction and attract tourists (Avraham, 2015, 2016). Moreover, governmental quality influences on social media have configured trust, impacting the extent of approved adaptation (Aladwani & Dwivedi, 2018). The governments engage with consumers on social media platforms, with the literature suggesting that the city government should employ a positive tone, as it is more feasible in encouraging citizen participation on social media (Zavattaro et al., 2015).

The literature also supports social media as a constructive vehicle in enabling accountability and transparency (Guillamón et al., 2016). It helps to increase the citizen's participation and collaboration in decision-making as well as improve public services (Guillamón et al., 2016). However, governments sometimes tend to fabricate social media posts to create strategic distractions (King et al., 2017). This strategy more often results in criticism of the regime together with its officials, as it limits dialogue and meaningful conversations between the citizens and the government (King et al., 2017).

In summary, the literature points out that various types of stakeholders diffuse city brand content through social media as part of their communication strategies. The government content on social media helps alter place image and build a quality brand to enable quality interaction and attract tourists. When the content is painted with a positive tone, it is more feasible in evoking citizen participation on social media. This presents an oversight on social media usage in city branding policy, therefore influencing how the city will attract and retain business.

Resident engagement through social media

Residents have increasingly become an active part of regional marketing as well as place branding, owing to their voiced, graphic, and behavioural languages of an area (Taecharungroj, 2019). Social media provides visitors and residents with an opportunity to show their views about a place through dense informal networks (Jeuring & Haartsen, 2017). The literature demonstrates that social media communication is a civic responsibility for residents to support holistic place branding strategies (Jeuring & Haartsen, 2017). Further, the legitimacy of place branding depends on the relationship between efficiency and advertisements (Martin & Capelli, 2017). Brands become more authentic when the advertisements are tailored to target populaces during the promotion of local products through co-branding efforts with the target public (Schivinski et al.,

2021). Likewise, resident engagement through local community events in place branding initiatives enhances the place's attractiveness to soothe the residents (Insch & Walters, 2018). As a result, the satisfaction of the residents contributes to raising the quality of life and building a sense of belonging and community, promoting the place branding processes of the region (Insch & Walters, 2018; Martin & Capelli, 2017).

Another aspect of the literature supports that social media allows for the creation and distribution of individual narratives by the residents that contribute to place branding (Hudak, 2019). This branch of the literature notes that digital platform has enabled residents to effectively partake in sharing their place impressions as well as experiences in more meaningful ways, therefore, allowing for collaborative place branding (Hudak, 2019). Classifying residents as the primary online place-brand ambassadors means that they are vital in enhancing competitiveness in tourist destinations (Schivinski et al., 2020). Moreover, user-generated content on social media allows local residents to be connected with tourists (Taecharungroj, 2019). This form of engagement enhances the trading of commodities between the locals and tourists (Uchinaka et al., 2019), allowing for the development of a shared economy besides building cohesion and harmony.

Place branding alignment begins when individual residents make use of placemaking materials, such as practices and institutions, leading to the formation of their mental associations with the area (Kavaratzis & Kalandides, 2015). These interactions constitute the brand meaning of this place. As consumers, the literature notes that for effective place branding, the place branding process must be participatory and interactive in order to stimulate co-created destination varieties (Kavaratzis, 2017). Therefore, the co-created brand needs to incorporate both internal and external locality issues that touch on market challenges for effective economy sharing and satisfaction (Kavaratzis, 2017).

In summary, residents have a civic responsibility to support comprehensive municipal branding plans through social media communication. The literature is consistent in showing that inhabitant's participation in local community events as part of place branding campaigns improves the city's appeal. As a result, the level of resident satisfaction with a place has an impact on the quality of life and the creation of a sense of belonging and community. The scholarly literature further supports that for effective economy sharing and pleasure, the co-created brand must contain internal and external localised issues that touch on market challenges through residents.

8.4. Sharing economy in city branding

The role of social media in sharing economy

The literature acknowledges social media as an important factor in sharing economy in relation to place branding (Fierro & Aranburu, 2019; Schivinski et al., 2020). Social media allow users to modify and create a collaborative and participatory environment (Laurell & Sandström, 2017). Actors in the sharing economy use the platform to gather knowledge about the market as well as non-market domains of the industry (Cui et al., 2020). The progression of technology and the increasing economic digitisation has made sharing to be a new consumer's role, whose behaviour has transformed from having to using (Cui et al., 2020). For example, the progression of technology makes economic digitisation easier for meeting participants' diverse needs due to automatic matching as well as sorting technology, thus ensuring efficiency and scale (Cui et al., 2020). Therefore, social media helps generate value to cities and locations when communication has a high quality by allowing brands to communicate with their consumers (Kucharska, 2017).

Sharing economy in the context of place branding is also characterised by online collaboration, online sharing, and social commerce[4] (Key, 2017). The use of social media promotes sharing economy because individuals in peer groups encourage each other to try similar things (Key, 2017). An individual is more likely to choose to visit and explore a city as a result of the social influence,[5] perhaps on the basis of their peers (Lutz et al., 2018). Online sharing in the context of city branding involves information sharing regarding the place, such as status updates, links, videos, and photos (Fierro & Aranburu, 2019; Palm et al., 2019). The literature, likewise, supports that social media also play an important role in mediating sharing economy transactions that allow the scaling of sharing activities by connecting consumers and locations (Eckhardt et al., 2019). As an example, positive reviews from such platforms build the reputation and enable the competition for customers as the destination city.

Further aspects of sharing economy in the literature include collaborative economy or consumption (Schivinski et al., 2020), which refers to the organisation of peer-to-peer sharing of items and services, which is strengthened via the advancement of digital platforms (Zmyślony et al., 2020). The universal nature of the collaborative economy has enabled sharing economy corporations like Airbnb, Uber, and Couchsurfing to establish a presence in cities and consequently to support co-branding (Fierro & Aranburu, 2019). The success of these firms can be chiefly credited to the international marketing strategies they adopt to appeal to local cities.

In summary, the scholarly literature agrees that online cooperation, online sharing, social commerce, and consumer ideology are all characteristics of the sharing economy in the context of place branding. The fact that individuals in peer groups encourage each other to attempt similar things suggests that the collaborative use of social media encourages the growth of the sharing economy. As a result, in the context of city branding, the literature supports that social media play a crucial strategic role in facilitating sharing economy transactions by connecting consumers and venues, allowing for the scalability of sharing activities.

Sharing economy fostering city branding

The literature approaches the role of sharing economy in place branding regarding several aspects, including the culture of the residents and the correct implementation of digital platforms to foster communication (Fierro &

Aranburu, 2019). The culture of the residents is understood as "a system, a dynamic whole that creates and is created by people, places, and practices, and that the system and its components are inseparable and engaged in mutual determination" (Causadias, 2020, p. 311). The system organises its components and vice versa (Causadias, 2020). Individuals establish their culture via communal practices in a particular place, while culture shapes their practices and the ways they build their place (Causadias, 2020). In this case, the culture of residents includes the customs and practices of target residents. Residents can serve as brand ambassadors, as well as being citizens and also voters (Banerjee, 2020), and therefore they are one of the significant stakeholders in a given place. This stream of the literature supports that the engagement with residents is essential in achieving the goals of place branding. The success of place branding relies on capturing the emotional side of the residents living in this place through developing a trust-focused relationship between the residents and this place (Banerjee, 2020). Such techniques are easily extended on social media (Czarnecka & Schivinski, 2019), further facilitating shared consumption and economy.

The resident's satisfaction can play a vital role in economic sharing, as well as in legitimising the strategies for developing this place (Zenker & Braun, 2017). The literature indicates that residents can only support the phenomenon or activity when there are positive impacts rather than negative impacts associated with the development of a place (Zmyślony et al., 2020). Therefore, the failure of incorporating the resident culture into the process of developing a strong city brand strategy can result in immense resistance from the residents (Zmyślony et al., 2020).

Cities, like products, compete with others to attract investments as well as tourists in the hospitality industry, which means tourists have to be marketed through a positive brand image (Glińska & Rudolf, 2019). For example, Airbnb markets itself in Texas with a less aggressive hotel room pricing that targets to benefit all consumers, which are the primary actors in the sharing economy (Zervas et al., 2017). In the city branding context, sharing economy is central to the promotion of such a positive image (Eckhardt et al., 2019). In a visitor economy, culture, attractions, infrastructure, accessibility, events, and heritage contribute to a successful destination in light of visitation or tourism (Grimmer & Vorobjovas-Pinta, 2019). The literature also supports that the impact of image branding by the sharing economy is the driver of the emerging sharing cities (Salvia et al., 2019). The assets to be shared include rides, accommodation facilities, and tools or competencies (Salvia et al., 2019). City configuration in size, accessibility, public space availability, social norms, habits, or even traditions shape how sharing occurs (Salvia et al., 2019).

In hospitality, the sharing economy actors like Airbnb and Uber are vital in connecting people to their destination cities by assuring top-notch shared rides and housing and accommodation services free of shared accommodation abuses (Zervas et al., 2017). Social media is linked to the success of this positive-image branding and setting it apart from a city's hospitality sector (Palm et al., 2019).

Hence, the literature supports that cities can utilise sharing concept to foster their economic growth, job creation, sociocultural development, and environmental sustainability, which involves, for example, crowdfunding to support the city objectives (Lindström, 2020). Also, development is realised by citizens' creation of demands as a stimulator to the growth of sharing activities, inspiring innovative activities (Rutkowska-Gurak & Adamska, 2019). A collaborative approach in this sense means engaging residents in crowdsourcing proposals and for objectives alignment (Rutkowska-Gurak & Adamska, 2019).

The literature further highlights that sharing cities employ smart technologies to connect several users to the idling assets for sharing by a bigger population instead of individual-owning (Salvia et al., 2019). Therefore, social media plays the role of linking to as many consumers as possible (Palm et al., 2019). The impacts of sharing economy on a city need to be controlled locally by its authorities to ensure sustainable and smart development that links all city's stakeholders and strengthens access to the underused assets (Rutkowska-Gurak & Adamska, 2019). However, this takes care of the potential conflicting interest of stakeholders (Rutkowska-Gurak & Adamska, 2019; Vith et al., 2019). In contrast, literature records various challenges of sharing concepts. As an urban phenomenon, there are issues like ethical tensions and moral dilemmas (Vith et al., 2019). Accommodation sharing has created problems for a city's image like non-compliance with current zoning codes, noise disturbances, straining real estate, and taxation difficulties (Morell & Espelt, 2019).

Scholars have also addressed an increase in the growth of digital sharing platforms utilised by people and cities. The development of digital sharing corporations has touched a status that is disrupting established industries across the globe (Fierro & Aranburu, 2019). Some have described the growth as volatile and remarkable, as with the case of Airbnb and Uber, two overall podiums for peer-to-peer hospitality services as well as ride services (Sutherland & Jarrahi, 2018). Therefore, the inflow of visitors to a city has become susceptible to the strategic interruption resulting from sharing platforms, including Airbnb (Fierro & Aranburu, 2019). The propagation of the sharing economy companies and platforms will reach a level where it can ultimately become an unavoidable and critical part of the international economy. However, this development would influence a country's technological potential, including institutional considerations, economic sustainability, human capital quality, and labour market laws (Lechman, 2013).

The literature indicates the significance of digital economy sharing for sustainability in terms of using new digital sharing economy practices to influence the usual consumption patterns since the inexpensive, available marketplace of sharing moves consumption from a possession routine to more access-based practices (Sutherland & Jarrahi, 2018). As a result, digital economy sharing has a substantial potential that can save natural resources because of the increased use of current assets and the stimulation of resource-efficient options. The literature further extends the idea that the sharing economy of cities produces a constructive social impact. Along with economic inspirations, social incentives drive engagement in the sharing economy (Sutherland & Jarrahi, 2018). The sharing practice can link individuals as well as encourage social cohesion in cities. Finally, social media sharing enhances the bringing of the economy to the status of social practices where individuals serve as economic drivers within their social bonds with the city (Sutherland & Jarrahi, 2018).

In summary, the scholarly literature is conclusive regarding the significance of the sharing economy in place branding facilitated by the advancement of social media. This is discussed in the literature in terms of numerous factors, including resident culture and the proper implementation of digital platforms to facilitate communication. In the perspective of city branding, the literature defines that the sharing economy is critical to promoting a favourable brand image of a place. The literature suggests that cities may use the sharing concept to help them grow economically, create jobs, develop socioculturally, and maintain the environmental sustainability. As a result, the effects of the sharing economy on a city must be managed by local authorities to ensure sustainable and innovative growth of the city, which can connect multiple city stakeholders and improve their access to underutilised assets.

8.5. Conclusion

The literature review has revealed that the brand of a place is a crucial consideration for people who want to visit the region. Despite the different interpretations of what place branding entails, there is a common understanding that place branding aims at boosting the outlook of a region (Braun et al., 2018). This idea implies that through place branding, city governments can create an environment that provides opportunities to people from different regions (Martínez-Ariño, 2018). Such opportunities promote the economic activities of the city since more people visiting a region means increased business activities (Cleave et al., 2016). Some of the people that can affect a place's brand include tourists and businesspersons, who leverage opportunities available in a specific region to advance their economic agenda.

The scholarly literature supports the idea that stakeholders, especially, the citizens, play an essential role in the economic growth of a city. City governments can engage in the economic activities in the territory to ensure that such practices are conducted in an acceptable manner that drives economic growth (Eshuis & Klijn, 2017). Residents, who are consumers of the economic services in the city, have an integral responsibility of guaranteeing that their conduct meets the required standards that characterise interactions in a metropolitan environment (Wassler et al., 2019). The collaboration of the different stakeholders is of great importance since it avails an atmosphere where people can coexist in the same place without the challenges, especially people from a diverse range of backgrounds (Acuti et al., 2019).

Importantly, the literature has established that social media is a significant form of digital technology that facilitates the efforts of place branding (Lund et al., 2018). Through social media, people can communicate a wide range of matters, such as normal socialisation and topics relating to the economy (Geissinger et al., 2020). In promoting the concept of sharing economy, city residents can use social media to exchange the assets and other valuables available for lease, rent, borrowing, and gifting. Such information can be accessed by potential users of the advertised products, hence, connecting people from different parts of the city (Palm et al., 2019). This peer-to-peer connection encourages sharing economy by linking up individuals (Cui et al., 2020). Social media engagement can happen to the government or to the residents in a given place (Xu & Saxton, 2019). In this case, city authorities engage in social media as brand managers whose role is to guarantee that the reputation of a place is maintained. In contrast, city residents engage in social media platforms as consumers who are either providing or looking for the available opportunities in the place.

The culture of residents dictates the success of sharing economy in cities (Fierro & Aranburu, 2019). Essentially, metropolitan places such as cities are characterised by people originating from diverse backgrounds in search of opportunities (Kavaratzis, 2017). City residents may practice different cultural practices based on their upbringing, which can affect sharing economy either positively or negatively. Having people from cultures that do not embrace some of the aspects of sharing economy such as leasing, gifting, and lending means that the involvement of these individuals in sharing economy may not create the best to achieve a flourishing city economy (Fierro & Aranburu, 2019). This idea signifies that cultures, as the key components of sharing economy, shape how people interact and create opportunities for each other as peer-to-peer market players (Fierro & Aranburu, 2019).

In summary, the current literature review highlights how sharing economy promotes place branding by having residents of a specific region engaged in social media to create and foster opportunities. Sharing economy grows the confidence of people who want to visit the city, which in turn attracts different talents from other regions. These talents are the ones that build and promote the brand of a city, allowing this place to not only have strong physical and functional attributes but also appealing personality traits. Essentially, a functional and appealing city is better placed to continue attracting more people, which is an aspect that cultivates the economy of a place.

Notes

1 Physical attributes are the brand's distinguishing characteristics, such as its name, term, sign, symbols, design, packaging, or any combination of these (Li, 2017).
2 Functional attributes are tangible advantages of using a product or service (Li, 2017).
3 Personality traits are the intangible social and psychological aspects of a brand's meaning related to citizens' beliefs and ambitions (Li, 2017).
4 Social influences are individuals who adapt their behaviour to match the needs of a social context, which is referred to as social influence. Conformity, socialisation, peer pressure, obedience, leadership, persuasion, sales, and marketing are examples of conformity (Rivis & Sheeran, 2003).

5 Social commerce is the purchasing and selling of goods or services directly within a social media platform. This strategy goes beyond social media's conventional function in discovery by encouraging consumers to finish the entire purchase process without leaving their favourite apps (Liang & Turban, 2011).

References

Acuti, D., Grazzini, L., Mazzoli, V., & Aiello, G. (2019). Stakeholder engagement in green place branding: A focus on user-generated content. *Corporate Social Responsibility and Environmental Management, 26*(2), 492–501. https://doi.org/10.1002/csr.1703

Aladwani, A. M., & Dwivedi, Y. K. (2018). Towards a theory of sociocitizenry: Quality anticipation, trust configuration, and approved adaptation of governmental social media. *International Journal of Information Management, 43*, 261–272. https://doi.org/10.1016/j.ijinfomgt.2018.08.009

Ashworth, G. J., Kavaratzis, M., & Warnaby, G. (2015). The need to rethink place branding. In *Rethinking place branding* (pp. 1–11). Springer.

Avraham, E. (2015). Destination image repair during crisis: Attracting tourism during the Arab Spring uprisings. *Tourism Management, 47*, 224–232. https://doi.org/10.1016/j.tourman.2014.10.003

Avraham, E. (2016). Destination marketing and image repair during tourism crises: The case of Egypt. *Journal of Hospitality and Tourism Management, 28*, 41–48. https://doi.org/10.1016/j.jhtm.2016.04.004

Banerjee, S. (2020). Factors impacting state branding communication success: A mediating and multigroup analysis. *Place Branding and Public Diplomacy*, 1–19. https://doi.org/10.1057/s41254-020-00175-2

Boisen, M., Terlouw, K., Groote, P., & Couwenberg, O. (2018). Reframing place promotion, place marketing, and place branding-moving beyond conceptual confusion. *Cities, 80*, 4–11. https://doi.org/10.1016/j.cities.2017.08.021

Braun, E. (2012). Putting city branding into practice. *Journal of brand management, 19*(4), 257–267.

Braun, E., Eshuis, J., Klijn, E. H., & Zenker, S. (2018). Improving place reputation: Do an open place brand process and an identity-image match pay off? *Cities, 80*, 22–28.

Casidy, R., Helmi, J., & Bridson, K. (2019). Drivers and inhibitors of national stakeholder engagement with place brand identity. *European Journal of Marketing*, 1445–1465. https://doi.org/10.1108/EJM-04-2017-0275

Causadias, J. M. (2020). What is culture? Systems of people, places, and practices. *Applied Developmental Science, 24*(4), 310–322. https://doi.org/10.1080/10888691.2020.1789360

Cleave, E., Arku, G., Sadler, R., & Gilliland, J. (2016). The role of place branding in local and regional economic development: Bridging the gap between policy and practicality. *Regional Studies, Regional Science, 3*(1), 207–228. https://doi.org/10.1080/21681376.2016.1163506

Cleave, E., Arku, G., Sadler, R., & Kyeremeh, E. (2017). Place marketing, place branding, and social media: Perspectives of municipal practitioners. *Growth and Change, 48*(4), 1012–1033. https://doi.org/10.1111/grow.12189

Cui, L., Hou, Y., Liu, Y., & Zhang, L. (2020). Text mining to explore the influencing factors of sharing economy driven digital platforms to promote social and economic development. *Information Technology for Development*, 1–23. https://doi.org/10.1080/02681102.2020.1815636

Czarnecka, B., & Schivinski, B. (2019). Do consumers acculturated to global consumer culture buy more impulsively? The moderating role of attitudes towards and beliefs about advertising. *Journal of Global Marketing, 32*(4), 219–238. https://doi.org/10.1080/08911762.2019.1600094

de Oliveira, G. F., & Rabechini Jr, R. (2019). Stakeholder management influence on trust in a project: A quantitative study. *International Journal of Project Management, 37*(1), 131–144. https://doi.org/10.1016/j.ijproman.2018.11.001

Eckhardt, G. M., Houston, M. B., Jiang, B., Lamberton, C., Rindfleisch, A., & Zervas, G. (2019). Marketing in the sharing economy. *Journal of Marketing, 83*(5), 5–27. https://doi.org/10.1177/0022242919861929

Eshuis, J., & Klijn, E. H. (2017). City branding as a governance strategy. *The Handbook of New Urban Studies*, 92–105. https://doi.org/10.4324/9780203145159

Eugenio-Vela, J. D. S., Ginesta, X., & Kavaratzis, M. (2020). The critical role of stakeholder engagement in a place branding strategy: A case study of the Empordà brand. *European Planning Studies, 28*(7), 1393–1412. https://doi.org/10.1080/09654313.2019.1701294

Fan, H. (2014). Strategic communication of megacity brands: Challenges and solutions. In *Branding Chinese mega-cities*. Edward Elgar Publishing.

Ferilli, G., Sacco, P. L., Teti, E., & Buscema, M. (2016). Top corporate brands and the global structure of country brand positioning: An AutoCM ANN approach. *Expert Systems with Applications, 66*, 62–75. https://doi.org/10.1016/j.eswa.2016.08.054

Fierro, A., & Aranburu, I. (2019). Airbnb branding: Heritage as a branding element in the sharing economy. *Sustainability, 11*(1), 74.

Foroudi, P., Gupta, S., Kitchen, P., Foroudi, M. M., & Nguyen, B. (2016). A framework of place branding, place image, and place reputation. *Qualitative Market Research: An International Journal*, 241–264. https://doi.org/10.1108/QMR-02-2016-0020

Geissinger, A., Laurell, C., Öberg, C., Sandström, C., Sick, N., & Suseno, Y. (2020). Social media analytics for knowledge acquisition of market and non-market perceptions in the sharing economy. *Journal of Knowledge Management*, 500–512. https://doi.org/10.1108/JKM-01-2020-0038

Glińska, E., & Rudolf, W. (2019). City brand personality projected by municipalities from Central and Eastern Europe Countries—a comparison of Facebook usage. *Sustainability, 11*(19), 5440.

Goulart Sztejnberg, R., & Giovanardi, M. (2017). The ambiguity of place branding consultancy: working with stakeholders in Rio de Janeiro. *Journal of Marketing Management, 33*(5–6), 421–445. https://doi.org/10.1080/0267257X.2017.1319404

Govers, R. (2015). Rethinking virtual and online place branding. In *Rethinking place branding* (pp. 73–83). Springer.

Grimmer, L., & Vorobjovas-Pinta, O. (2019). From the sharing economy to the visitor economy: The impact on small retailers. *International Journal of Tourism Cities*, 90–98. https://doi.org/10.1108/IJTC-01-2019-0015

Guillamón, M. D., Ríos, A. M., Gesuele, B., & Metallo, C. (2016). Factors influencing social media use in local governments: The case of Italy and Spain. *Government Information Quarterly, 33*(3), 460–471. https://doi.org/10.1016/j.giq.2016.06.005

Gupta, S., Schivinski, B., & Brzozowska-Woś, M. (2017). Antecedents and consequences of brand loyalty. *Handel Wewnętrzny*, 200–212.

Hankinson, G. (2015). Rethinking the place branding construct. In *Rethinking place branding* (pp. 13–31). Springer.

Hanna, S. A., & Rowley, J. (2015). Rethinking strategic place branding in the digital age. In *Rethinking place branding* (pp. 85–100). Springer.

Hudak, K. C. (2019). Resident stories and digital storytelling for participatory place branding. *Place Branding and Public Diplomacy*, *15*(2), 97–108. https://doi.org/10.1057/s41254-019-00117-7

Insch, A., & Walters, T. (2018). Challenging assumptions about residents' engagement with place branding. *Place Branding and Public Diplomacy*, *14*(3), 152–162. https://doi.org/10.1057/s41254-017-0067-5

Jeuring, J. H. G., & Haartsen, T. (2017). Destination branding by residents: The role of perceived responsibility in positive and negative word-of-mouth. *Tourism Planning & Development*, *14*(2), 240–259. https://doi.org/10.1080/21568316.2016.1214171

Jonas, J. M., Boha, J., Sörhammar, D., & Moeslein, K. M. (2018). Stakeholder engagement in intra-and inter-organizational innovation. *Journal of Service Management*, 399–421. https://doi.org/10.1108/JOSM-09-2016-0239

Kavaratzis, M. (2017). The participatory place branding process for tourism: Linking visitors and residents through the city brand. In *Tourism in the city* (pp. 93–107). Springer.

Kavaratzis, M., & Hatch, M. J. (2013). The dynamics of place brands: An identity-based approach to place branding theory. *Marketing Theory*, *13*(1), 69–86.

Kavaratzis, M., & Kalandides, A. (2015). Rethinking the place brand: The interactive formation of place brands and the role of participatory place branding. *Environment and Planning A*, *47*(6), 1368–1382. https://doi.org/10.1177/0308518X15594918

Keller, K. L. (2003). Understanding brands, branding and brand equity. *Interactive Marketing*, *5*(1), 7–20.

Key, T. M. (2017). Domains of digital marketing channels in the sharing economy. *Journal of Marketing Channels*, *24*(1–2), 27–38. https://doi.org/10.1080/1046669X.2017.1346977

King, G., Pan, J., & Roberts, M. E. (2017). How the Chinese government fabricates social media posts for strategic distraction, not engaged argument. *American Political Science Review*, *111*(3), 484–501. https://doi.org/10.1017/S0003055417000144

Kolotouchkina, O., & Seisdedos, G. (2018). Place branding strategies in the context of new smart cities: Songdo IBD, Masdar and Skolkovo. *Place Branding and Public Diplomacy*, *14*(2), 115–124. https://doi.org/10.1057/s41254-017-0078-2

Kucharska, W. (2017). Consumer social network brand identification and personal branding. How do social network users choose among brand sites? *Cogent Business & Management*, *4*(1), 1315879. https://doi.org/10.1080/23311975.2017.1315879

Kucharska, W. (2019). Online brand communities' contribution to digital business models. *Journal of Research in Interactive Marketing*, 437–463. https://doi.org/10.1108/JRIM-05-2018-0063

Kucharska, W., Flisikowski, K., & Confente, I. (2018). Do global brands contribute to the economy of their country of origin? A dynamic spatial approach. *Journal of Product & Brand Management*, 768–780. https://doi.org/10.1108/JPBM-10-2017-1641

Laurell, C., & Sandström, C. (2017). The sharing economy in social media: Analyzing tensions between market and non-market logics. *Technological Forecasting and Social Change*, *125*, 58–65. https://doi.org/10.1016/j.techfore.2017.05.038

Lechman, E. (2013). New technologies adoption and diffusion patterns in developing countries. An empirical study for the period 2000–2011. *Equilibrium: Quarterly Journal of Economics and Economic Policy*, *8*(4), 79–106. https://doi.org/10.12775/EQUIL.2013.028

Lechman, E. (2016). *ICT diffusion in developing countries*. Springer.

Lechman, E. (2018). Networks externalities as social phenomenon in the process ICT diffusion. *Economics and Sociology, 11*(1), 22–43. https://doi.org/10.14254/2071-789X.2018/11-1/2

Li, X. (2017). From Beijing to Rio: Rebranding China via the modern Olympic Games. *The Journal of International Communication, 23*(2), 252–271.

Li, X., & Feng, J. (2021a). Empowerment or disempowerment: Exploring stakeholder engagement in nation branding through a mixed method approach to social network analysis. *Public Relations Review, 47*(3), 102024. https://doi.org/10.1016/j.pubrev.2021.102024

Li, X., & Feng, J. (2021b). Nation branding through the lens of soccer: Using a sports nation branding framework to explore the case of China. *European Journal of Cultural Studies*, 1–21. https://doi.org/10.1177/13675494211011179

Liang, T. P., & Turban, E. (2011). Introduction to the special issue social commerce: A research framework for social commerce. *International Journal of Electronic Commerce, 16*(2), 5–14. https://doi.org/10.2753JEC1086-4415160201

Light, A., & Miskelly, C. (2019). Platforms, scales and networks: Meshing a local sustainable sharing economy. *Computer Supported Cooperative Work (CSCW), 28*(3), 591–626. https://doi.org/10.1007/s10606-019-09352-1

Lindström, K. N. (2020). Ambivalence in the evolution of a community-based tourism sharing concept: A public governance approach. *Scandinavian Journal of Hospitality and Tourism, 20*(3), 302–315. https://doi.org/10.1080/15022250.2020.1786455

Lucarelli, A. (2018). Place branding as urban policy: The (im) political place branding. *Cities, 80*, 12–21. https://doi.org/10.1016/j.cities.2017.08.004

Lund, N. F., Cohen, S. A., & Scarles, C. (2018). The power of social media storytelling in destination branding. *Journal of Destination Marketing & Management, 8*, 271–280.

Lutz, C., Hoffmann, C. P., Bucher, E., & Fieseler, C. (2018). The role of privacy concerns in the sharing economy. *Information, Communication & Society, 21*(10), 1472–1492. https://doi.org/10.1080/1369118X.2017.1339726

Martin, E., & Capelli, S. (2017). Region brand legitimacy: Towards a participatory approach involving residents of a place. *Public Management Review, 19*(6), 820–844. https://doi.org/10.1080/14719037.2016.1210908

Martínez-Ariño, J. (2018). Conceptualising the role of cities in the governance of religious diversity in Europe. *Current Sociology, 66*(5), 810–827. https://doi.org/10.1177/0011392117745942

Morell, M. F., & Espelt, R. (2019). A framework to assess the sustainability of platform economy: The case of Barcelona ecosystem. *Sustainability, 11*(22), 6450. https://doi.org/10.3390/su11226450

Ntounis, N., & Kavaratzis, M. (2017). Re-branding the high street: The place branding process and reflections from three UK towns. *Journal of Place Management and Development*, 392–403. https://doi.org/10.1108/JPMD-12-2015-0056

Palm, J., Södergren, K., & Bocken, N. (2019). The role of cities in the sharing economy: Exploring modes of governance in urban sharing practices. *Energies, 12*(24), 4737. https://doi.org/10.3390/en12244737

Paniagua, J., & Korzynski, P. (2017). Social media crowdsourcing. In *Encyclopedia of creativity, invention, innovation and entrepreneurship* (pp. 1170–1157). Springer. https://doi.org/10.1007/978-3-319-15347-6_200009

Richelieu, A. (2018). A sport-oriented place branding strategy for cities, regions and countries. *Sport, Business and Management: An International Journal*, 354–374. https://doi.org/10.1108/SBM-02-2018-0010

Ripoll Gonzalez, L., & Lester, L. (2018). "All for one, one for all": Communicative processes of cocreation of place brands through inclusive and horizontal stakeholder collaborative networks. *Communication & Society, 31*(4), 59–78. https://doi.org/10.15581/003.31.4.59-76

Rivis, A., & Sheeran, P. (2003). Social influences and the theory of planned behaviour: Evidence for a direct relationship between prototypes and young people's exercise behaviour. *Psychology and Health, 18*(5), 567–583. https://doi.org/10.1080/0887044032000069883

Rutkowska-Gurak, A., & Adamska, A. (2019). Sharing economy and the city. *International Journal of Management and Economics, 55*(4), 346–368. https://doi.org/10.2478/ijme-2019-0026

Salvia, G., Morello, E., & Arcidiacono, A. (2019). *Sharing cities shaping cities*. Multidisciplinary Digital Publishing Institute.

Schivinski, B. (2019). Eliciting brand-related social media engagement: A conditional inference tree framework. *Journal of Business Research*, 594–602. https://doi.org/10.1016/j.jbusres.2019.08.045

Schivinski, B., Langaro, D., Fernandes, T., & Guzmán, F. (2020). Social media brand engagement in the context of collaborative consumption: The case of AIRBNB. *Journal of Brand Management, 27*(6), 645–661. https://doi.org/10.1057/s41262-020-00207-5

Schivinski, B., Langaro, D., & Shaw, C. (2019). The influence of social media communication on consumer's attitudes and behavioral intentions concerning brand-sponsored events. *Event Management, 23*(6), 835–853. https://doi.org/10.3727/152599518X15403853721268

Schivinski, B., Łukasik, P., & Dabrowski, D. (2015). User-generated images and its impact on consumer-based brand equity and on purchase intention. *Logistyka, 2*, 1054–1061.

Schivinski, B., Muntinga, D. G., Pontes, H. M., & Lukasik, P. (2021). Influencing COBRAs: The effects of brand equity on the consumer's propensity to engage with brand-related content on social media. *Journal of Strategic Marketing, 29*(1), 1–23. https://doi.org/10.1080/0965254X.2019.1572641

Scholz, J., & Smith, A. N. (2019). Branding in the age of social media firestorms: How to create brand value by fighting back online. *Journal of Marketing Management, 35*(11–12), 1100–1134. https://doi.org/10.1080/0267257X.2019.1620839

Schor, J. B., & Fitzmaurice, C. J. (2015). Collaborating and connecting: The emergence of the sharing economy. In *Handbook of research on sustainable consumption* (pp. 410–425). Edward Elgar Publishing.Sevin, E. (2016). Branding cities in the age of social media: A comparative assessment of local government performance. In *Social media and local governments* (pp. 301–320). Springer.

Shirvani-Dastgerdi, A., & De-Luca, G. (2019). Boosting city image for creation of a certain city brand. *Geographica Pannonica, 23*(1), 23–31.

Sutherland, W., & Jarrahi, M. H. (2018). The sharing economy and digital platforms: A review and research agenda. *International Journal of Information Management, 43*, 328–341. https://doi.org/10.1016/j.ijinfomgt.2018.07.004

Taecharungroj, V. (2019). User-generated place brand identity: Harnessing the power of content on social media platforms. *Journal of Place Management and Development*, 39–70. https://doi.org/10.1108/JPMD-11-2017-0117

Uchinaka, S., Yoganathan, V., & Osburg, V. S. (2019). Classifying residents' roles as online place-ambassadors. *Tourism Management, 71*, 137–150. https://doi.org/10.1016/j.tourman.2018.10.008

Vith, S., Oberg, A., Höllerer, M. A., & Meyer, R. E. (2019). Envisioning the "sharing city": Governance strategies for the sharing economy. *Journal of Business Ethics, 159*(4), 1023–1046. https://doi.org/10.1007/s10551-019-04242-4

Wassler, P., Wang, L., & Hung, K. (2019). Identity and destination branding among residents: How does brand self-congruity influence brand attitude and ambassadorial behavior? *International Journal of Tourism Research, 21*(4), 437–446.

Weber, R. (2010). Selling city futures: The financialization of urban redevelopment policy. *Economic geography, 86*(3), 251-274.

Xu, W., & Saxton, G. D. (2019). Does stakeholder engagement pay off on social media? A social capital perspective. *Nonprofit and Voluntary Sector Quarterly, 48*(1), 28–49.

Zavattaro, S. M., French, P. E., & Mohanty, S. D. (2015). A sentiment analysis of US local government tweets: The connection between tone and citizen involvement. *Government Information Quarterly, 32*(3), 333–341. https://doi.org/10.1016/j.giq.2015.03.003

Zenker, S., & Braun, E. (2017). Questioning a "one size fits all" city brand. *Journal of Place Management and Development*, 270–287. https://doi.org/10.1108/JPMD-04-2016-0018

Zervas, G., Proserpio, D., & Byers, J. W. (2017). The rise of the sharing economy: Estimating the impact of Airbnb on the hotel industry. *Journal of Marketing Research, 54*(5), 687–705. https://doi.org/10.1509/jmr.15.0204

Zmyślony, P., Leszczyński, G., Waligora, A., & Alejziak, W. (2020). The sharing economy and sustainability of urban destinations in the (over) tourism context: The social capital theory perspective. *Sustainability, 12*(6), 2310. https://doi.org/10.3390/su12062310

Index

Note: Page numbers in *italics* indicate a figure and page numbers in **bold** indicate a table on the corresponding page.